Leading the Immortals

The Story of Lieutenant Colonel
Hüseyin Avni, Commander of the 57th
Regiment at Gallipoli

By
Hüseyin Avni Tanman
Ahmet Yurttakal

Translated from Turkish by
Emre Özmen

Gosling Press

This edition Copyright Gosling Press 2024
All rights reserved.

ISBN 978-1-874351-34-4 (Hardback)
ISBN 978-1-874351-35-1 (Paperback)

Gosling Press
www.goslingpress.co.uk

'I hold the memory of the fallen Lieutenant Colonel Avni, the virtuous, devoted and distinguished commander of the 57th Regiment, in the highest regard.'

Mustafa Kemal Atatürk

ABOUT THE AUTHORS

Hüseyin Avni Tanman
He is the great-grandson of Lieutenant Colonel Hüseyin Avni Bey. He graduated from Bilkent University with a degree in Banking and Finance and earned a master's degree from Imperial College London with a thesis titled 'Rural Development in Bafa Lake, Kapıkırı Village, Türkiye.' He has actively participated in several nongovernmental organisations focusing on environmental and agricultural issues. Presently, he is a business owner in the tourism and service industry. Aside from his professional pursuits, he is a sailing enthusiast and an amateur historian. He is married and has two children.

Ahmet Yurttakal
A graduate of Çanakkale 18th March University, Faculty of Education, he earned his master's degree from the same university in the Department of History. His master's thesis focused on the evacuation of the Gallipoli Peninsula during the Gallipoli Campaign. He is the author of several books in Turkish about Gallipoli, including *Cevat Çobanlı Paşa, A Gallipoli Hero* (2014 and 2018) and *From Suez to Gallipoli: Memories of Reserve Officer Münim Mustafa* (2018). He has contributed to numerous research projects on Gallipoli Campaign and its battlefields, presenting papers at various symposiums, congresses, and panels. His articles have been published in various books, national magazines and websites. He is married and has two children.

Translator's Note

In translating this book from Turkish, the areas that posed the most potential challenges were proper nouns and place names. For Turkish place names used by both sides but spelt differently, I included their English spellings in parentheses when these names first appear in the text, while retaining the original Turkish spellings to give readers an authentic sense of how these names appeared in Turkish sources. Also, especially in the quotes, I provided the English equivalent along with the Turkish name in square brackets. For more obscure place names that even Turkish readers might not immediately recognise and that have no direct English equivalent, I gave additional information about their locations on the battlefield in the footnotes.

Apart from providing information about certain names and terms, I have also taken the liberty of going beyond my primary task by adding footnotes that provide historical context which I felt was necessary but not included in the original text. Any notes added by me are marked with the abbreviation 't.n.' (translator's note), while those without this label are original footnotes from the text.

Emre Özmen
Ankara, July 2024

Contents

About the Authors		ii
Translator's Note		iii
Contents		iv
List of Illustrations		v
Introduction		viii
Preface		xi
Acknowledgements		xiv
Chapter One	EARLY YEARS	1
Chapter Two	AT GALLIPOLI	9
Chapter Three	THE LOSS OF AVNİ BEY	153
Chapter Four	LETTERS	176
Chapter Five	THE FAMILY	184
BIBLIOGRAPHY		200
INDEX		204

ILLUSTRATIONS

1	Lieutenant Hüseyin Avni. 'Hūseyin Avni from 2nd Company, 18th Regiment in Shkodra. 1310 [1894]	2
2	Geometry book used by Hüseyin Avni in 1887–1888	3
3	Hüseyin Avni's sons Fehmi (left) and Naci. Stip, 1904	5
4	Officers of the 8th Division, 1914	8
5	Major Hüseyin Avni, head of the 3rd Branch of the 7th Corps headquarters in Skopje, 1912	12
6	Deployment of the 19th Division headquarters and the 57th Regiment in Eceabat	14
7	Combined British-French fleet.	16
8	Headquarters of Mustafa Kemal's 19th Division in April 1915	19
9	Then and now: Lifeboats advancing towards Arıburnu	20
10	Anzac Cove, the main landing site at Arıburnu.	20
11	Landing at Anzac Cove	23
12	Looking across North Beach from Plugge's Plateau.	27
13	The defence on the first day	30
14	Officers of the 16th Battalion	33
15	Captain McDonald's binoculars	38
16	The Sphinx and the Allied encampment.	40
17	Situation of the 57th Regiment and other units on 28 April	53
18	Lieutenant Patterson's map	56
19	Notes on the map written by Avni and Kemal.	57
20	Lieutenant Penistan James Patterson	58
21	The prayer book found on Lieutenant Patterson on 29 April	59
22	Hüseyin Avni's Silver Liyakat Medal with Swords and its patent	63
23	Turkish map showing the situation on the evening of 1 May	65
24	An example of sketch maps drawn by the battalion commanders at Avni's request on 2 May.	66
25	Spoils of war in a Turkish trench at Anzac	68
26	Enver Paşa's visit to Gallipoli (24–25 September 1915)	80
27	The pith helmet captured by the 57th Regiment on the night of 14/15 May	85
28	Northern Group HQ, Kemal Yeri	88

29	Map showing the disposition of Turkish troops at Anzac on 20 May 1915	97
30	Collecting the dead in no-man's land on 24 May 1915	100
31	The British whistle that Avni gave to İzzettin	101
32	Colonel Mustafa Kemal in a trench west of Baby 700, June 1915	108
33	Map showing the opposing lines at Anzac	112
34	Map from the war diary of the 19th Division showing the front held by the division at Anzac in June 1915	114
35	A Turkish trench at Anzac	116
36	Entrance of a covered trench at Gallipoli	120
37	Major Zeki on the old battlefield in 1919	133
38	Lieutenant Greig in a watercolour painting illustrating the fight at the crater on 12 July 1915	138
39	Turkish map showing opposing lines at Anzac after August fighting.	145
40	A watercolour portrait of Hüseyin Avni	146
41	A communication trench leading to Lone Pine	149
42	Lieutenant Colonel Hüseyin Avni in early 1915	154
43	Map showing the front and headquarters of the 57th Regiment on 16 August 1915	156
44	The war diary entry about Avni's loss, 13 August 1915	157
45	Hüseyin Avni's kabalak hat	159
46	'Living Dead' column of the 9th issue of Ottoman War Magazine	161
47	Hüseyin Avni's tunic	162
48	Hüseyin Avni's kabalak hat and felt cone	163
49	Hüseyin Avni's ceremonial sabre	165
50	Sketch showing the location of the regimental headquarters and the disposition of the battalions	166
51	Cemetery and monument in the gully behind Mortar Ridge, 1919	169
52	Avni's headquarters and important spots within Çatal Dere	169
53	Close-up view of the cemetery and the monument in the gully	170
54	Commemorations of the 37th anniversary of the Battles of Suvla and Conkbayırı	172
55	Hüseyin Avni's grave in 1973	173
56	The early version of Hüseyin Avni's grave	174
57	Tekin Arıburun's last visit to his father in 1992	174

58	Hüseyin Avni's grave in 2019	175
59	Senior Captain Hüseyin Avni and his children Fehmi and Melek, 1907	178
60	Photos of Mehmet Fehmi and Melek	182
61	Mehmet Fehmi, 1917	189
62	The photograph of Fehmi 1919	190
63	Melek & Hakkı	191
64	One Turkish Lira signed by Gazi Mustafa Kemal Atatürk	192
65	Avni's wife Fatmatüzzehra Arıburun	193
66	Lieutenant Mehmet Tekin with Fatmatüzzehra and Melek	194
67	Lieutenant Tekin Arıburun in England in 1928	195
68	Engagement ceremony of Tekin and Perihan Arıburun 1940	196
69	Commander of the Turkish Air Force General Tekin Arıburun	199
70	Perihan Arıburun and Tekin Arıburun. Ankara, 1990	199

INTRODUCTION

My grandfather Tekin Arıburun, son of Avni Bey[1], and my grandmother, Perihan Arıburun, who lived in Ankara, used to follow a special tradition when they visited our home in İstanbul, especially on my birthday. They would bring along a gift, or send one if they couldn't be with us in person, and it would always be signed, 'Your fallen great-grandfather.' These gifts took various forms: sometimes a pencil case, other times a handful of soil or a few pinecones from Gallipoli, and sometimes a simple greeting card. It was a custom for them to visit Gallipoli for the anniversaries of either 18 March or 25 April. Since I was born in May, I remember they'd often stop in İstanbul to see us on their way back to Ankara from Gallipoli. This is how I came to be instilled with love and respect for my greatgrandfather Hüseyin Avni Bey, whose name I bear.
The house my grandfather and his family lived in on Haydar Street in the Fatih district of İstanbul was heavily damaged during the great fire of 1918. They watched their whole neighbourhood burn to the ground from the house of their relatives in Üsküdar, which they happened to be visiting that day. Unfortunately, a great portion of Avni Bey's belongings were lost in the fire. The relics that you will find in this book are the items my grandfather was able to save on that day and then preserved with great care.

Tekin Arıburun never wrote his memoirs. Apart from being an important figure both in Turkish Air Force history and in Turkish political history, he was the son-in-law of Naci Eldeniz Paşa,[2] who was the teacher of Mustafa Kemal Atatürk at the Military Academy. Naci Paşa hosted Kaiser Wilhelm II during his visit to İstanbul in 1917 and was appointed personal aide-de-camp to Sultan Mehmed VI in July 1918, retaining the position until April 1920. He sympathised with the Nationalist movement and ultimately joined Mustafa Kemal, serving as a corps commander during the Greco-Turkish War of 1919-1922. My grandfather always refrained from sharing what he had heard from his father-in-law, one of

---

[1] 'Bey' was a title used in the Ottoman Army for officers holding the ranks of major, lieutenant colonel, and colonel.
[2] 'Paşa' (Pasha) was a title for generals in the Ottoman Army and was also used for high-ranking civilian state officials.

the close witnesses both to Kemal Paşa's departure to Anatolia in 1919 and the subsequent events that led to the birth of the Turkish Republic. Even though he was part of Atatürk's inner circle, he regarded his professional experiences as 'classified information' and felt it would be inappropriate to disclose family-related memories. It is also possible that he chose not to remember certain parts of them. Whenever he shared the memories he deemed suitable to narrate, much like giving a history lesson, my grandmother Perihan or my mother would take notes to ensure that they wouldn't be lost to time.

Following my grandfather's passing, my mother took over a portion of his library and his entire collection of papers, which included numerous photographs, notes, and a variety of documents. These materials remained untouched in boxes for a considerable time. As we sorted through the documents and had individuals who could read the old Turkish alphabet translate them, it was revealed that among them were undiscovered letters of Avni Bey. During the process, we also realised that my grandfather had a habit of jotting down notes and drawing sketches within the books he read. As we compiled these materials and began working on them, we discovered the potential to dig deep into Avni Bey's personal life and military career, moving beyond the widely known information that he was the heroic, fallen commander of the Ottoman 57th Infantry Regiment.

In May 2023, with my book 'Hüseyin Avni Bey' in hand, Ahmet and I were walking the 'Silt Spur' trenches at Anzac, exploring the details of the landing using maps. From there, we headed towards the Lone Pine Memorial. While we were discussing the Australian attack on 6 August, a group of British visitors walking the battlefield with their guide, Peter Hart, caught my eye. I already knew Peter from his books. I approached him, introduced myself, and as soon as he saw the book, he said, 'You should translate this into English. We don't know enough about your side of the story, and this would be a great opportunity.' I replied, 'I'd love to, but I don't know any publishers.' He then said, 'Hold on,' and called over his friend, John Wilson, who was one of the visitors in the group. After a quick introduction, John mentioned 'Gosling Press,' and within five minutes, everything was settled.

In this book, we have tried to create a comprehensive portrait of Avni Bey and offer new insights into the history of the Gallipoli Campaign by using official records alongside papers held in the family archive. Avni Bey was the commander of the 57th Regiment, which halted the Anzac advance near Conkbayırı (Chunuk Bair) on 25 April 1915. His regiment fought in some of the fiercest and bloodiest battles at iconic places such as The Nek and Quinn's Post, and later across famous Anzac positions Steele's and Courtney's Posts, making the 57th one of the Ottoman regiments with the heaviest casualties throughout the campaign. This translation provides a valuable opportunity to gain a comprehensive view of Avni Bey and his regiment s actions at Gallipoli. I hope with this book, Hüseyin Avni Bey will receive better recognition as a heroic figure and a loving father.

Hüseyin Avni Tanman

PREFACE

The Ottoman 57th Infantry Regiment is distinguished from other Ottoman units that saw action at Gallipoli in two respects. Firstly, it was one of the two units, the other being the 27th Infantry Regiment, that frustrated the Allied operational plans at Anzac on the day of the landings. Secondly, the regiment is identified with Lieutenant Colonel Mustafa Kemal Bey, the commander of the 9th Infantry Division, who would later be known as 'Atatürk.' The 57th Regiment also stood out as one of the Ottoman units that remained on the front until the end of the Gallipoli Campaign.

Raised at Yarçeşme Barracks in Tekirdağ (formerly known as Rodosto) on 20 January 1915, the 57th Regiment arrived in Maydos (modern-day Eceabat) on the Gallipoli Peninsula just a month later, on 25 February 1915. Under the leadership of Avni Bey, the regiment conducted battle drills day and night in preparation for the defence of the Peninsula. When the news of the Allied landings was received in the small hours of 25 April 1915, it was rapidly deployed to the front by Lieutenant Colonel Mustafa Kemal Bey and pushed back the Anzac troops advancing up onto Conkbayırı (Chunuk Bair). The 57th suffered heavy casualties, particularly in the early stages of the campaign, fully adhering to Mustafa Kemal Bey's famous order, 'I don't order you to attack; I order you to die.' This would lead to its recognition in Turkish historiography as the 'Regiment of the Fallen.' Avni Bey described how his men 'fought as if in a race' and commended their valour, saying: 'With hearts full of faith, they attacked a cowardly enemy, who could not stand against cold steel, and demonstrated the might of the Ottoman bayonet, inflicting severe casualties and forcing him to retreat.'

Avni Bey was a typical example of the officers leading from the front. On one occasion, he led his men personally in a bayonet attack, holding his sword while shouting religious expressions 'Allah' and 'La ilahe illallah.'[3] He was so committed that, in one message, he wrote: 'The enemy is in the gully right now. Hopefully, will blow their brains out

---

[3] While 'Allah Allah' has been the battle cry of the Turkish Army for centuries, the expression 'La ilahe illallah', meaning 'There's no deity but Allah,' is considered the faith's cornerstone in Islam, the foundation of a Muslim's religious devotion. (t.n.)

with grenades.' For his actions 'at the risk of his life in combat' he was eventually promoted to the rank of lieutenant colonel personally by Enver Paşa, the Ottoman War Minister and the Deputy Commander-in-Chief, and temporarily assumed command of the right flank of the Ottoman garrison at Anzac alongside his regiment, commanding a force nearly equivalent to a division. Possibly due to his bold attitude in battle, Avni Bey was popular among his subordinates, as evidenced by the message of an Ottoman officer named Captain Kamil: 'In yesterday's routine order, I read about your promotion to the rank of lieutenant colonel by the Deputy Commander-in-Chief. Words cannot express the joy this news brings to my heart.' His death on 13 August 1915, the second day of the Islamic feast Ramazan Bayramı (Eid al-Fitr), deeply saddened the officers and men on the front, including Colonel Mustafa Kemal Bey, then commander of the Anafartalar (Suvla) Group. In his account of the campaign, Mustafa Kemal wrote, 'I hold the memory of the fallen Lieutenant Colonel Hüseyin Avni, the virtuous, devoted, and distinguished commander of the 57th Regiment, the cornerstone of the victory at Arıburnu, in the highest regard.' Major İzzettin Bey (later known as General İzzettin Çalışlar), Mustafa Kemal's chief of staff, also commended him in his memoirs, referring to him as 'the gallant commander of the glorious 57th Regiment.'

The lack of a comprehensive biographical study about a prominent figure like Avni Bey is primarily due to limited available resources. Some years ago, I wrote an article for a Turkish history magazine about his death, based on two documents I found in the Turkish State Archives, but questions regarding how and where exactly he was killed remained largely unanswered. As a result of long-term research, or perhaps more accurately, owing to the sacrifice of Avni Bey, I crossed paths with his grandchildren, Hüseyin Avni Tanman and Fatma Gülru Tanman. When I saw that they had carefully preserved the information and documents I had long sought in their family archive, I felt an excitement and joy that I still cannot describe. Our first step together that day marked the beginning of a journey to discover more about Avni Bey, a figure widely known as a fallen Gallipoli hero, yet whose biography remained incomplete for decades.

In writing the book, we primarily relied on Tekin Arıburun's archive and notes taken by family members during their conversations with him as the main sources of biographical information about Avni Bey.

Furthermore, the war diary of the 57th Regiment, as well as foreign archives and sources, contributed to our understanding of Avni Bey's role as a soldier. We closely examined these sources on a day-to-day basis, aiming to provide a thorough and detailed account of the events. Through extensive research, especially in Turkish archives, we were able to gain access to a wealth of valuable materials. These ranged from Avni Bey's Military Academy class notes to the personal identification booklet found in his personnel file. Regrettably, we couldn't access documents about Avni Bey's military career before Gallipoli, as well as the record of his personal belongings and papers found on him after his death, which would have been of great importance to us. During the writing process, we also conducted field research at Gallipoli, exploring the trenches, headquarters, and tunnels marked on various Ottoman and Anzac maps.

The book is organised into five chapters. The first chapter covers Avni Bey's family history and the early stages of his military career until his service in Tekirdağ. In the second chapter, we look into his involvement in the Gallipoli Campaign from the day he assumed command of the 57th Regiment until 10 August 1915, providing a day-by-day account accompanied by maps and pictures. In the third chapter, we provide the details that emerged for the first time about when and where Avni Bey was killed, where his headquarters was and the uniform he was wearing at the moment of his death. Avni Bey's letters sent to his family from Gallipoli, along with emotional letters and postcards from his children, which are being published for the first time, are compiled in the fourth chapter. The final chapter of the book deals with the news of Avni Bey's death and the difficulties experienced by his family.

We believe this book will engage anyone with an interest in the history of the Gallipoli Campaign, and the reader will discover the story of a heroic Turkish regiment commander and the gallant actions of his unit.
Ahmet Yurttakal

ACKNOWLEDGEMENTS

We received support from many individuals and institutions in producing this book. We thank the staff of the Turkish State Archives, Turkish Naval Museum Command, Turkish Military Academy, Turkish Ministry of National Defence Archive Services Directorate, Turkish General Directorate of Mapping, as well as the former president of ATASE, retired Brigadier General Necdet Tuna, for his invaluable support throughout our research and for facilitating our access to the war diaries and documents of the 57th Regiment. We would also like to thank Colonel Ömer Faruk Aslan, Museum Director of the İstanbul Military Museum and Cultural Site Command, along with İlkay Karatepe, Erkan Sönmez, Salim Üstün, Rıdvan Önal. We also appreciate the contributions of Cem Demirci, Bulut Ek, and Niels Morsink for their meticulous photography of Hüseyin Avni's belongings at the İstanbul Military Museum and Cultural Site. Additionally, we thank Yücel Demirel and Dilek Cansel for their assistance in transliterating and reading the Ottoman Turkish documents.

For their knowledge and expertise, we would like to thank: F. Gülru Tanman, Prof. Dr. M. Baha Tanman, Hakan Arıburun, Bintuğ Arıburun, Şahin Aldoğan, Muzaffer Albayrak, Tuncay Yılmazer, Gültekin Yıldız, Mesut Uyar, M. Fatih Baş, M. Onur Yurdal, İzzeddin Çalışlar, Murat Söylemez, Mehmet Akif Erdoğan, Fatih Güldal, Zeynep Çulha ve Sabahattin İnceoğulları. We are grateful to our families for their patience, understanding and moral support.

Finally, we would like to thank Peter Hart and John Wilson/Gosling Press for their interest and efforts in bringing this book to publication in the shortest time possible, along with all the friends who, though not named individually, contributed to it.

We remember all the fallen and veterans with deep gratitude, recognising that 'the breath we take today is thanks to someone's last breath.'

Hüseyin Avni Tanman & Ahmet Yurttakal

Chapter One
EARLY YEARS

Hüseyin Avni's family tree traces back to the Oghuz tribes, who migrated from Central Asia to Anatolia in the thirteenth century and settled in Alaiye (Alanya). One of his ancestors, *Kadı* (judge) Hacı Abdülkerim, participated in the conquest of Rumelia during the reign of Sultan Murat II. As a reward for his actions, the town of Debar, on the Albania-Macedonia border, and the villages of Trebishte (Lower Trebishte and Upper Trebishte) were given to him as *arpalık*.[4] Hacı Abdülkerim had stipulated in his will that his eldest son to continue the family line should pursue scholarly endeavours, while the second son should join the military. In the family, it has been passed down by word of mouth until today that the descendants of the son affiliated with the 'scholarly class' are known as *Kadıoğulları* (sons of judge), whereas the lineage of the son associated with the 'military class' is called *Cebecioğulları* (sons of the armourer).

Ali was born in Debar in the mid-nineteenth century as a member of *Cebecioğulları* family and was orphaned at a young age. His uncle, seeking a portion of his father's inheritance, stirred unrest and sought to harm him. The family's butler, a faithful man, saved Ali by whisking him away, keeping him hidden and protected for some time before taking him to Bitola, where he was apprenticed to a watchmaker. Ali, who would take over the shop from his master years later, married Fatma, a midwife in Bitola, in the late 1860s. The newlywed couple's first child, Şaban, was born in 1869, followed by the birth of Hüseyin Avni in 1871. Şaban would pass away at a young age.

Lieutenant Hüseyin Avni
Hüseyin Avni began his military education at the Bitola Military Middle School before advancing to the Bitola Military High School. He graduated from the Military Academy, which he had entered in 1889, on 6 May 1892 as a second lieutenant (service number: 1308-94).[5] He was known for his courageous attitude and resolute decision-making.

---

[4] Arpalık was a type of appanage given to the Ottoman elite or senior commanders. (t.n.)
[5] '1308' (1892) represents the year of his graduation while '94' denotes his class rank. (t.n.)

1. Lieutenant Hüseyin Avni. 'Hüseyin Avni from 2nd Company, 18th Regiment in Shkodra. 1310 [1894].' (Hüseyin Avni Tanman Collection)

Standing between 1.70–1.75 metres tall, he had brown hair and hazel eyes.

After graduating, he was initially assigned to the 3rd Army. Shortly after, on 15 May 1892, transferred to the 2nd Company, 3rd Battalion, 18th Regiment under the same army, headquartered in Gjirokastër, a border outpost in Albania. He received the 5th Class Order of the Mecidiye in 1894 for his distinguished service there.

On 8 August 1895, Avni was promoted to first lieutenant and appointed to the 4th Company, 3rd Ergiri Battalion, 33rd *Redif* (Reserve) Regiment of the 3rd Army. On 23 May 1897, he was appointed as the adjutant of the 20th *Redif* Pristina Brigade and took part in the Greco-Turkish War of 1897. After serving in Ergiri and Pristina, his next stop would be Stip in Northern Macedonia. After his promotion to captain on 10 January 1898, he was given command of the 1st Company, 2nd Stip Battalion, 38th *Redif* Regiment. Six years had passed since he left Bitola when he received the news of the death of his father, the watchmaker Ali. While in Stip, Avni crossed paths with Captain Haşmet, an army officer who would later become his close friend. This friendship ultimately led Avni to meet Fatmatüzzehra, one of Haşmet's sisters, and their subsequent marriage in 1899. Fatmatüzzehra was the daughter of Sadık from İstanbul, who served as a lieutenant in Gazi Osman Paşa's headquarters

2. Geometry book used by Hüseyin Avni in 1887–1888. The handwriting reads: 'The geometry book of Hüseyin Avni, fourth year student at Manastır Military Middle School.' The name 'Hussein Avni,' written with Latin letters, can also be seen. (Hüseyin Avni Tanman Collection)

during the Siege of Plevna in 1877.[6] From the union of Avni and Fatmatüzzehra, two sons, Naci and Mehmet Fehmi (later known as Mehmet Tekin) were born in 1900 and 1903 respectively, both in Stip. Naci passed away at the age of five.

Avni was promoted to senior captain on 22 August 1904 and transferred to the 3rd Battalion of the 90th Regiment. On 9 April 1906, his daughter Melek was born in Kocani, Northern Macedonia. On 2 June 1908, he was promoted to major and assumed command of the 3rd Battalion, 17th Regiment in Bitola, and the family moved from Stip to Bitola.

After serving in this position for three years in Bitola, he was transferred to the 3rd Branch of the 7th Corps headquarters in Skopje on 11 July 1912. At that time, Avni and his family were uncertain about moving to Skopje due to the escalating unrest in the Balkans. Fatmatüzzehra's sister, Semine, resided with their mother, Paşa, in Skopje's Köprülü (Veles). However, Avni opposed Fatmatüzzehra's desire to be close to her mother and sister. Since he foresaw the events that may occur in the Balkans, he believed it would be safer for the entire family to move to İstanbul, the Ottoman capital, rather than Skopje. His paternal relatives had already departed Debar and settled in İstanbul. Eventually, in August 1912, Fatmatüzzehra moved to İstanbul, taking her children and her mother-in-law, Fatma, with her. They settled as tenants in the mansion of Avni's uncle, İsmail Sami, at No.29, on Değirmen Street of Fatih district for a monthly fee of nine silver mecidiyes[7].

The outbreak of the Balkan War on 16 October 1912 validated Avni's foresight. Semine, along with her husband İbrahim and their children Salim Tevfik and Mehmet Şerif Abdullah, also migrated to İstanbul. The family reunited in the capital when Fatmatüzzehra's father, Sadık, passed away, and her mother, Paşa, moved in with Semine. Mehmet Fehmi began second grade at Saliha Sultan Primary School, while Melek was

---

[6] Osman Nuri Paşa (1832–1900). Ottoman field marshal. Famous defender of Plevna during the Russo-Turkish War of 1877–1878. One of the most respected and distinguished military leaders in the Ottoman Turkish military history. (t.n.)

[7] Ottoman currency subunit. One Ottoman Lira in gold was worth five silvermecidiyes. (t.n.)

3. Hüseyin Avni's sons Mehmet Fehmi (left) and Naci. Stip, 1904. (Hüseyin Avni Tanman Collection)

not yet of school age. Avni's family, however, had to wait until the end of the Balkan War in 1913 to be reunited.

Tekirdağ Days[8]

After a lengthy separation of over a year, Avni returned to İstanbul following the end of the Balkan War. He enjoyed a reunion with his family until he was assigned to his new duty as deputy commander of the 23rd Regiment stationed in Ayvalık[9] on 12 January 1914. Avni, who departed for Ayvalık in late January, reunited with his family once again in July when he returned to İstanbul on leave. Shortly after, all leave was cancelled upon the declaration of a general mobilisation on 2 August, and the 23rd Regiment received orders to move to Tekirdağ. Avni bought a ticket for travel from İstanbul to Bandırma[10] to join his regiment that had departed from Ayvalık and was en route to Soma.[11]

When Mehmet Fehmi, who had been longing for his father over the past three years, insisted on remaining with him for a while longer, Avni did not deny his son's request and decided to take him along. He also brought a relative with him to take Mehmet Fehmi back to İstanbul. On the evening of 11 August, they all boarded the Biga[12] ferry to Bandırma. An unfortunate incident occurred during the journey, and Avni's binoculars were stolen. Well aware of the importance of equipment for a soldier in wartime conditions, he promptly reported the situation to the ferry's authorities. Despite exhaustive searches and his protests, the binoculars could not be found.

The 23rd Regiment, having completed its mobilisation following the order from the 3rd Corps, departed from Ayvalık on 11 August 1914 and marched to Soma. There Avni joined his regiment and later travelled back to Bandırma by railway. After spending a few more days with Fehmi, he sent him off to İstanbul with his close relative before his unit's departure to Tekirdağ. On the same day, the regiment departed from Bandırma by ferry, reached Tekirdağ on 25 August 1914, and was bivouacked in the

---

[8] A city located in Eastern Thrace, in western Turkey. Formerly known as Rodosto. (t.n.)
[9] A district of Balıkesir province on the western coast of Turkey. (t.n.)
[10] A district of Balıkesir province, located on the southern coast of the Marmara Sea. (t.n.)
[11] A district of Manisa province in western Anatolia. (t.n.)
[12] A district of Çanakkale on the southern coast of Marmara Sea. (t.n.)

area known as Aşıklar, under the command of Lieutenant Colonel Hüseyin Recai. When the area of responsibility of the 3rd Corps expanded with the order sent by the 1st Army Command on 19 October 1914, the location of the units changed. The 23rd Regiment departed from Tekirdağ on 26 October 1914 and arrived in Çorlu[13] on the evening of 27 October. The headquarters of the 8th Division to which Avni's regiment was attached, the 8th Field Artillery Regiment, the field ambulance and the divisional field hospital were also deployed there.[14]

In Command of a Depot Regiment
In early November, the 3rd Corps decided to establish a depot regiment with the fourth companies of the depot battalions of the 8th Division. This new unit would be named the Soma Depot Regiment. On 9 November 1914, Avni was tasked by Colonel Ali Rıza (Sedes), the commander of the 8th Division, with procuring the necessary clothing and supplies for this new organisation from Soma. Two days later, Avni moved there. Upon his return, he took on the task of training the new regiment and ensuring its combat readiness.

---

[13] A district of Tekirdağ on the western coast of the Marmara Sea. This was an important supply centre during the campaign. (t.n.)
[14] Şükrü Erkal, Alpaslan Orhon and Muhterem Saral, *Birinci Dünya Savaşı'nda Çanakkale Cephesi (04 Haziran 1915 – 09 Ocak 1916), Vol. 5, Book 1* (Ankara: Genelkurmay Askerî Tarih ve Stratejik Etüt Başkanlığı Yayınları, 2012), 49–52.

4. Officers of the 8th Division, 1914. 1, 8th Division Commander Colonel Ali Rıza (Sedes); 2, 22nd Regiment Commander Major İbrahim Hakkı; 3, 24th Regiment Commander Major Mehmet Nuri (Conker); 4, 23rd Regiment Commander Lieutenant Colonel Recai; 5, Deputy Commander of the 23rd Regiment Major Hüseyin Avni. (Necmettin Özçelik Collection).

Chapter Two
AT GALLIPOLI

The Formation of the 57th Regiment

After the decision to create the 19th Infantry Division in Tekirdağ, Lieutenant Colonel Mustafa Kemal was given its command on 20 January 1915 and arrived in Tekirdağ four days later. The formation of the division was completed by 1 February 1915. The 1st Battalion of the 57th Regiment was formed with men from the fourth company of each of the three battalions of the 19th Regiment, 7th Division. Likewise, the 2nd Battalion was raised using men from the fourth company of each of the three battalions of the Soma Depot Regiment. The 3rd Battalion, on the other hand, consisted of men from the first, second, and third companies of each of the three battalions of the Soma Depot Regiment. The average strength of the battalions was 750 men.[15] The battalion commanding officers were Captain Zeki for the 1st Battalion, Captain Ata for the 2nd Battalion, and Captain Ali Hayri for the 3rd Battalion.[16] A machine gun company was formed by transferring the machine gun company of the 20th Regiment to the 57th.

Since the regiment had just been raised, it faced significant shortages of equipment and material. Kemal reported the lack of equipment that he had identified to the 3rd Corps on 16 February:

> The men are either barefoot or will end up barefoot after a short march. Some of them tie their makeshift bags made of sacks or cloth to their backs with ropes, which will no doubt break after covering a short distance. There is a need for coats, clothing, blankets, and tents, as the men sleep in the open during the winter. This situation is particularly challenging in rainy weather.[17]

---

[15] Arzu Tunç et al., eds., *Çanakkale Muharebelerinde 19. Tümen Cerideleri, Vol. 1*, (Ankara: Genelkurmay Askerî Tarih ve Stratejik Etüt Başkanlığı Yayınları, 2015), 6.
[16] The full names of these officers are: Ahmet Zeki Soydemir, Mehmet Ata Erçıkan, Ali Hayri Arıburnu.
[17] Arzu Tunç et al., eds., *Çanakkale Muharebelerinde 19. Tümen Cerideleri, Vol. 1*, 19–20.

On 22 February, Avni, who had been commanding the Soma Depot Regiment, was appointed as the commander of the 57th Regiment. Once the formation was complete, Avni instructed his battalions to prepare for combat and began training and educating the men.

The 57th Arrives on the Peninsula

On 19 February 1915, a combined British and French fleet bombarded the forts at the entrance of the Dardanelles, namely Seddülbahir, Kumkale, and Orhaniye. Following the bombardment, 3rd Corps Commander Esat (Bülkat) Paşa ordered the 19th Division to be prepared to be deployed to Gallipoli in case of a landing attempt. That very night, the division informed corps via an encrypted message that it was fully ready for action.[18] The awaited order arrived on 23 February when Esat instructed the 57th Regiment to move to Eceabat. In the meantime, an organisational arrangement had been made in the 57th Regiment. The 2nd Battalion of the 57th Regiment (formerly part of the 20th Regiment), was replaced with the 2nd Battalion, 58th Regiment, while the 1st Battalion (formerly part of the 19th Regiment) remained in its place. The 3rd Battalion, 57th Regiment (formerly part of the 21st Regiment) was replaced by the 1st Battalion, 59th Regiment. The 58th and 59th Regiments were transferred to İstanbul, and their place would be taken by the 72nd Regiment from the 24th Division and the 77th Regiment from the 26th Division.[19]

On Tuesday, 23 February, the 57th Regiment was presented with regimental Colours. After the ceremony, Avni inspected his unit, and the battalions transferred their equipment from the barracks to the pier. The

---

[18] Arzu Tunç et al., eds., *Çanakkale Muharebelerinde 19. Tümen Cerideleri*, Vol. 1, 22–23.
[19] Arzu Tunç et al., eds., *Çanakkale Muharebelerinde 19. Tümen Cerideleri*, Vol. 1, 27–28.

steamers *Reşitpaşa*,[20] *Millet*,[21] and *Halep*[22] had been allocated for the transportation of the regiment.[23] Although the departure was planned for the same day, it was not possible due to adverse weather conditions. Esat was insistent on the regiment moving to Eceabat as soon as possible, issuing one order after another. He instructed the division headquarters to go to Eceabat by a small ship if the weather was still unfavourable the next day. If that wasn't possible, he ordered a few officers to take the train to Uzunköprü and then proceed to Eceabat by stagecoach.[24]

Next day, with the weather relatively good in the morning, the order to move came early. The battalions marched from the barracks in Yarçeşme to the Tekirdağ pier at 07:30, reaching the pier in two hours with a brisk pace. The equipment, which was brought to the pier the day before, was loaded onto the ships at 07:50, followed by the riding horses and pack mules at 09:40. As the wind, initially calm in the early morning, gradually strengthened, the embarkation became more difficult and was completed with the help of steamboats and barges. It took until 20:00 to embark all men and equipment onto the ships. *Reşitpaşa* had been assigned to accommodate the headquarters of the 19th Division and the 57th Regiment, along with the men from the 1st and 2nd battalions. The 3/57th, Machine Gun Company, Mountain Battery, and divisional field hospital were embarked on *Halep*, while the Field Artillery Battalion, Field Bakery Platoon, and Field Ambulance were accommodated on *Millet*.[25] At 22:50, the ships departed the Tekirdağ pier bound for Çanakkale. Mustafa Kemal and Hüseyin Avni whiled away their journey

---

[20] Previously named *Port Antonio*, built in Newcastle by Sir Raylton Dixon & Co. in 1901, the ship had a gross tonnage of 4,458, a length of 112.8 m, and a beam of 14.1 m. Purchased by the Donanma Cemiyeti (Ottoman Naval Association) in 1911. Served as a troop ship to transport soldiers and wounded during the Gallipoli Campaign.
[21] Served as a troop ship during the early stages of the Gallipoli Campaign. Sunk by Russian warships while waiting to receive coal in the Port Karadeniz Ereğli in the Black Sea on 9 May 1915.
[22] Previously named *Aberdeen*, built in Glasgow by Robert Napier & Sons in 1881, was purchased in 1906. Served as a troop ship during the Gallipoli Campaign. Sunk by the British submarine E-11 on 15 August 1915.
[23] ATASE: BDH 5384-183-H1-1-2; Arzu Tunç et al., eds., *Çanakkale Muharebelerinde 19. Tümen Cerideleri, Vol. 1*, 31.
[24] Arzu Tunç et al., eds., *Çanakkale Muharebelerinde 19. Tümen Cerideleri, Vol. 1*, 32–33.
[25] Arzu Tunç et al., eds., *Çanakkale Muharebelerinde 19. Tümen Cerideleri, Vol. 1*, 34.

5. Major Hüseyin Avni, head of the 3rd Branch of the 7th Corps headquarters in Skopje, 1912. (Hüseyin Avni Tanman Collection)

conversing on the deck of the *Reşitpaşa*.

At 07:00, all three steamers had arrived at the Kilye pier north of Eceabat, but the 57th Regiment was delayed in disembarking due to insufficient preparation by the Dardanelles Fortified Area Command. After waiting one and a half hours, the 1/57th finally began to disembark, followed by the 2/57th. Both battalions immediately commenced preparations for establishing the bivouac west of Eceabat, marching along the coast.[26] Without delay, Hüseyin Avni proceeded to the division headquarters and joined Mustafa Kemal for a meeting.[27] Later, the 1/57th and 2/57th battalions, along with the quick-firing battery and the engineer company assigned from the 9th Division, were stationed at Çamburnu,[28] while the 3/57th occupied houses in Eceabat.

At this time, the 57th Regiment totalled 2,728 personnel – 48 officers and 2,680 other ranks. The regiment was armed with 4 machine guns, 2,250 rifles, and 451 boxes of ammunition.[29] Following the arrival of reinforcements in early March, the regiment's total strength increased to 3,767, 49 of whom were officers. In addition to the 4 machine guns, the regiment now had 3,000 rifles, 534 boxes of ammunition, and 439 hand grenades.[30]

Getting Ready for Action
Before the major attack on 18 March, the Allied forces conducted occasional small-scale landing operations to destroy Turkish defences and carried out reconnaissance missions. At sunrise on 4 March, seven battleships and three cruisers appeared at the entrance of the strait. After heavily bombarding Seddülbahir and Kumkale, they landed 60 men at Seddülbahir and 400 men at Kumkale to demolish the guns of the forts. The 57th Regiment was ordered to quickly move from Çamburnu to Sarafim Farm[31] to reinforce the defence of the landing places. Avni

---

[26] ATASE: BDH 5384-183-H1-1-2.
[27] Arzu Tunç et al., eds., *Çanakkale Muharebelerinde 19. Tümen Cerideleri*, Vol. 1, 35.
[28] Çamburnu is located at the southern entrance of Eceabat. During the campaign, a hospital was established here – along with a cemetery. (t.n.)
[29] Arzu Tunç et al., eds., *Çanakkale Muharebelerinde 19. Tümen Cerideleri*, Vol. 1, 90.
[30] Arzu Tunç et al., eds., *Çanakkale Muharebelerinde 19. Tümen Cerideleri*, Vol. 1, 393.
[31] Located approximately 7km west of Kilitbahir village, this was an important reserve and rest area during the campaign. (t.n.)

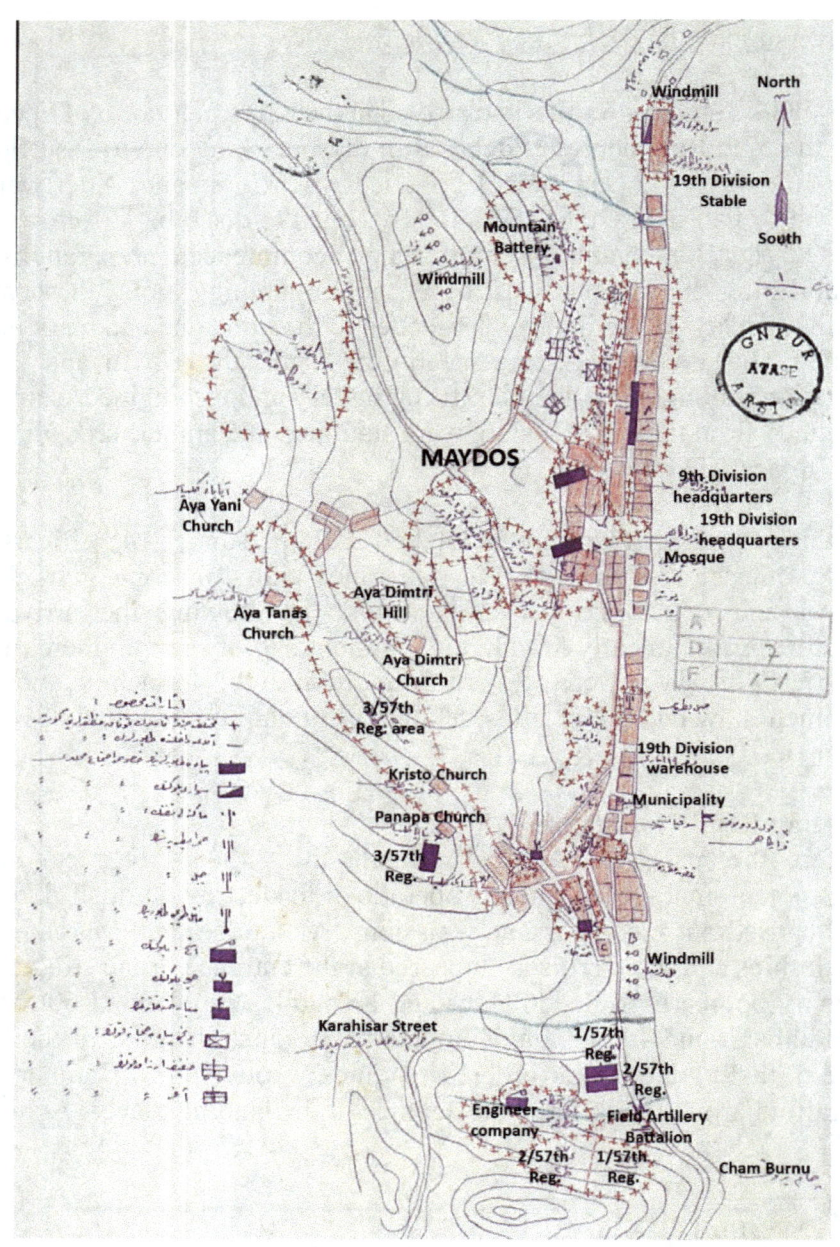

6. Deployment of the 19th Division headquarters and the 57th Regiment in Eceabat. (*Çanakkale Muharebelerinde 19. Tümen Cerideleri*, vol. 2, appendix 8)

mounted his horse and galloped to Krithia village (today's Alçıtepe) to meet with the 19th Division Chief of Staff, Lütfi. He describes the day as follows:

> Yesterday, in the absence of the division commander, the regiment was ordered to parade at 13:00 by Chief of Staff Lütfi Bey. The regiment commander was instructed to proceed quickly to Krithia to receive further orders, while the regiment stand by at Sarafim Farm. Before setting of at 13:20, I designated Captain Ata Efendi[32], the commander of the 2nd Battalion, as my deputy and ordered him to wait at Sarafim Farm. The whole regiment assembled in the southwest square and formed into a marching column. At 16:00 the regiment reached the ordered place. Upon arriving in Krithia, I ordered the regiment, in accordance with the instructions from the chief of staff, to advance to the rear of Achi Baba, north of Krithia, and wait there for further orders (this order was written at 15:30 and received at 17:00). Following this, the regiment re-formed into a marching column precisely at 17:07. Arriving at Achi Baba, the regiment was instructed to remain there until the situation was clarified. Having received the 'back' order, I re-joined the regiment at 21:06. In a mere five minutes, the regiment was ready in marching column. When the leading parties reached Sarafim Farm, they encountered the 77th Regiment, which blocked the road, causing a one-hour delay in our return to our accommodation. Eventually, we reached our destination.
>
> Since the road was covered without any breaks during the march, sixteen men suffered foot injuries, and four fell ill. Additionally, seven men did not return to their companies, with three of them joining later in the morning. No incidents occurred with the pack animals.[33]

---

[32] 'Efendi' was a title used in the Ottoman Army for NCOs and officers holding the ranks of lieutenant, first lieutenant, and captain.

[33] ATASE: BDH 5384-183-H1-1-6.

7. Combined British-French fleet.

Until 18 March 1915, the Allied fleet continued its minesweeping and bombardment operations. At 08:15 on 18 March, the signal flag unfurled from the dreadnought *Queen Elizabeth*, marking the beginning of the final big push. However, 18 March proved to be a grim day for the Allies, as three ships were sunk and four others heavily damaged. Following the Allies' defeat, anticipation grew for a potential landing on the Turkish side. The training of the 57th Regiment, still stationed in Eceabat, intensified gradually. A battle drill took place on Sunday, 28 March, to evaluate the effectiveness of the rigorous training. The men were tasked with reacting to a scenario where the enemy was positioned near the town of Gallipoli. At 08:10, the companies formed up in platoon formation and marched towards Cumalı village via Yalova village. The drill ended in the evening, and the regiment returned to Eceabat.[34]

On 4 April, the regiment was informed that Esat Paşa, the commander of the 3rd Army Corps, would conduct an inspection. Esat was scheduled to arrive in Eceabat at 08:00 the following morning to see the men at the training square at Çamburnu. Beforehand, Mustafa Kemal notified his regiments of the importance of maintaining discipline and order during the inspection to ensure Esat's satisfaction. However, although Esat and his company arrived in Eceabat, they were unable to conduct the inspection due to rainy and northerly weather. During this time, the training of the 57th Regiment was primarily concentrated at Çamburnu and the area west of Karahisar Street in Eceabat.[35] The regiment now had a total strength of 3,687 personnel, including 49 officers, and was armed with 4 machine guns, 3,000 rifles, 572 boxes of ammunition, and 830 hand grenades.[36]

---

[34] ATASE: BDH 5384-183-H1-1-14.
[35] Arzu Tunç et al., eds., *Çanakkale Muharebelerinde 19. Tümen Cerideleri, Vol. 1*, 379–381.
[36] ATASE: ATAZB, Kls: 41, G:3ai.

Early in April, the 19th Division was designated as the army's general reserve, with instructions to be prepared for deployment around the town of Gallipoli or the Asiatic side, depending on the location of the actual Allied landing operation. After being assigned as army reserve, it was decided to redeploy the division. Accordingly, one regiment and the mountain artillery battalion would be stationed in the vicinity of Bigalı (Boghali) village, another regiment would be positioned around Mal Tepe, and the remaining forces would stay in Eceabat. The new deployment of the division was as follows:

57th Regiment in bivouac just west of Bigalı,
The 3rd Mountain Artillery Battalion, 39th Field Artillery Regiment and the 77th Regiment in bivouac north of Mal Tepe,
The 1st Battalion, 77th Regiment watching the coast from Koyun Limanı to Suvla Azmak,
The 72nd Regiment in bivouac around Söğütlü Çeşme, south of Bigalı Dere, on the Eceabat-Yalova road,
1st Field Artillery Battalion, at the farm to the east of Sarıkız Tepe, north of Bigalı Dere,
The 2nd Field Artillery Battalion was between the 72nd and 77th Regiments, around the Telakki District, on the Bigalı-Eceabat road.
The Mountain Battery at the Yel Değirmeni Düzü (Windmill Flat) near Bigalı,
The Engineer Company, Signal (Telegraph) Platoon and Cavalry Company in Bigalı village,
The Field Ambulance at the farm, and the Field Hospital in Eceabat.[37]

The 57th Regiment continued with battle drills on Thursday, 15 April. The day's drill began with Hüseyin Avni having the regiment march in the direction of Yalova-Cumalı villages. The battalions were spread out along the ridges north of Yalova village, deployed in dominant positions as if there were Allied forces on the opposite hills, and a manoeuvre was

---

[37] ATASE: BDH 5384-183-H1-1-19; Erkan-ı Harbiye Kaymakamı İzzettin, 'Çanakkale Muharebeleri Hatıralarından 12 Nisan 331 Günü' *Askerî Mecmua*, 10, (1336/1920); Mustafa Kemal, *Arıburnu Muharebeleri Raporu*, ed. S. Akgül et al. (Ankara: Genelkurmay Askerî Tarih ve Stratejik Etüt Başkanlığı Yayınları, 2011), 12–13; Şükrü Erkal, Alpaslan Orhon & Muhterem Saral, *Birinci Dünya Savaşı'nda Çanakkale Cephesi, Vol. 5, Book 1*, 210.

conducted in preparation for a potential landing operation.[38] On Saturday, 17 April, the regiment conducted its usual battle drills, this time at Sarafim Farm. While drills were ongoing, a British plane dropped two bombs, destroying some tents in the bivouac of the 26th Regiment and causing a few casualties. The plane was repelled by fire from the 57th Regiment's Machine Gun Company.[39]

Two days later, the regiment carried out one last battle drill in the general directions of Bigalı-Turşun and Mal Tepe-Suvla-Turşun. The manoeuvre took place near Uzunhıdırlı-Sivli (Yolağzı) village,[40] where the troops spread out over the terrain and then retreated.[41] On the same day, another change occurred in the deployment of the 19th Division, with Mustafa Kemal and the division headquarters moving to the Yel Değirmeni Düzü (Windmill Flat) near Bigalı.[42]

The Glorious Defence of Arıburnu
The severe defeat suffered on 18 March shocked Britain and France deeply, prompting the decision to carry out an amphibious operation to break through the Dardanelles. To pave the way for the navy to reach İstanbul, the mine lines in the strait had to be cleared. The primary obstacle to this operation lay in a network of forts and batteries lining both shores of the Dardanelles. To overcome this, the capture of the Kilitbahir Plateau, providing a commanding view over the Anatolian defences, was necessary. Accordingly, two separate landings at Seddülbahir and Arıburnu were planned. Although initially aimed for 23 April 1915 (St. George's Day), adverse weather conditions necessitated a postponement to 25 April. The Australian and New

---

[38] Arzu Tunç et al., eds., *Çanakkale Muharebelerinde 19. Tümen Cerideleri, Vol. 2*, (Ankara: Genelkurmay Askerî Tarih ve Stratejik Etüt Başkanlığı Yayınları, 2015), 3.
[39] Arzu Tunç et al., eds., *Çanakkale Muharebelerinde 19. Tümen Cerideleri, Vol. 2*, 5.
[40] Uzunhıdırlı was a settlement located in the east of Suvla Plain, between the villages of Kumköy and Yolağzı. Today there is a lake with the same name here. (t.n.)
[41] Arzu Tunç et al., eds., *Çanakkale Muharebelerinde 19. Tümen Cerideleri, Vol. 2*, 6–9.
[42] ATASE: BDH 5384-183-H1-1-19; Erkan-ı Harbiye Kaymakamı İzzettin, 'Çanakkale Muharebeleri Hatıralarından 12 Nisan 331 Günü' *Askerî Mecmua*, 10, (1336/1920); Mustafa Kemal, Arıburnu Muharebeleri Raporu, Genelkurmay Askerî Tarih ve Stratejik Etüt Başkanlığı Yayınları, Ankara 2011, 12–13; Şükrü Erkal, Alpaslan Orhon and Muhterem Saral, *Birinci Dünya Savaşı'nda Çanakkale Cephesi, Vol. 5, Book 1*, 210.

8. Headquarters of Mustafa Kemal's 19th Division in April 1915, photographed in May 1969. (Şahin Aldoğan Collection)

Zealand Army Corps, set to land at Arıburnu, was tasked with securing the roads leading to Gallipoli-Maydos (Eceabat) and Bigalı-Kocadere (Kurija Dere). Their objective also included advancing on Mal Tepe and entrenching in that area. The primary objective for the covering force during the landing would be to secure positions in squares 224, 237, and 238 on the Peninsula maps to facilitate the landing of the main body.[43]

On the night of 24/25 April 1915, the moon was due to set at 02:57. Leveraging the moonlight, 1,500 Australians forming the first wave boarded lifeboats shortly after 01:30. The ships edged towards the shore with the lifeboats alongside them, steaming at a speed of 5 miles. Around 02:00, two men from the 8th Company of the 27th Regiment, Bigalı İdris (from Biga) and Gelibolulu Cemil (from Gallipoli), were the first to notice the ships. The commander of the 8th Company, Captain Faik,

---

[43] Cecil Faber Aspinall Oglander, *Büyük Harbin Tarihi Çanakkale*; *Gelibolu Askerî Harekâtı, Vol. 1*, trans. Metin Martı (İstanbul: Arma Yayınları), 458.

9. Then and now: Lifeboats advancing towards Arıburnu. (Murat Söylemez Collection)

10. Anzac Cove, the main landing site at Arıburnu.

reported this first to the 2/27th battalion at Kaba Tepe by telephone. Upon receiving the news, the 9th Division immediately put all reserves on full alert. At 05:17, Colonel Halil Sami, the commander of the 9th Division, notified the 3rd Corps that numerous Allied warships and transports had been sighted both to the north and south of Kaba Tepe, as well as off Arıburnu and Ağıl Dere (Aghyl Dere). Additionally, he reported that 'the enemy had landed on the shores of Arıburnu.'[44] Meanwhile, the commander of the 77th Regiment, Major Saip, stationed near Mal Tepe, reached out to the 19th Division telephone centre at 05:10 and reported 'hearing infantry fire from the ridges of Arıburnu.'[45] The news of the landing had now reached all troops on the Peninsula. Halil Sami sent the report he had given to the 3rd Corps to the 19th Division as well: 'Please be informed that news of the enemy's landing attempt was received. The enemy brought numerous warships and transports close to the area between Arıburnu and Kaba Tepe and are now landing troops at Arıburnu.'[46]

Upon receiving the report from Halil Sami, Cavalry Lieutenant Vahit, the aide-de-camp to the 19th Division, ran and handed it to Mustafa Kemal. A flurry of activity had now started at the division headquarters. The aide then immediately woke up the Chief of Staff, Major İzzettin, and informed him of the situation. İzzettin hastily dressed and made his way to the commander. While conferring with Mustafa Kemal at the headquarters, the sounds of gun and rifle fire began to echo from the Arıburnu and Kaba Tepe area.[47] The 57th, 77th and 72nd regiments were telephoned and ordered to prepare for action.[48] Without delay, Kemal contacted the commander of the 3rd Corps, Esat, whose headquarters were located in the town of Gallipoli. Kemal reported the arrival of numerous transports escorted by armoured cruisers at Seddülbahir, Arıburnu, and Saros. Receiving no response, he called Esat once more and conveyed the news of the Allied landing around Arıburnu, at Zığındere (Gully Ravine), and the enemy's occupation of Tekke Burnu.

---

[44] Reşat Hallı, Muhterem Saral and Remzi Yiğitgüden, *Birinci Dünya Savaşı'nda Çanakkale Cephesi (04 Haziran 1915 – 09 Ocak 1916), Vol. 5, Book 2* (Ankara: Genelkurmay Askerî Tarih ve Stratejik Etüt Başkanlığı Yayınları, 2012), 19–20.
[45] Reşat Hallı, Muhterem Saral and Remzi Yiğitgüden, *Birinci Dünya Savaşı'nda Çanakkale Cephesi (04 Haziran 1915 – 09 Ocak 1916), Vol. 5, Book 2*, 71.
[46] Arzu Tunç et al., eds., *Çanakkale Muharebelerinde 19. Tümen Cerideleri, Vol. 2*, 16.
[47] Erkan-ı Harbiye Kaymakamı İzzettin, 'Çanakkale Muharebeleri Hatıralarından 12 Nisan 331 Günü' *Askerî Mecmua*, 10, (1336/1920), 2.
[48] Mustafa Kemal, *Arıburnu Muharebeleri Raporu*, 38.

He also informed him that he would advance towards Arıburnu with the 57th Regiment to counter the landing.[49]

Going into Action: March from Bigalı to Conkbayırı

At 06:00, Kemal notified the divisional cavalry company of the landing and issued orders for immediate readiness. He also ordered the company to dispatch two separate patrols to conduct reconnaissance in the vicinity of Kaba Tepe and Kum Tepe. The patrol, composed of five cavalrymen under the command of Lieutenant Rasim, moved towards Kaba Tepe, while another party under Lieutenant Reşit set out for Kum Tepe. Additionally, four cavalrymen under Lieutenant Necati, tasked with establishing communication between the 9th Division and the 19th Division, were summoned to the division headquarters. The cavalry would spread out across the Arıburnu area and relay front line news to Kemal.[50]

While the 57th Regiment had been on alert at the bivouac near Bigalı for two hours, Lieutenant Vahit delivered the division commander's order to Hüseyin Avni at 07:05:

> Prepare to move with your regiment and report to the division commander to receive further orders.[51]

Avni went straight to the division headquarters, where he found the division commander engrossed in studying the map. Kemal showed Avni on the map the location of the landing and informed him that they would move soon. Once the final preparations were made, the officers of the mountain battery, the divisional medical officer, the aide, and the adjutant gathered at the parade ground.[52]

After a short wait, the cavalry company, the 57th Regiment, the mountain battery, and a medical detachment received the order to move:

---

[49] Esat Bülkat, *Çanakkale Hatıraları 3. Kitap* [unpublished typescript] (İstanbul: Harp Akademiler Kütüphanesi, 1950), 518.
[50] Sermet Atacanlı, *Arıburnu'nun İlk Müdafaası* (İstanbul: Türkiye İş Bankası Kültür Yayınları, 2015), 277–278.
[51] ATASE: BDH 5384-183- H1-1-22a.
[52] Mustafa Kemal, *Arıburnu Muharebeleri Raporu*, 16.

1. Enemy's landing attempt around Arıburnu is more serious than his efforts elsewhere.
2. The Cavalry Company, 57th Regiment, mountain battery, and a medical detachment will advance to the ridges west of Kocadere.
3. The rest of the division will remain in bivouac, ready for immediate action.
4. Initially, I will accompany the detachment moving against the enemy. If necessary, I will return to the division.
5. Keep in contact with the division's chief of staff, who will remain at the headquarters.
6. The headquarters is on the ridge next to the mill east of Bigalı village.
Commander of the 19th Division
Lieutenant Colonel Mustafa Kemal[53]

11. Landing at Anzac Cove.

At 07:39, the 57th Regiment started marching north, making its way through Bigalı Dere. By this time, a signal (telephone) detachment had also joined the regiment. Before leaving, Kemal got in touch with the 3rd Corps once again. In the message he sent, he mentioned the lack of intelligence regarding the number of enemy troops landed between Kaba

---
[53] ATASE: BDH 5384-183-H1-1-22a.

Tepe and Arıburnu, and that he had dispatched the divisional cavalry company to the western ridges of Kocadere. Kemal also stated he would move in that direction with the 57th Regiment and a mountain battery to prevent the loss of the mentioned ridges. He assured that if the situation required the engagement of a large portion of the division, he would return to the divisional headquarters.[54]

Kemal, his staff and an infantry company, was at the front of the marching column. Following closely, about 200 metres behind, was the 2/57th, accompanied by Hüseyin Avni. Behind this battalion was the mountain battery, followed by the 1/57th, and bringing up the rear was the 3/57th. The divisional train remained in Bigalı, while the combat equipment moved along with the battalions. The commanders of the mountain battery and the field artillery battalion subsequently joined the march. As the troops advanced, a British plane persistently followed, and was eventually driven away by rifle fire.[55] Around this time, news began to arrive from the patrols sent to Arıburnu. Deputy Reserve Officer[56] Hasan Reşit reported the situation as follows: 'The enemy has made serious landings from Ağıl Dere and Arıburnu and continues to do so. Several transport ships, five battleships and cruisers are observed. Kabatepe is currently held by the 2nd Battalion, 27th Regiment of the 9th Division. The fighting is ongoing at Kocaçimen Dağı [Koja Chemen Dagh/Hill 971].'[57] Arıburnu was now in the hands of the landed troops, who were confronted by the 27th Regiment. Captain Faik, commander of the 8th Company, 27th Regiment, was first to counter the landing but was wounded and sent to the rear.[58]

'You Have Your Bayonets!'
Arriving at Kurtgeçidi (Kurt Ketchede) via Kocaçimen by 10:00, Kemal left the detachment behind and quickly descended to Conkbayırı. There,

---

[54] Arzu Tunç et al., eds., *Çanakkale Muharebelerinde 19. Tümen Cerideleri*, Vol. 2, 24.
[55] ATASE: BDH 5384-183-H1-1-22a, BDH 5384-183-H1-1-23.
[56] Shortly after the war broke out, the Ottoman Military Academy had been suspended. To meet the army's demand for platoon commanders, university graduates from civilian backgrounds were recruited. A Reserve Officer Training Centre was established in İstanbul at the outset of the war for this purpose. Those who completed the training were assigned to units as 'deputy reserve officers' and were promoted to the rank of 'reserve officer' if they performed well within six months. (t.n.)
[57] ATASE: ATAZB, Kls: 41, G:3ak.
[58] Arzu Tunç et al., eds., *Çanakkale Muharebelerinde 19. Tümen Cerideleri*, Vol. 2, 25.

he encountered a scattered party of 15 men from the 27th Regiment, out of ammunition, retreating under heavy pressure from the advancing Australians. Kemal stopped them and shouted, 'You cannot run from the enemy! If you haven't got any ammunition, you have your bayonets!' He immediately made them fix bayonets and lie down on the ground. Meanwhile, the head of the main column had arrived at Kör Dere.[59] Kemal ordered Captain Ata, the commander of the 2/57th Battalion, to launch an attack on the Anzac troops from Hill 261 (Hill 161) with his entire battalion. He also had the mountain battery took a position at Suyatağı (Su Yatagha), east of Conkbayırı, and commenced firing on the Anzacs.[60]

By 10:24, the 27th Regiment was engaged in combat on the left flank, 800 metres from the ridges occupied by the Allied forces, along a 1.5 kilometre front stretching between Arıburnu and Kaba Tepe. Simultaneously, the 57th Regiment launched its attack from the right flank, starting from a distance of 600 metres.[61] The 1/57th, bolstered by the drills and training under Hüseyin Avni, boldly dashed forward, advancing from Dik Dere[62] towards Baby 700. The Chief of Staff İzzettin vividly recounted the famous counter-attack of the 57th Regiment under a rain of shrapnel: 'The barrage of fire from the enemy ships was relentless and stifling. Countless large shells seemed to assail the Turkish soldiers ferociously, aiming to thwart their advance towards the sea. The craters opened by the shells were vast enough to bury an entire company.'[63] The bombardment became increasingly intense, with shells tearing into the earth and leaving behind enormous craters. Lieutenant Alaattin, Avni's aide, later described the scene: 'In the beginning, we were very anxious about the relentless fire from the enemy ships. My God, what a terrible bombardment that was! The shells were massive, each the size of a man. Wherever they landed and exploded, they left craters 13–15 yards deep and 4 yards wide, often deeper than a man's height. There were numerous times when my commander and I found ourselves trapped under mounds of earth thrown up by explosions. Just as we were about to lose our breath, another shell would explode, hurling

---

[59] The deep gully just east of Conkbayırı. (t.n)
[60] Mustafa Kemal, *Arıburnu Muharebeleri Raporu*, 17.
[61] Arzu Tunç et al., eds., *Çanakkale Muharebelerinde 19. Tümen Cerideleri*, Vol. 2, 28.
[62] Second gully to the east of Battleship Hill. (t.n)
[63] CBA: 01000140-1.

us out from beneath the debris. The shells were making a terrible whistling sound as they flew past. At first, I would loudly recite the Shahada, the declaration of faith, whenever I heard the sound. The commander noticed this and said, 'Son, it's better to recite it quietly in your heart before you heard the whistle. When you hear it, keep your heart calm and be thankful. We only hear the whistle of these huge shells after they have passed over us. And if our time hasn't come yet, there's no need to worry. If one shell buries us, another will come along and bring us back to the surface.'[64] Unable to resist the counterattacks, the Anzacs began to fall back. At 11.30, the 1/57th had advanced 400 to 500 metres from its starting position, with the 2/57th in support. Although the attack initially pressed home, Mustafa Kemal was still worried about the rapidity. He thought the battalion on the right flank was advancing too slowly and wanted to accelerate the advance on the left to reach the landing beach as soon as possible. Hüseyin Avni immediately issued the orders to the battalions accordingly, saying: 'There is no time to waste in defending the homeland.'[65]

At 11:45, Captain Ata reported that the 1st Battalion on the left flank was advancing slowly. In response, Hüseyin Avni warned Captain Zeki that the 2/57th Battalion was complaining about the slow pace of the attack. He ordered Zeki to increase the pace and maintain contact with the 2/57th. Zeki then led the two reserve companies forward himself. Meanwhile, the 3/57th, which was held in reserve, was ordered to prepare for defence.[66] At 11:50, in a report sent from '600 metres north of Arıburnu,' Kemal stated that 'the Allied force of more than two regiments could not withstand the attacks and fled.' He also mentioned that he had moved the remainder of his division closer to Kocadere and would use them if necessary.[67] By 12:00, the 2/57th was positioned on the right flank and the 1st Battalion on the left flank, with two companies from the 3rd Battalion held in reserve and two companies supporting the attacking battalions. As the battle intensified and ammunition began to run low,

---

[64] Tekin Arıburun, 'Arıburun Savaşlarının 66. Yıldönümünde Kahraman Kumandan Şehit Hüseyin Avni Bey'i Anarken,' *Yeni Düşünce Dergisi,* 5-13, (1981): 11.
[65] ATASE: BDH 5384-183-H2-1-1.
[66] TASE: BDH 5384-183-H1-1-23a, BDH 5384-183-H1-1-24.
[67] Arzu Tunç et al., eds., *Çanakkale Muharebelerinde 19. Tümen Cerideleri, Vol. 2,* 31.

Avni, responding to Ata's demand, requested additional supplies from the ammunition column near Kocadere.⁶³

12. Looking across North Beach from Plugge's Plateau.

By 13:45, the 57th Regiment was ramping up the pressure. The gap between the opposing sides had shrunk to 350 metres. Three additional companies from the 2nd Battalion were thrown into the battle, leaving only one company as a reserve. Zeki was wounded leading the attack of his unit, and Captain Osman Nuri, commander of the 1st Company, assumed command. When the 2/57th began suffering from the machine gun fire, Avni had First Lieutenant Ali Ratıb, the commander of the machine gun company, open fire upon the Anzacs with his two machine guns. Around the same time, the remaining reserves from the 3rd Battalion also joined the battle from the gully west of Battleship Hill. Shortly after, the hill was firmly in Turkish hands, and the Anzacs, never

---

⁶⁸ ATASE: BDH 5384-183-H1-1-24; Arzu Tunç et al., eds., *Çanakkale Muharebelerinde 19. Tümen Cerideleri, Vol. 2.* 37.

to set foot on it for the remainder of the campaign, were pushed back to Baby 700.[69]

At 16:00, the two companies on the left flank of the regiment kept pushing forward until they were engaged in close combat. In the thick scrub, ferocious fighting raged just 20 metres apart, with both sides fiercely contesting the ground. Suddenly, shells from the mountain battery began falling among the advancing companies, wounding First Lieutenant Fahri, the regimental aide, and three other officers. The friendly fire ceased only after Avni intervened, urgently relaying a warning to the battery to stop firing on their own troops.[70] Meanwhile, the Anzacs organised a counter-attack against the 2/57th but were forced to retreat with heavy loss. Avni later described his men in the fighting: 'With hearts full of faith, they attacked a cowardly enemy, who could not stand against cold steel, and demonstrated the might of the Ottoman bayonet, inflicting severe casualties and forcing him to retreat.'[71] Captain Ata reported that he had committed the 3rd Company to the battle, leaving the battalion without any reserves. In response, Hüseyin Avni reinforced both the 2/57th and 3/57th with an additional company each and ordered the attack to continue. The fierce fighting at Baby 700 resulted in heavy casualties for the regiment, including four wounded officers.[72]

By 17:00, the regiment had advanced 500 metres from its starting position in the morning. Now the entire regiment, including the machine gun company, with the exception of two companies held in reserve, was engaged, When Mustafa Kemal reported that the Allies were boarding lifeboats and retreating to their ships, another company went forward with the bayonet. Avni, led the attack on The Nek himself, with sword in hand, shouting religious battle cries 'Allah' and 'La ilahe illallah'. He later described the scene: 'The enemy, already inclined to flee, was running towards Korku Deresi [Monash Valley]. The area between Düz Tepe [Battleship Hill] and Cesaret Tepe [The Nek] was completely filled with enemy corpses. We advanced as far as Korku Deresi and remained

---

[69] ATASE: BDH 5384-183-H1-1-24a, BDH 5384-183-H2-1-2, BDH 5384-183-H2-1-2a.
[70] ATASE: BDH 5384-183-H2-1-2a, BDH 5384-183-H2-1–3.
[71] CBA: 01000140-1.
[72] ATASE: BDH 5384-183-H2-1–3, BDH 5384-183-H2-1–3a; CB. Arşivi 01000140-1.

there.'

It was now dark, and the Australians and New Zealanders found themselves trapped with nowhere to go. The landing force were driven to the southern portion of Russell's Top, forced to retreat into Monash Valley on the left, and surrounded on all sides. Avni dispatched the 3/57th Battalion's aide, Sabri, to the right to ensure the regiment's connection with other units that flank, and the regimental aide, Alaattin, to the left to establish communication with the 3/72nd. Simultaneously, he sent a strong patrol, led by a reserve officer, to Monash Valley.[73]

As of 18:10, the 2/57th was positioned on the right flank and the 1/57th on the left, both reinforced by two companies from the 3rd Battalion. By 18:30, the battalions began advancing again. At 19:48, Avni reported to the division that the Allied troops had retreated to their 'last line' and that the entire regiment was now on the front line. He stated his intention to launch a night attack after forming a reserve force with three companies he could assemble. The attack commenced around 21:00. A battalion from the 72nd Regiment reinforced the regiment's left flank. Avni had the 2/57th attack Hain Tepe [Plugge's Plateau] from the right flank 'to completely destroy the enemy and prevent them from boarding the boats.' However, the darkness and rough terrain caused the companies to become disorganised, resulting in a loss of contact with the right flank. Around this time, reports came in that 'reinforcements had arrived from the rear and ammunition had been sent from the division.'

By 23:00, the 57th Regiment held the first line with its 10 companies. Its right flank extended to The Nek, while the left flank reached near Courtney's Post. The 6th and 10th companies were stationed at Kabak Sırt, while the regiment's machine gun company was positioned south of Baby 700. Avni had established his command post at the head of the Mule Valley behind Chessboard, less than 100 metres from the Allied position. Word came that Kemal had reached Baby 700 around 23:00. Despite Avni's efforts to meet and brief him, they couldn't connect in person. Instead, they communicated through Captain Ata. İzzettin later wrote in his memoirs:

To see both the situation at the front line and the men, the division

---

[73] CB. Arşivi 01000140-1.

commander, his aides, and I headed to Düz Tepe [Battleship Hill] from Conkbayırı, following the summit route. When we arrived

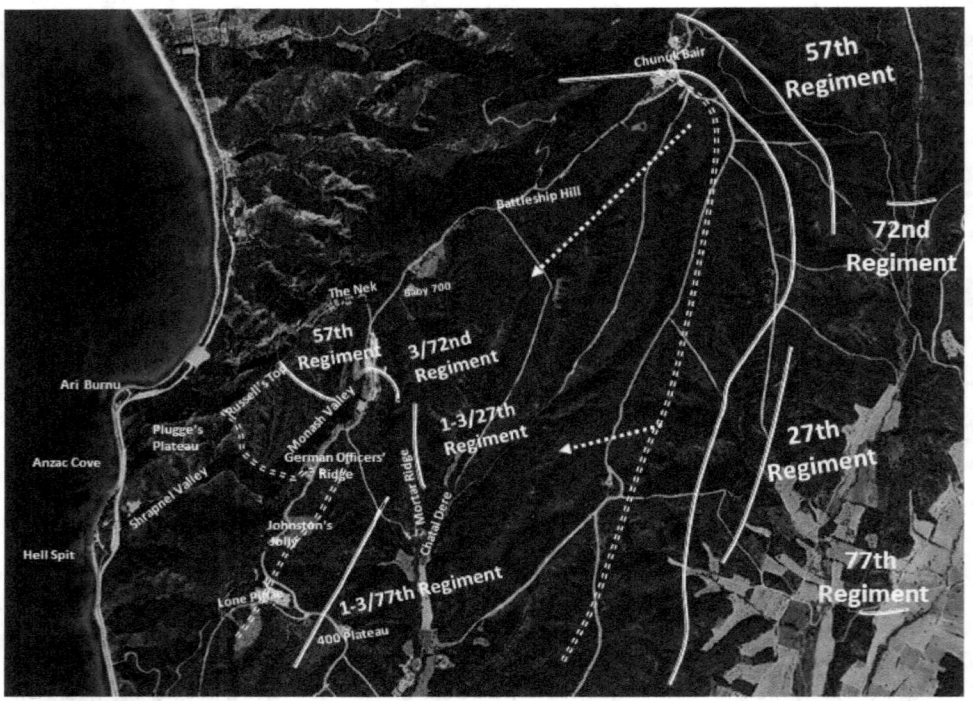

13. The defence on the first day. The visual illustrates the initial encounter with the Allies near Conkbayırı and the subsequent fighting on the night of 25 April, as the regiments advanced towards Arıburnu.

there, we saw many dead bodies on the ground. These were Australian soldiers who died in the early fighting. The scene remained unchanged as we continued on our way. Here and there our fallen lay among the enemy dead. The stretcher bearers of the 57th Regiment were carrying the wounded, assisted by men from the division's field ambulance. We came upon a reserve company and began chatting with the men. The firing line ahead was very close. Suddenly, an intense firing broke out, with bullets flying dangerously near us, causing confusion among the men. The distance to the enemy was so close that even the slightest whisper or sound from our side prompted the Australians to open fire in that direction immediately. For this reason, we had to speak in a very low voice, avoid lighting matches, and refrain from smoking. Due to the darkness, it was possible to see the situation of neither the firing line nor the opposing side. 2nd Battalion Commander, Ata Efendi, one of the closest battalion commanders, arrived. We received briefing from him. He said that the number of dead and wounded was high, the companies were reduced to half strength, and a significant number of officers were out of combat. Through Ata Efendi, the regiment's commander was told that the current line must be held firmly and not a single step should be taken back.[74]

The 27th and 57th Regiments were attacking three Australian brigades. The 27th Regiment engaged with two battalions totalling 2,000 men, while the 57th Regiment fought with three battalions totalling 2,500 men against 12 battalions from three brigades, consisting of approximately 12,000 men. The fourth companies of the 57th Regiment's battalions did not participate on the first day as they had not yet completed their organisation and training.

İzzettin later described the actions and moral situation of the 57th Regiment as follows:

> Our force was one-third the strength of the Australians that we forced to retreat. Our artillery support comprised Fethi Efendi's mountain battery positioned at Suyatağı and the mountain battery accompanying the 27th Regiment, which was deployed around Sancak Tepe.[75] These two batteries were quite ineffective when compared to the overwhelming fire from the ships. Therefore, we owe this success, which laid the first foundation stone of the Arıburnu Front, to the miraculous bravery and courage of our men and the heroism and sacrifices of our officers. The success rested upon the intuitive leadership of the commander of the 27th Regiment and the swift decision-making of the commander of the 19th Division to secure Conkbayırı with at least one regiment, as well as the dynamic attack by the 57th Regiment, driven by the

---

[74] Erkan-ı Harbiye Kaymakamı İzzettin, 'Çanakkale Muharebeleri Hatıralarından 12 Nisan 331 Günü' *Askerî Mecmua*, 10, (1336/1920).
[75] The hill immediately north of Scrubby Knoll. (t.n.)

division commander. The commitment and piety displayed by men on that day were truly remarkable and admirable.[76]

In his account, Mustafa Kemal praised the actions of the 57th on the first day, stating:

> Thanks to the resistance of the 57th Regiment, which broke the enemy's determination and will with its lion-hearted attack on 25 April 1915, the enemy's efforts were thwarted. It was the extraordinary service and sacrifices of the 57th and then the 27th Regiments, which were very effective in the movement and attack on the enemy's flank from Conkbayırı and made this tactical move a spectacular success, truly deserving a place in our military history.[77]

First Prisoners: McDonald, Elston and Lushington
The situation was grave for the Anzac battalions, which had given ground in the face of the 57th Regiment's counterattacks, necessitating immediate support for the 3rd Australian Brigade. Landing around 16:00, Lieutenant Colonel Harold Pope, commander of the 16th Battalion, and his adjutant, Captain Ronald McDonald, promptly went to see Colonel John Monash, commander of the 4th Brigade. Monash took them to General Alexander Godley's headquarters on the beach. There, Pope was ordered to quickly move his battalion, find the 3rd Brigade headquarters, and reinforce Colonel Ewen Sinclair-MacLagan. Following these orders, Pope led his battalion through Monash Valley towards The Nek.

Pope was at the front with a guide provided by the 4th Brigade headquarters. McDonald was moving back and forth between the front and back of his walking column. Private Reginald Francis Lushington described the journey:

> Night had fallen and A and B companies of the 16th were proceeding to take up a position where there was a wide gap in the Anzac front line. We had landed on the beach in the late

---

[76] Erkan-ı Harbiye Kaymakamı İzzettin, 'Çanakkale Muharebeleri Hatıralarından 12 Nisan 331 Günü' *Askerî Mecmua*, 10, (1336/1920).
[77] Mustafa Kemal, *Arıburnu Muharebeleri Raporu*, 39-71.

14. A group portrait of the 16th Battalion officers, featuring Lieutenant Colonel Pope (seated, 5th from left), his adjutant Captain McDonald (seated, 6th from left), and Lieutenant William Ernest Elston (standing, far back, 4th from right). (AWM: P05772.003)

afternoon. Wounded were lying by the hundred in long lines against the face of the cliff. Here they were protected from the shrapnel bursting overhead and from innumerable spent bullets which fell by no means harmlessly on the beach. As darkness began to close in we filed along the bed of what was afterwards known as Monash Valley. Turning a sharp bend, we received our first shock. 'Halt! Hands up!' The hoarse challenge of the sentry was full of menace. The startling suddenness of it made the blood run cold. The password and countersign, 'Birdwood-Australia,' were exchanged and we continued on our way.[78]

After a while, McDonald realised that the rear of the battalion was no longer following them. The unit had been split in two by an Indian mountain artillery unit marching in a different direction through Monash Valley, and those who fell behind lost in the dense scrub. When McDonald informed Pope, who was at the front with the guide, that the

---

[78] T. H. Bolton 'A Forgotten Hero of Gallipoli.' *Western Mail*, 23 April 1953.

companies were lost, Pope decided to continue the march and sent the guide back to search for the missing half of the battalion.[79]

McDonald, along with A Company's 1st Platoon Commander Lieutenant William Elston[80] and Lushington, remained with Pope as they continued their search for the 3rd Brigade headquarters. They mistakenly headed towards a hill and ended up at a firing line on the slope of a steep ridge instead of their intended destination. This spot, later named 'Pope's Hill' after him, was a small hill surrounded by cliffs. At the hilltop, they encountered a sergeant major from the 11th Battalion and a few scattered soldiers on the ridge. The column halted, and Pope moved forward to the firing line to assess the situation. Meanwhile, McDonald sought to gather information about the whereabouts of the men of the 3rd Brigade. He was informed by the sergeant major that they were at the furthest left flank of the 3rd Brigade, with Indian troops further left, and that the Brigade headquarters lay somewhere in the valley, but contact had been lost.[81] Following the information received, McDonald went to the far left of the firing line, found Pope and explained the situation. Pope then made the decision to conduct reconnaissance and establish communication with the anticipated Indian troops. He instructed Lieutenant Elston and his men to reconnoitre the direction he pointed, locate the Indians, and gather information. Lushington recounted:

> Captain McDonald joined Lieutenant Elston in the lead and we proceeded cautiously along what appeared to be a goat track about two or three feet below the edge of the ridge. This track turned up on to the flat summit just before reaching a right-angle turn where the slope changed to a vertical cliff. This was afterwards called the Bloody Angle. Filing along the flat ground at the edge of the ridge, we had gone only about 50 yards further when from some bushes ahead there came a challenge in a foreign tongue. But they failed to give the password. *Honi! Honi! Honi!* (pronounced ho-ne with the accent on the first syllable) screamed the challengers. 'Australians, British, friends,' anything but the correct password

---

[79] AWM: 30 B1/22.
[80] Lieutenant William Ernest Elston, a 45-year-old farmer at the time of his re-enlistment, returned to Australia via Egypt after his release following the armistice in November 1918. He was promoted to the rank of captain before retiring from the army.
[81] AWM: 30 B1/22.

was given in reply by the two officers. 'Give the password Tipperary' we shouted to them. But all was in vain. We conjured in our minds the spectacle of two friendly units destroying each other through a misunderstanding.'[82]

Since it was dark, it was not possible to discern who was in the bushes. As Elston and McDonald walked forward to talk to the 'Indian' soldiers, they heard voices that abruptly ceased. At this moment, Lushington stepped forward and said that he wanted to go voluntarily, and since he knew Tamil, he could communicate with the Indians. Lushington moved through the bushes, attempting to speak and called out to Pope. When Pope approached the barely visible shadows in the dark, a scuffle broke out, and he threw himself down the slope. He immediately got up from where he had fallen and quickly climbed up. When he reached his company, he said, out of breath, 'These may be Turks, not Indians.' Despite calling out for McDonald, Elston, and Lushington, there was no response. The silence, which lasted a few seconds, was broken by Lushington's shout: 'Fire! These are Turks!'[83] Bullets flew from both sides, tearing through the bushes. What the Anzacs thought were Indian troops was actually the patrol that Avni had sent to Monash Valley around 17:00. Avni later described the incident:

> We were aware of the British presence in Korku Deresi [Monash Valley]. At one point, our patrol encountered a British platoon of about fifty men. Initially, the patrol aimed their rifles at them and demanded their surrender. The British, fearing a sudden attack, initially wished to surrender. However, upon realising the distance between them, they swiftly aimed their rifles and opened fire. In response, the patrol quickly took cover and returned fire, killing a good number of them. Others fled.'[84]

Captain McDonald, Lieutenant Elston and Private Lushington were among the first prisoners of the 57th Regiment. McDonald later recounted:

---

[82] T. H. Bolton 'A Forgotten Hero of Gallipoli.' *Western Mail*, 23 April 1953.
[83] T. H. Bolton 'A Forgotten Hero of Gallipoli.' *Western Mail*, 23 April 1953.
[84] CBA: 01000140-1.

> We could see Elston, in the dusk, talking with somebody. Almost immediately, a call came for a senior officer. The colonel started to move forward, but I went in his place calling as I went 'I'm the adjutant and I'll come.' I moved forward and a man kneeling covered me with his rifle. He had a scarf wrapped round his head, (resembling, very much, a puggaree) I raised one hand and walked towards him saying, 'I'm a British officer, I want your *burrashaid*.' He rose and put his rifle down. Immediately I was seized by two men who rose out of the undergrowth, and I was surrounded by quite a considerable party with fixed bayonets, some of whom started running to where the Colonel had been. I was thrown down and my revolver was taken from me. I was then taken quickly ahead where I joined Elston and Lushington, who were in a similar plight. We were then taken ahead to where an officer with some Turks was posted in a small hollow. I was searched and all my equipment and papers were taken away. Our men opened heavy fire on us and we were hurried away behind a hill where we found a considerable force of Turks. Turkish reinforcements were arriving at the time, with machine guns. I was questioned by a Turkish officer as to my name, rank, and unit, and they wanted to know also our brigade and division. I answered these in French.[85]

It was Avni who questioned McDonald, the most senior of the prisoners brought to the 57th Regiment headquarters. Avni asked in French about the names, ranks, regiments, divisions, and brigades of the prisoners, as well as the number of troops that had landed and the expected reinforcements. McDonald replied he was only a regimental officer and consequently knew nothing, but suggested there could be a force of 20,000 men. When asked if he knew the dispositions of the troops that had landed, McDonald replied, 'If I did, I should not be here.' Avni gave the following details in his report:

> Two British officers and a sergeant major were captured by the patrols in Korku Deresi [Monash Valley]. The prisoners were treated well and were questioned about their strength. It was understood that the enemy force at Arıburnu was around 20,000.

---

[85] National Archives of Australia, B2455, https://www.naa.gov.au/

The prisoners were handed over to Hasan Fehmi Efendi, imam[86] of the 3rd Battalion, who attacked the enemy fiercely among the men with a rifle in his hand and were sent to the division.[87]

Avni took McDonald's binoculars as a souvenir.[88] Later on, the prisoners, along with important documents such as maps, letters, and orders, were handed over to Hasan Fehmi, Imam of the 3/57th, and sent to Mustafa Kemal, who had arrived at Battleship Hill. Major İzzettin offered cigarettes to the prisoners. During a brief interrogation, it was learned that five brigades were assigned to Anzac sector. Of these, three brigades had landed that day, two had been decimated, and only one brigade remained intact. After questioning the prisoners, Kemal informed Esat at 23:30 that a captain, a lieutenant, and a private had been captured and would be sent to the corps. Due to the lack of available guards to accompany the prisoners, they had to wait at the division headquarters for a while longer.[89]

The prisoners were each given a hat by the Turks and taken to the 3rd Corps headquarters at Mal Tepe at 02:00. They were given food and tents and were allowed to rest. The person who questioned them on the morning was Major Kemal (Ohrili Kemal), the Head of the Operations

---

[86] İmams in the Ottoman Army held a role similar to that of British Army chaplains. Each battalion had an imam, while each regiment was assigned a müftü, who held a higher rank. While their primary duty was to provide religious guidance, they were sometimes required to assume command in the absence of officers. (t.n.)

[87] CBA: 01000140-1.

[88] Thirty years later, McDonald wished to visit the battlefield where he had fought, accompanied by his wife. He applied to the Turkish General Staff for permission. Lieutenant Colonel Tekin Arıburun, then a teacher at the Air Force Academy, arranged for the retired Anzac officer and his wife to visit the battlefield. Upon their return from Gallipoli, Tekin Arıburun hosted them at his home. While sitting in the living room, McDonald noticed a large photograph of Hüseyin Avni on the wall. He couldn't believe his eyes and excitedly said to his wife, 'It's this officer who took us prisoner!' Tekin Arıburun then revealed that the officer in the photo was his father. He opened a display case in the room and took out a bone-covered prayer book and a pair of binoculars. McDonald was astonished; the binoculars were his. These were the very binoculars Hüseyin Avni had taken from him when he was captured and brought to the headquarters in Kesik Dere (Mule Valley) on the evening of 25 April.

[89] Arzu Tunç et al., eds., *Çanakkale Muharebelerinde 19. Tümen Cerideleri, Vol. 2*, 49; Erkan-ı Harbiye Kaymakamı İzzettin, 'Çanakkale Muharebeleri Hatıralarından 12 Nisan 331 Günü' *Askerî Mecmua*, 10, (1336/1920).

Office of the 3rd Corps headquarters. The map of the Gallipoli Peninsula standing orders by General Ian Hamilton,

15. Captain McDonald's binoculars taken by Hüseyin Avni as a souvenir of war on 25 April. 'R. T. A. McDonald, 11.21.14' can be read on the binoculars and under its case. (Hüseyin Avni Tanman Collection)

the field message book, the pay book, and the letters from McDonald's family hidden among the pages of his pay book were examined and then sent to Esat. After the interrogation, the four prisoners, including Fred Ashton, a bugler from the 11th Battalion captured by the 27th Regiment, were transported to the town of Gallipoli on a steamer from Kilye. McDonald gives a description of the subsequent events:

> We were next interviewed, by Esat Paşa, He did not examine us but gave us a breakfast instead. We were then moved off to the coast, where we saw a considerable number of Turkish wounded being embarked and a considerable number of irregular troops being brought from the Asiatic shore in every sort of craft. We were mobbed by these irregulars, who went for us with their knives, our guard and some Turkish officers beat them off and we were put in

a tent under a very strong guard. We were embarked almost immediately on a ferry steamer and were sent to the seaport of Gallipoli. Observed great numbers of horse, guns and foot moving by road through Gallipoli. All well-equipped and first class troops – impossible to estimate numbers which were considerable. We were housed here and were given food.[90]

There Lushington, Ashton and French other ranks were separated from the officers.[91]

Day Two: 26 April 1915
The men, having fought tirelessly for 14 hours, were both hungry and exhausted. While food was being supplied from the depot at Bigalı, delivering it to the front at night proved difficult. Captain Ali Hayri, commander of the 3rd Battalion, suggested using the iron rations due to the lack of bread. Avni agreed, allowing for the use of one day's ration if necessary to keep the men from going hungry. At midnight, he reported the 57th Regiment's situation to the division commander:

> The casualties are quite high, but I could not get full information. Three officers were confirmed killed[92] and five wounded. We are very close to the enemy, and I am currently reconnoitring the ground around me. I will report back with more details, but we are far from your location. We have advanced beyond the point the enemy reached this morning and are now near the sea. We are attempting to establish contact with the battalions on our right and left. I can barely hold the front with the men I have. The 72nd Regiment on our left complaining that the enemy is digging trenches. The 72nd is isolated, and the enemy is in very broken terrain. If a well-organised unit is sent, we can unite with the 72nd Regiment and attack from the left flank. In any case, we need a

---

[90] AWM: 30 B1/22.
[91] Captain McDonald and Lieutenant Elston were sent first to İstanbul and then to the Afyon prison camp. Privates Lushington and Ashton were taken to the prison camp in Yeşilköy, İstanbul. After the armistice in 1918, they were all released and repatriated to Australia.
[92] These officers were 2nd Battalion 6th Company Commander Captain Hacı Mehmet, 3rd Battalion 11th Company Commander Captain Ahmet Avni, and 3rd Battalion 11th Company platoon commander Lieutenant Mehmet Sabri.

well-organised force. I only have one reserve company left.[93]

Kemal was more optimistic. He advised that the regiment should avoid getting so close to the front that they would be forced into a bayonet attack, stating that the Anzacs were on the verge of retreat and that they would launch an attack with all available reserves. He also mentioned that reinforcements from the corps would arrive within a few hours.[94] Thus, while the battalions used the cover of darkness to fortify their positions, the supply of ammunition and food continued until morning.

As dawn broke, it became evident that the Allied troops had not withdrawn but had instead positioned themselves along Russell's Top and Walker's Ridge. Despite several attacks throughout the night, the Anzacs remained firmly in place. The 57th Regiment was positioned at The Nek, as well as Chessboard and Quinn's Post. Except for the company guarding the regimental Colours, the entire regiment was no more than 200 metres away from the enemy. On the left flank, the Anzacs' attempt to advance had resulted in a retreat towards the woods in the rear.

16. The Sphinx and the Allied encampment.

---

[93] ATASE: BDH 5384-183-H2-1-5a.
[94] ATASE: BDH 5384-183-H2-1-5a.

At daybreak, the Allied navy began a heavy bombardment. With naval support, the Anzacs attempted to attack the 57th Regiment's positions with a force of more than a battalion, aiming for Conkbayırı via Battleship Hill. This attack was halted within an hour, thanks to Avni's bold interventions. Mustafa Kemal summarised the situation in his report to the corps as follows:

> The entire 77th Regiment and parts of the 27th Regiment's left flank have scattered, falling back on their own accord. The 57th Regiment on the right is also being overwhelmed by the enfilading fire from the enemy's superior infantry force and warships. The enemy has landed artillery. I am trying to continue defending as much as I can.'[95]

When it became difficult to hold the trenches due to the intense bombardment, some surviving soldiers began to retreat. In a note to the division at 08:02, Avni wrote,

> The enemy has begun to advance violently from both flanks. We are suffering casualties among officers and men. I have no reserves left. I will have to retreat slowly.

Kemal quickly responded:

> Try to hold your position. If you must, you can retreat east to the right of the 27th Regiment.[96]

Two companies of the 2nd Battalion of the 57th Regiment at Kabak Sırt were buried by explosions from shells hurled by warships, killing most of the men. The officers and men who survived this hellfire lost consciousness and hearing and would have to undergo treatment for a long time.[97] Witnessing this, other soldiers at The Nek also began to retreat. Avni immediately dispatched the 4th Company of the 1st Battalion at Baby 700, to intervene and stop the retreat, but they too were

---

[95] Reşat Hallı, Muhterem Saral, and Remzi Yiğitgüden, *Birinci Dünya Savaşı'nda Çanakkale Cephesi, Vol. 5, Book 2*, 84.
[96] ATASE: BDH 5384-183-H2-1-6a.
[97] Mustafa Kemal, *Arıburnu Muharebeleri Raporu*, 82.

unable to maintain their position amidst the ongoing bombardment. When the men he asked about the situation said, 'Sir, the enemy rushed us from the right,' Avni ordered the machine gun company to establish a defensive line on the ridge (Top Bayırı), immediately east of Baby 700, as a last resort. Due to the intense bombardment, the company could only take position on the relatively sheltered eastern slopes of the ridge. Avni then tasked the commander of the 2nd Battalion with rallying the retreating men and ensuring the orderly withdrawal of the left flank.[98] İzzettin later recounted the events:

> I was at the artillery battalion's observation post at Suyatağı, keeping watch and periodically visiting the observation post at Conkbayırı, where I had a clear view of the right of the front and Arıburnu beach. I maintained contact with the regiment commanders, received battle reports, and relayed the information and my observations to the division commander at Kemal Yeri [Scrubby Knoll] by phone. We had a telephone line between Kemal Yeri and Suyatağı, which we used to notify dispatch riders of our needs, but it broke down frequently. The attack began with intense rifle and machine gun fire echoing around us. Then the naval bombardment from the sea reached its peak. Numerous enemy shells dropped near Suyatağı, but most were falling inside Kör Dere behind us. Initially, the combat equipment and divisional ammunition column deployed there suffered considerable losses. They were only able to avoid further casualties by moving closer to the northern ridges of Suyatağı.[99]

The 57th Regiment was retreating gradually, and the terrain and dense scrub made it difficult to maintain order, causing the soldiers to scatter. As the right flank moved back towards Suyatağı, Avni personally went there to gather the dispersed soldiers and prevent a general retreat. He assembled the soldiers he found and established two posts: one between Conkbayırı and Suyatağı, and the other at the pass north of Conkbayırı, this effectively stopped the chaotic retreat and kept the men together.[100]

---

[98] CBA: 01000140-1.
[99] Erkan-ı Harbiye Kaymakamı İzzettin, 'Çanakkale Muharebeleri Hatıralarından 12 Nisan 331 Günü' *Askerî Mecmua*, Issue 10, Matbaayı Askeriye, İstanbul 1336.
[100] ATASE: BDH 5384-183-H2-1-6a; CBA: 01000140-1.

At 12:40, the 57th Regiment's withdrawal continued eastward. Meanwhile, many transport ships were approaching and leaving Arıburnu, with the landing proceeding rapidly. During this time, Avni wrote to the division, expressing his concern about a potential night attack by the Anzacs. He noted that his regiment was unable to take their positions, was isolated, and that he only had a single company from the 3rd Battalion of the 72nd Regiment with him.[101] The number of available men in the 57th Regiment had fallen to 500. Ten officers were wounded and nine had been killed. The loss of officers and sergeants further damaged the morale of the men. The battalions were intermixed, so only one battalion could be formed from the remaining soldiers, with two companies held in reserve. Because of the lack of officers, Avni appointed Hasan Fehmi, the imam of the 3rd Battalion, as the commander of these companies. He sent one company to the right flank as a reserve force and positioned the other two in the direction of Battleship Hill.[102]

Avni then called the division commander to explain the situation:

> If there is a desire for a strong attack on the enemy, I propose we get our forces organised first, they have been marching for 48 hours and are disorganised due to officer losses. Launching the attack with newly arrived fresh troops would be the best move. So far, we've lost nine officers killed and ten wounded. Casualties among the men are high, but I am still awaiting comprehensive information.[103]

Kemal quickly replied by dispatching two companies to Avni's command and reassured him that additional reinforcements were on their way. He requested the regiment to hold their position for the time being.[104]

'The Gallantry Displayed is Admirable'

Sunset gave the regiments a chance to reorganise. Ammunition was replenished with supplies from Kocadere village, and hot meals were distributed. The defensive lines were also fortified in the moonlight. At 19:07, Kemal sent a message to the 57th Regiment, praising their

---

[101] ATASE: BDH 5384-183-H2-1-7.
[102] CBA: 01000140-1.
[103] ATASE: BDH 5384-183-H2-1-7, BDH 5384-183-H2-1-7a.
[104] ATASE: BDH 5384-183-H2-1-7a.

bravery: 'The gallantry displayed in your successful attacks and fight against a superior enemy over the past two days is truly admirable. Congratulations to all of you.' He also added that another attack would be launched at dawn.[105] However, Avni did not see eye to eye with Kemal about the attack:

> To the Division Command
> 26/27 April 1915
>
> At sunset today, an order was received from the division regarding an operation to be carried out against the enemy at dawn. However, it is hoped that there will be a change in our current situation. The regiment had fought continuously until morning, and the battalions were completely mixed together from the day's battle. With the last reserve company from the 2nd Battalion sent forward to counter the enemy's fierce attacks, the regiment found itself in a grave situation. The front was expanding everywhere, and news was coming from all directions that the enemy was pushing on. The regiment awaited the arrival of two battalions of reserves from division, but our hope was in vain.
>
> As the regiment received orders to retreat, we opened heavy fire to mask our withdrawal. Following this, the enemy began to retreat across our entire front. Only one company on the right flank faced resistance. When we reinforced this company with the newly formed 4th Company, the enemy heavily bombarded our right flank, burying two companies (one from 2nd Battalion, other from 3rd Battalion) in the trenches. No survivors. The reinforcing 4th Company, seeing this, ceased firing and retreated due to the enemy's encircling movement, which quickly turned into a rout. The bombardment continued violently across the entire front, and the rout of one company spread to the others. Despite our efforts, the regiment could not be held in place.
>
> The regiment, initially in a strong position, fell back under heavy enemy bombardment. The withdrawal was only stopped at the line where we started our first attack, gathering only about 150–300 soldiers. The regiment remained disorganised until evening, with

---

[105] ATASE: BDH 5384-183-H2-1–8.

only two companies of a hundred men each. The morale of these men is broken, and they are in a disordered state. We could not establish contact with the 20th Regiment until this evening. We learned from a private we sent that only the 3rd Battalion of this regiment was positioned behind the artillery as a reserve.

Given this situation, it is obvious that the regiment cannot participate in tomorrow's operation. The soldiers cannot fight effectively unless they are put into order. Nine of our already few officers have been killed, and ten wounded. There are many casualties among the corporals and sergeants as well. If this regiment joins the attack, the disorder may spread to other units. Therefore, I respectfully request the division commander to carry out the operation with another unit, and give the 57th Regiment time to rest and reorganise at the second line.

The regiment's commander Avni Bey injured his foot during the retreat and could not come to the phone, so he sent me as his proxy. Ata

Commander of the 2nd Battalion 57th Regiment

Since the order given today must be executed by dawn and we are unable to carry it out, we are waiting for the commander's response on whether he can authorise it. Our lines have not yet been handed over to any other unit.[106]

Kemal agreed with the requests, reinforcing the 57th Regiment with two companies from the 3rd Battalion of the 77th Regiment. He pulled the 57th back from the front line and assigned the regiment as the reserve for the arriving 64th Regiment.[107] Kemal also sent İzzettin to assess the situation on the ground. Touring the front of the 57th Regiment, İzzettin found the terrain highly challenging. However, he believed it was unlikely that the Allies would attempt a breakout in such difficult terrain. Meanwhile, the regiment was positioned about 500 metres from the

---

[106] ATASE: BDH 5384-183-H2-1-8, BDH 5384-183-H2-1-8a, BDH 5384-183-H2-1-9.
[107] Arzu Tunç et al., eds., *Çanakkale Muharebelerinde 19. Tümen Cerideleri, Vol. 2*, 73.

Anzac line. Despite being scattered, the arrival of two companies from the 77th Regiment had helped restore the spirits.[108]

By the end of the second day, the 19th Division's deployment at Anzac was: The 57th Regiment held positions on Battleship Hill and the ridge to the south, blocking the route towards Conkbayırı. The 27th Regiment occupied Mortar Ridge and blocked the Mal Tepe-Eceabat direction. The 72nd Regiment was on the southernmost flank, at Pine Ridge, while two companies from its 3rd Battalion served as divisional reserve at Conkbayırı. Two companies from the 3/77th were positioned in the Azmak Dere-Ejelmer Bay region. The 2/27th remained at Kaba Tepe. Some of the division artillery was in Suyatağı, but most of it was on the eastern slopes of the Third Ridge (Gun Ridge) around Scrubby Knoll. In addition, a mixed light battery was deployed at Kaba Tepe and a four-gun siege battery was deployed at Palamutluk Sırtı (Olive Grove) to the south of Kaba Tepe.[109]

'Success Comes from God'
While the Anzac Corps kept bringing soldiers, guns, ammunition, and supplies ashore, the 3rd Corps deployed newly arrived field guns in different places to prevent further reinforcements and, most importantly, try to drive the Anzacs into the sea. Meanwhile, Avni spent the night reorganising his regiment. The 1/57th had taken such heavy losses that it had to be disbanded, and had hardly any officers left. The remaining men were merged into two battalions, the 2nd and 3rd. In preparation for the morning attack, a silent advance was made first to Baby 700 and then towards The Nek. Reinforcements consisting of two infantry regiments and a mountain battalion had now arrived.

According to the divisional order issued at 05:00, the 64th Regiment would advance on the right flank, starting from the 57th Regiment's position, with the 57th in close support. The 19th Division Mountain Artillery Battery would target the landing site, while the mountain batteries of 7th and 9th Divisions would also provide support for the attack.[110]

---

[108] Arzu Tunç et al., eds., *Çanakkale Muharebelerinde 19. Tümen Cerideleri*, Vol. 2, 77.
[109] Reşat Hallı, Muhterem Saral, and Remzi Yiğitgüden, *Birinci Dünya Savaşı'nda Çanakkale Cephesi*, Vol. 5, Book 2, 85.
[110] ATASE: BDH 5384-183-H2-1-9a, BDH 5384-183-H2-1-10.

Once again, the task had fallen to the 57th Regiment when the deployment of the 64th Regiment to the front was delayed. Avni ordered his 2nd and 3rd battalions to attack at dawn. The 3/57th attacked from the right, and the 2/57th from the left towards Monash Valley. At 07:00, the 1st and 3rd Battalions of the 64th Regiment finally arrived at the front. Avni had the 1/64th attack from the right towards Walker's Ridge, while the 3/64th was sent directly to the left of the 2/57th via Mortar Ridge. Subsequently, two companies from the 3rd Battalion of the 20th Regiment arrived behind Mortar Ridge. Meanwhile, the division's batteries began pouring shrapnel over the beach.[111] The 1/64th had taken cover in trenches previously dug by the 57th Regiment to protect themselves from Allied infantry fire, artillery, and naval bombardment.

To maintain the attack's momentum, Avni ordered the battalion to leave the trenches. However, the battalion remained inactive and suffered heavy losses under the bombardment.[112] The attack had eventually come to a standstill. At 14.55, bugle calls were heard everywhere, and the attack resumed across the entire front. After 16:45, reports indicated that the Anzac troops had pushed into Monash Valley. This was confirmed by a report jointly signed by Captain Ata and Captain Ali Hayri, the two battalion commanders of the 57th Regiment, and Osman Nuri, the commander of the 1/64th: 'The enemy has been repelled from our front. With sufficient force, we should be able to drive him into the sea.'[113]

Allied warships, using seaplane observation, bombarded Turkish positions throughout the day to protect their troops. The fire was so intense that 'nothing could live above ground in a section fired at.'[114] At around 17:25, the attack renewed again with all available forces. Only one trench was captured on the Allied right flank. Although the final objective was not reached, Avni remained hopeful: 'The men are fighting spiritedly. The battalions that joined my regiment are fighting as if they were competing with each other. Success comes from God.'[115] The

---

[111] ATASE: BDH 5384-183-H2-1-10.
[112] CBA: 01000140-1.
[113] ATASE: BDH 5384-183-H2-1-11, BDH 5334-183-H2-1-11a.
[114] Ellis Ashmead Bartlett, *Çanakkale Gerçeği*. Trans. Yüzbaşı Rahmi, Ed. Muzaffer Albayrak (İstanbul: Yeditepe Yayınevi, 2007), 122.
[115] ATASE: BDH 5384-183-H2-1-12.

reinforcements that arrived had rekindled the spirit of the men and İzzettin later recounted:

> The men of the 57th Regiment fought with a special kind of enthusiasm, driven by their aspiration for martyrdom and the belief in their passage to heaven. After the attacks, we found laundry scattered across the ground. These were old, soiled clothes discarded by religious heroes who sought to enter heaven in clean attire. They had donned clean underwear before the fight. Such warriors could indeed be revered as veterans until their final embrace of martyrdom. The spirit of the 57th Regiment was incredibly high, thanks to Major Avni Bey and his officers, who focused heavily on this aspect before the battle. The regiment frequently gathered for prayers in the training squares of Çamburnu at Eceabat, igniting a fervour of faith within both officers and men.'[116]

As the evening sun cast long shadows over the battlefield, two fresh companies from the 3rd Battalion of the 20th Regiment arrived. They were immediately dispatched to reinforce the 1/64th opposite Walker's Ridge. By 18:15, the sound of bugles pierced the air once more. Another attack was launched on the right flank. Simultaneously, the divisional reserve, the 33rd Regiment, moved into position on the left of the 57th Regiment. Avni himself came to the front line to command the battle. He encouraged his men, stating that the Allies' defensive power was weakened and that they should attack without hesitation, no matter what, in order to dismantle the remaining enemy force. Despite their fervour, the attacks failed to break through. Avni had the attack renewed with bugle calls once more. The soldiers repeatedly charged the deep, steep cliffs of Monash Valley, but were unable to descend the cliffs and were eventually forced to retreat under machine gun fire.[117]

One of these machine guns, positioned on the eastern edge of Russell's Top, was captured by the 3/57, allowing the battalion to advance as far as Shrapnel Valley. However, the 2/57 and 3/77 on the left could not descend into the valley in front of them because of intense machine gun

---

[116] Erkan-ı Harbiye Kaymakamı İzzettin, 'Çanakkale Muharebeleri Hatıralarından 12 Nisan 331 Günü' *Askerî Mecmua*, Issue 10, Matbaayı Askeriye, İstanbul 1336.
[117] ATASE: BDH 5384-183-H2-1-12a, BDH 5384-183-H2-1-13.

fire. Meanwhile, the 3/72 veered to the right and got mixed up with the 2/57 before they could attack the sandbag-fortified Anzac lines directly ahead.[118] Avni wrote in his report,

> I started the attack with bugle calls everywhere and hit the enemy with all my strength. A trench and a machine gun were captured on the right flank. We are currently continuing our attack. The enemy has been partially surrounded from the right. Success comes from God. Hopefully, a result will be achieved tonight.[119]

During the night, some of the troops managed to descend from Quinn's Post to Monash Valley. Although the first line trenches at Walker's Ridge were captured, the attackers couldn't advance any further. The attack, launched under heavy machine gun and rifle fire, saw battalions become disorganised again due to the darkness and the loss of officers and sergeants. The scattered attacking lines, unable to see ahead, mistakenly fired at each other, believing they were engaging the enemy. For this reason, Captain Ata had to order the advance with bayonet only.[120] The dispersed units were forced to remain in their positions for the night and had to be reorganised.

At midnight, the situation was critical. At 01:10 on 28 April, Lieutenant Colonel Şevki, commander of the 33rd Regiment, Major Saip, commander of the 77th Regiment, and Major Münir, commander of the 72nd Regiment, sent a joint report to the division. They explained that the desired success could not be achieved in the attacks due to the Allies attaching great importance to fortifying their lines, many officers were wounded, and that more forces were needed in any case.[121] Avni and the commander of the 64th Regiment, Major Servet, also made a similar statement to the division commander in another joint report:

> To the 19th Division Command
> 28 April 1915, 02:40

---

[118] CBA: 01000140-1.
[119] Burhan Sayılır, *Çanakkale Muharebelerinde 57. Piyade Alayı*, (İstanbul: Bağcılar Belediyesi), 211.
[120] ATASE: BDH 5384-183-H2-1-13a.
[121] Mustafa Kemal, *Arıburnu Muharebeleri Raporu*, 44.

Despite exhaustive efforts, our forces along the entire line are worn out, with units now intermingled and unable to advance. This is mainly due to the high toll of killed and wounded.

Regrettably, the men seem demoralised overall. All reserve forces have been depleted. There is a strong belief that deploying a well-organised force the size of a battalion would be sufficient to push the enemy back. We are hopeful that if the firing ceases everywhere and a fresh battalion is brought forward before morning, the final objective can be achieved. Otherwise, it is not possible to separate and mobilise such a mixed group of men in the dark.

The enemy is now completely encircled on three sides, with their rear facing the sea. His position in front of us is very steep and fortified. Since evening, we have only been able to capture only one enemy trench on the right flank. Urgent measures are required to address these pressing challenges.

Major Avni	Major Servet
Commander	Commander
of the 57th Regiment	of the 64th of Regiment[122]

Throughout the night, Avni and Servet commanded their troops from a place immediately behind the front line. Efforts were focused on deepening the trenches as much as possible and replenishing the depleted ammunition supplies. The fighting went on, especially on the 2/57th front. Of the five officers remaining in this battalion, two were killed, and three were wounded. As dawn broke, Mule Valley revealed itself filled with wounded. Although they received initial treatment from medical units, many had to endure prolonged waits behind the front line because of the shortage of transport vehicles and stretchers. The sight of wounded lying on the ground profoundly affected the morale of the men. Additionally, there was an urgent need to collect and bury the men who remained on the battlefield. Battalion commanders urgently emphasised the need for immediate burial of the fallen.[123]

---

[122] ATASE: BDH 5384-183-H2-1-14; Mustafa Kemal, *Arıburnu Muharebeleri Raporu*, 45.
[123] ATASE: BDH 5384-183-H2-1-14, BDH 5384-183-H2-1-15.

At 06:00, in his reply to the report sent by the 57th and 64th Regiments during the night, Kemal expressed his appreciation for their sacrifices. He instructed that the enemy not be allowed to advance a single step and that any gains be preserved. Additionally, he ordered the command of both regiments to be combined under Avni.[124]

In response to Kemal's order, Avni replied at 07:05 in the morning, assuring him that their positions were firmly held and that 'they would maintain them to the last breath, even if only one soldier remained.' That morning, 8 battleships, 2 cruisers, and 22 transport ships from the Allied fleet were observed off the coast of Arıburnu, with fresh troops continuing to come ashore. To counter further Allied operations, battalions were re-formed from the remaining officers and men. Captain Kadri remained as the only officer in the 2nd Battalion. Additionally, three officers from the 10th Company of the 20th Regiment, which reinforced the battalion, had been wounded.

Captain Ata requested that the 2nd Company of the 57th Regiment, guarding the regimental Colours and artillery, join the fighting. The company commander, Lieutenant Hasan,[125] left two squads to guard the Colours, which was with the 3/64th, and took the rest of the company to the front line.

Kemal decided to divide his front into three groups to facilitate command and control: Right Flank, Centre, and Left Flank. The newly established operational groups were as follows:
    Right Flank: Major Avni (57th Regiment, 64th Regiment, 3/72nd)
    Centre: Lieutenant Colonel Şefik (27th Regiment, a battalion from the 33rd Regiment)
    Left Flank: Lieutenant Colonel Şevki (72nd Regiment, 77th Regiment, 33rd Regiment, 125th Regiment)[126]

Five minutes after receiving the order, Avni informed the division that 'all the forces on the Right Flank were on the firing line, and the

---

[124] Mustafa Kemal, *Arıburnu Muharebeleri Raporu*, 47.
[125] Killed in action on 22 May 1915.
[126] ATASE: BDH 5384-183-H2-1-16.

defensive measures were not enough since there were no reserves left' and requested 'one battalion to be sent as a reserve force.' Thereupon, the 10th and 11th Companies from 3/77th were assigned to the Right Flank and sent to the north of Baby 700. Additionally, two of the regiment's machine guns were placed on this flank. Meanwhile, the weapons from the wounded and fallen along and behind the front line were collected and sent to the weapons depot in Bigalı village.[127]

The Anzacs kept up intense artillery and infantry fire all night. Most especially a gun behind MacLaurin's Hill poured on shrapnel until morning. Because of the high number of wounded, overnight the medical units ran out of bandages.[128] Both sides spent the night entrenching under fire. The shallow trenches, hastily dug like narrow channels, were not deep enough to offer proper protection. For this reason, Avni wanted to make sure his troops weren't all kept at the firing line. Thus, the battalions placed two companies at the front and kept the remaining two in the rear as a reserve. As the sun rose on 29 April, the intensity of the battle diminished. However, the Turkish divisional artillery kept battering the Anzac positions. At one point, reports were received that a group of Anzac soldiers had abandoned their trenches under the intense shelling. Some of them waved flags, pretending to surrender, hoping to divert the artillery fire and lure the Turks out of their trenches. The Turkish soldiers dashed forward, eliminated the flag-wavers, and captured the flags.

At 13:45 in the afternoon, an Allied attack was successfully repelled. Kemal expressed his satisfaction, stating, 'I am very pleased that you repelled the enemy's attack. Preserving our current situation depends on our right flank continuing the effort and sacrifice it has shown thus far.'

Acknowledging the delicate situation of the right flank, Kemal had positioned another battalion behind the regiment's own reserve as a divisional reserve to counter the threat of the Allies turning the right

---

[127] CBA: 01000140-1; Arzu Tunç et al., eds., *Çanakkale Muharebelerinde 19. Tümen Cerideleri, Vol. 2*, 115.
[128] ATASE: BDH 5384-183-H2-1-16a.

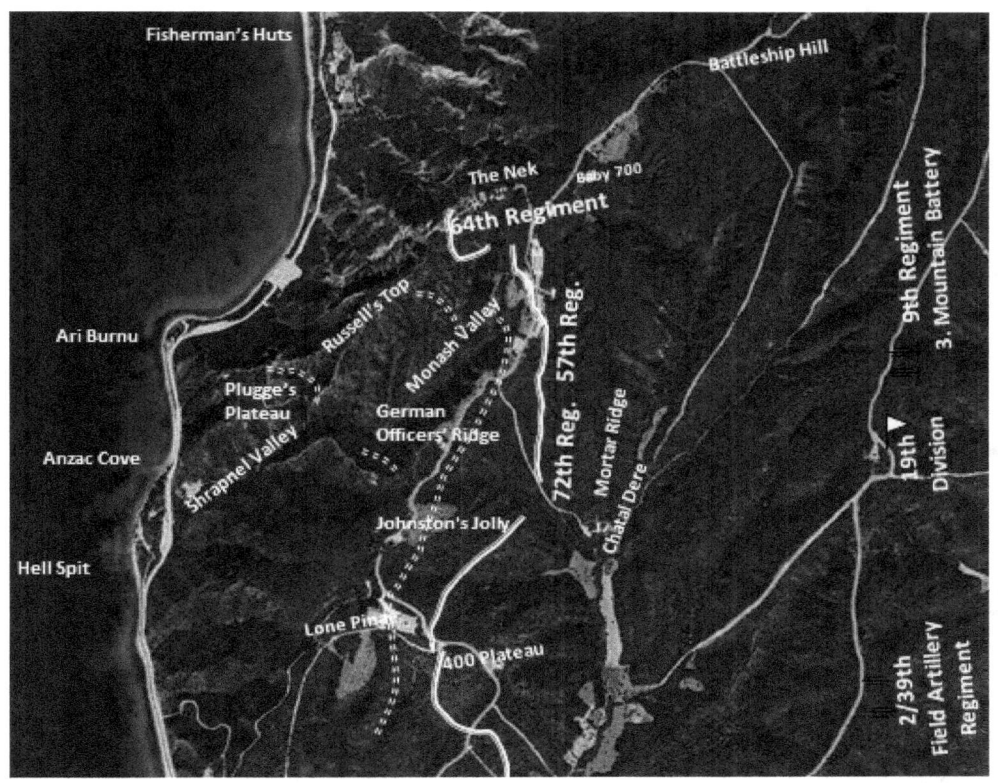

17. Situation of the 57th Regiment and other units on 28 April.

flank. Additionally, five battalions of infantry, machine guns, and some artillery were on the way.[129]

In the divisional order sent to all units on the evening of 29 April, Kemal stated that the arrival of these fresh forces would enable them to deliver a decisive blow to the Allies and added:

> In order to receive the well-deserved reward of your exemplary heroism for five days and five nights, I request you to continue your efforts to strengthen your position tonight to ensure the communication, command and control of your troops and to keep

---

[129] ATASE: BDH 5384-183-H2-1-19.

your reserve forces in a state where they can be used immediately when necessary. To provide your men with as much rest as possible, the officers must personally inspect the troops tonight to form an opinion.[130]

Upon receiving Kemal's order, Right Flank Commander Avni swiftly issued instructions for the defence of his sector to all units under his command. Instructions included fortifying trenches and creating reserve forces after deploying sufficient troops on the front line. Avni emphasised the prompt care for the wounded at dressing stations and their subsequent transfer to hospitals. He also stressed the collection and return of rucksacks belonging to fallen and surviving soldiers found scattered along roads and in forests by each unit. Avni strictly ordered the removal of dead or wounded immediately, especially taking advantage of the cover of darkness at night.[131]

Lieutenant Patterson's Prayer Book
Receiving the order to collect the dead and wounded, the 2/57th promptly set to work. On the first day, it was this battalion which had confronted the Anzacs advancing up onto Conkbayırı, launching an attack from Hill 161 towards Battleship Hill. Four days later, during the removal of the dead and wounded, they discovered the body of an Australian officer. Among his possessions were two maps and a prayer book, which Captain Ata collected. Ata inscribed on the back of one map: 'Note the stains of enemy's dirty blood and the lines drawn with a blue pen,' and passed it on to Avni. Avni examined the maps and found the name of the officer written in the upper left corner of 'Gallipoli Peninsula Map Number 1: Lieutenant Penistan James Patterson, 12th Battalion, 3rd Australian Infantry Brigade.'

The map contained various notes in the legend section and at the bottom left. Avni wrote a note on the back of the map addressed to the division commander:

> To esteemed commander of our Nineteenth Division as a humble souvenir: The Gallipoli Map Number 1, which was taken from the enemy officer captured by the Fifty-Seventh Regiment, who

---

[130] ATASE: BDH 5384-183-H2-1-19, BDH 5384-183-H2-1-19a.
[131] ATASE: BDH 5384-183-H2-1-20.

repulsed the enemy who landed at Arıburnu on the Gallipoli Peninsula, all the way to the beach on 25 April 1915.

Commander of the Right Flank and the 57th Regiment
Major Avni

Although Avni at first thought that the map was taken from a captured officer, he wrote a second note before sending it to the division commander:

To the Division Command
29 April 1915
From the southeast of Cesaret Tepe [The Nek]

I have the honour to present to our esteemed commander the maps numbered 1 and 3 of Gallipoli and Çanakkale, as a valuable and glorious historical souvenir. These have been found on one of the British army officers, many of whom were driven to the beach and killed by our regiment on the day the enemy landed troops.

Commander of the Right Flank and the 57th Regiment
Major Avni'[132]

Kemal was pleased with this present and decided to send it to Esat Paşa. He wrote a note next to Avni's: '30 April 1915. It is seen fit to present this souvenir to our esteemed corps commander Esat Paşa on behalf of the entire corps.'

---

[132] ATASE: BDH 5384-183-H2-1-19a.

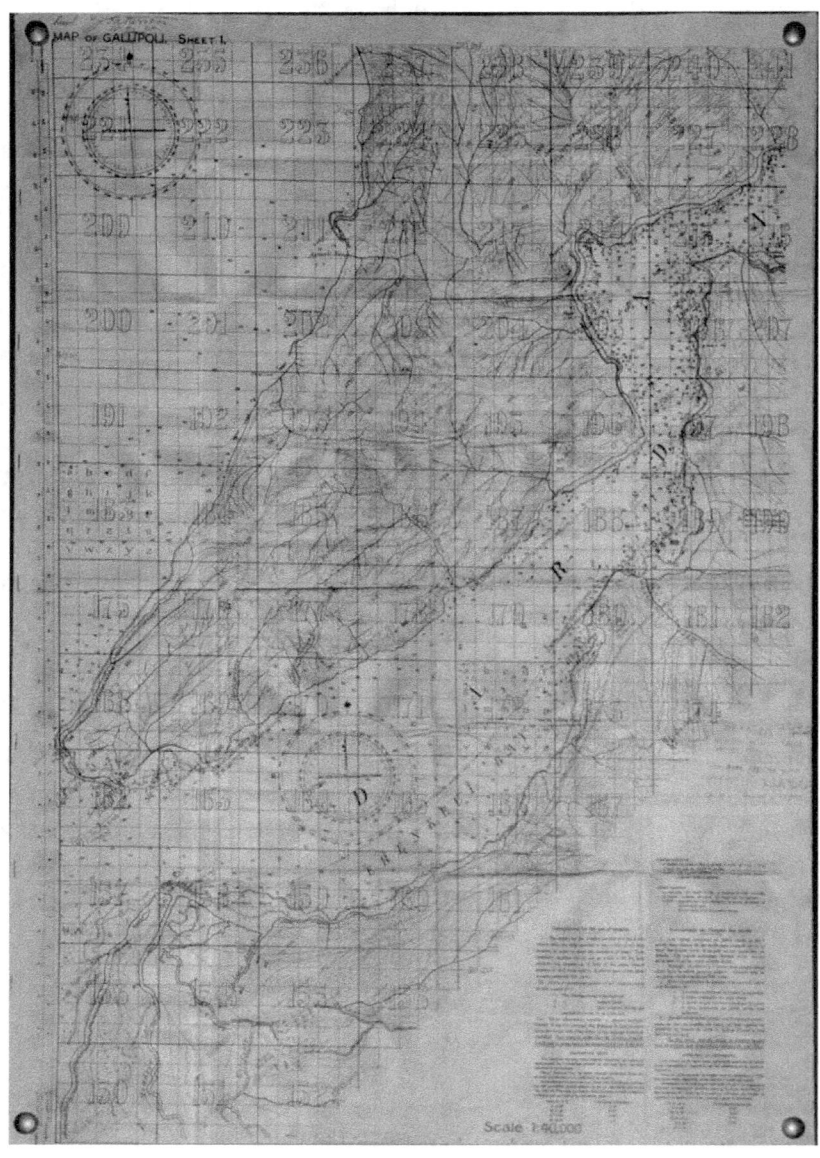

18. Lieutenant Patterson's map, presented by Avni to Kemal. (Turkish National Defence University Archive)

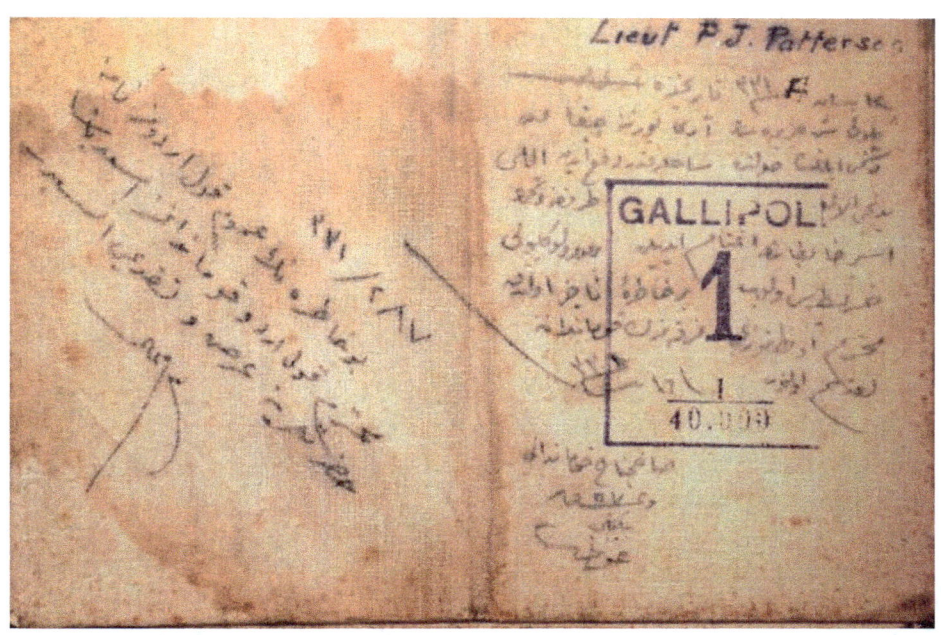

19. Notes on the map written by Avni and Kemal.

Avni kept Patterson's prayer book as a souvenir. The cover bore the signatures of five people and the date 7 December 1913. Four of the signatures, which were legible, belonged to James, G. Robinson, John F. Reading, and F. Rowlings.[133] These soldiers were all members of the 3rd Australian Brigade, having departed from Australia on the same ship and date, and were likely friends. G. Robinson and F. Rowlings emerged unscathed, while John F. Reading was wounded in the hand and foot on the first day.

---

[133] George Alfred Robinson, born in Adelaide in 1883, worked as a cook before the war. He enlisted on 19 August 1914, and served as a signaller at the 10th Battalion HQ.
John Forrest Reading, born in Reading, Bunbury, was a clerk before enlisting on 19 August 1914. Lance Corporal in E Company, 10th Battalion. He sustained wounds to his feet and wrists between 25–29 April and was subsequently evacuated to Alexandria on 30 April and later transferred to England.
Frederick Rowlings, born in 1894 in Servicetown, worked as a porter before the war. He served as a Private in C Company of the 11th Battalion. Due to various illnesses, he was removed from the front on 18 July 1915.

Patterson was part of the 1,500-man covering force that spearheaded the landings at 04:30 on 25 April. Leading his men, he ascended Walker's Ridge and advanced towards Battleship Hill where they were confronted by the 2/57th, who had arrived from Conkbayırı around 11:00. The 2/57th

20. Lieutenant Penistan James Patterson. (AWM H15819)

opened up with heavy rifle fire from about 320 metres away. Patterson and his party of 30 men moved northwest of the hill to provide support. It was during this engagement that Patterson was killed, between Battleship Hill and Baby 700.

This prayer book was likely given to Patterson by his father, a priest, in 1913, during his final year at Duntroon, possibly as a graduation gift. Patterson, known for his religious nature, marked the date of that day, 7 December 1913, inside the book. After his father's death in 1914, Patterson kept the prayer book with him. As a lieutenant in C Company of the 12th Battalion, he was first sent to Alexandria and then to LemNos. to prepare for the landing. While on the island, he was responsible for training scouts. It is believed that Robinson, Reading, and Rowlings were among the soldiers he trained, and they signed the prayer book as a souvenir. Patterson had bookmarked the page of the prayer book he was reading before boarding the pinnace or before he got ashore. His final prayer on that page, which he may have repeated until the last moments of his life, ends with these words: Oh Lord, we are ready and willing to pardon every one who has offended us. Yes, we pardon and wish well to all; and we hope to hear Thee say to us in our last moments: 'To-day shalt Thou be with me in Paradise.'[134]

---

[134] Luke 23:43.

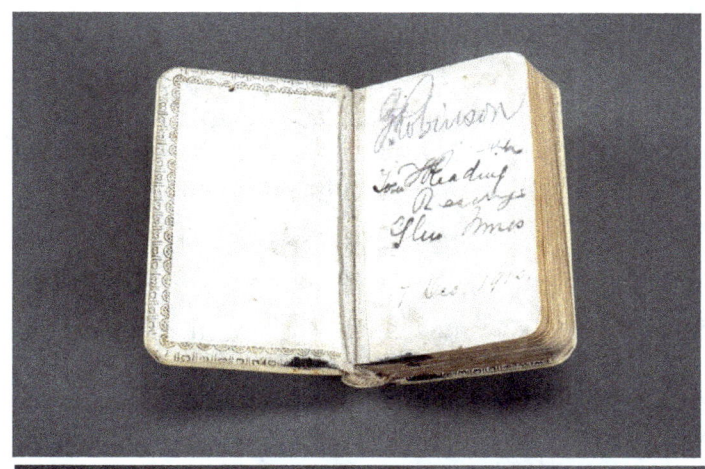

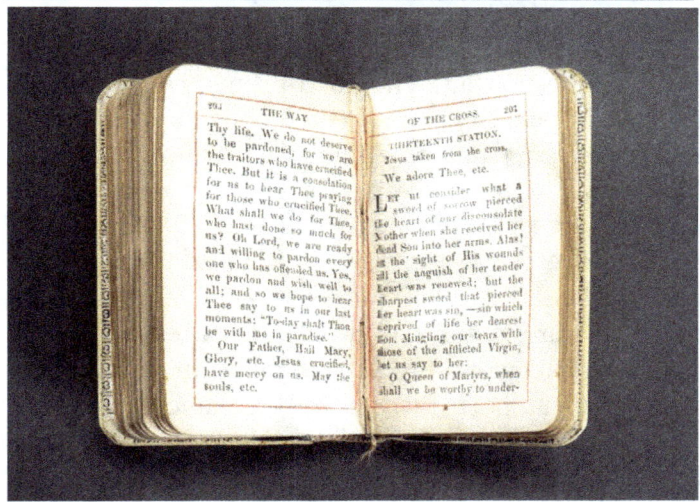

21. The prayer book found on Lieutenant Patterson on 29 April. The signatures of James Patterson and his comrades can be seen on the first page. (Hüseyin Avni Tanman Collection)

After the Campaign, a captain in charge of the archive records sent a letter to Patterson's mother, dated 18 March 1916, describing her son:

> Lieut. P. J. Patterson was gazetted to the Australian Imperial Force on the 15th August 1914 and posted to the 12th Battalion. Patterson was appointed Platoon Commander of No.1 Platoon. In addition,

he was responsible for the training of the Battalion Scouts, and they attained a high standard of efficiency under his control. His personality was a strong one, and his presence in the Battalion had undoubtedly a good effect on the Junior Officers. His tact and unfailing courtesy to all made an example for all Officers. While the 3rd Brigade was waiting at LemNos. Island (4 March to 12 April, 1915) Lieutenant Patterson's time was specially devoted to scout training.

He landed with the 12th Battalion on Gallipoli on Sunday 25 April 15. He came ashore in the first tow from the T.B. Destroyer *Ribble* (to which boat HQ and 'A' Coy. 12th Battalion had been transferred from H. M. Troopship *Devanha*). The boats from this tow beached at a point north of Anzac Cove, opposite Walker's Ridge; 'A' Coy. or portion of it No.1 Platoon being included, moved at once to the top of Walker's Ridge in the direction of Sari Bair. They had been subjected to rifle, machine gun and shrapnel fire between the troopship and the shore and when landing. During temporary halt on Walker's Ridge, the units on the left flank attempted to reorganise and also dug in to strengthen their position. Attacks were made on this flank by the Turkish Force and in order to assist the extreme left flank troops, the reorganised portions of 12th Battalion (portions of 'A' and 'D' Coys were here) moved forward again during the early afternoon. Lieut. Patterson was killed during this advance when leading his platoon. His action throughout has been marked by the same coolness and courage which had been a feature of his whole career in the 12th Battalion. His loss to the Battalion was a severe one; he was beloved by all ranks and all felt that they had lost a personal friend.'[135]

The title of Patterson's prayer book was/is *Flowers of Piety, Devotions and Prayers*. It is a pocket-sized prayer book with gilded page edges, printed in Austria in 1900. After Avni's death, this book was included among his personal belongings sent to home.

---

[135] https://recordsearch.naa.gov.au/SearchNRetrieve/Interface/ViewImage.aspx?B=8010260

Hüseyin Avni Receives Decoration

There was no action beyond rifle fire from both sides until the morning of 30 April 1915. When the sun rose, it revealed that the Allies had deepened their trenches, raised their parapets with sandbags, and reinforced them with timbers to prevent collapse. During the night, they had also dug closer to the right flank, nearing the 3/72nd front. In response, the 3/64th was moved from reserve and positioned behind the right flank, taking the place of the companies of the 77th Regiment. These companies were then tasked with entrenching north of the ridge west of Baby 700 and continuously monitoring the region from Sazli Dere onward.[136]

Despite the six days of attacks, the Allies couldn't be pushed into the sea and managed to consolidate their positions using the rugged terrain to their advantage. Kemal formulated a new plan of attack to dislodge the Allied troops. Accordingly, the strongest, the central, sector would be dealt with first, followed by a general assault to drive the entire force into the sea. In preparation for the offensive, two 1:25,000 scale maps prepared by the 3rd Corps were delivered to Avni at 06:25 in the morning. Kemal instructed that one copy remain with Avni, while the other be marked with trenches and sent back to the division.[137] During the meeting with the regimental commanders at Scrubby Knoll, the plan for the next day's attack was finalised and presented to Esat. Upon reviewing the plan, Esat remarked, 'I find the arrangements you have made for tomorrow morning's attack on the enemy appropriate.' He concluded his approval with the words, 'May God grant success.'[138]

The attack was scheduled to commence at 05:00 in the morning, starting with an artillery bombardment directed at targets personally designated by Kemal. Subsequently, the left and centre forces would assault the Allied right flank, which held significant dominance over the sea. Engineer companies would clear the Allies' entanglements, and dismounted cavalry elements would be dispatched to conduct reconnaissance across various sectors of the front. A surprise awaited Avni at the meeting at Scrubby Knoll – in recognition of his diligence

---

[136] CBA: 01000140-1.
[137] ATASE: BDH 5384-183-H2-1-20a.
[138] Arzu Tunç et al., eds., *Çanakkale Muharebelerinde 19. Tümen Cerideleri*, Vol. 2, 158.

and sacrifice during the relentless day and night fighting, he was awarded the Silver Liyakat Medal with Swords[139]. It was none other than Kemal who presented the medal with his sincere congratulations:

> To the 57th Regiment Command
> 30 April 1915, 15:30
>
> In recognition of your dedicated and diligent efforts, the Corps Command has sent you a Silver Liyakat Medal with Swords on behalf of the Sultan. I extend my sincere congratulations to you and expect that you will continue your selfless service, which is demonstrated in various ways every moment, by effectively leading in the ongoing day and night combat. Please promptly notify the deserving officers and other ranks under your command who are eligible to receive the War Medal, Imtiyaz Medal, and Liyakat Medal.
>
> Lieutenant Colonel Mustafa Kemal'[140]

'Never Surrender a Single Inch of Land to the Enemy'

The operation on 1 May commenced at 05:00 with a vigorous bombardment by Turkish batteries. Two mountain batteries positioned at Suyatağı targeted Russell's Top and the landing piers, while two others north of Scrubby Knoll aimed at Lone Pine and Johnston's Jolly. Additionally, two mountain batteries south of Scrubby Knoll fired at Steele's and Courtney's Posts. Field guns also contributed to the barrage across the Anzac position.[141] Under Avni's command, the right flank forces were positioned at The Nek and west of Mule Valley. The Central Group occupied Mortar Ridge, while the Left Flank Group was positioned at Johnston's Jolly and Lone Pine. Meanwhile, on the right flank, Avni impatiently awaited the designated attack time by phone. At 06:30, orders were finally issued for the 3/72nd and 3/57th Battalions to commence their assault, with the 2/57th in support.[142] The 3/72nd was

---

[139] The 'Medal of Merit' was the Ottoman Army's second-highest medal, available in both gold and silver versions.
[140] ATASE: BDH 5384-183-H2-1-22.
[141] Mustafa Kemal, *Arıburnu Muharebeleri Raporu*, 56–57.
[142] ATASE: BDH 5384-183-H3-1-1.

tasked with capturing a sandbag-fortified trench directly opposite, but the intense machine gun fire prevented the battalion from advancing into the

22. Hüseyin Avni's Silver Liyakat Medal with Swords and its patent. (Hüseyin Avni Tanman Collection)

trench, forcing them to descend into the gully. Avni then directed the 2nd Battalion to take the trench, but their efforts were also unsuccessful. Subsequently, another company from the 3/57th was deployed, but they too were scattered under heavy fire. Avni then ordered a company from 1/64th to attack, but they were also unable to make headway due to heavy machine gun fire. The Allied ships had now come into play, and the attack was checked across the front due to their overwhelming fire.

On the Monash Valley front, the 2/57th and 3/57th were unable to approach closer than 500 metres to the Anzac position. Despite the 14th Regiment advancing 200 metres towards its objective in the centre, it could proceed no further due to the fire from numerous enemy machine guns at Steele's Post. Additionally, under heavy bombardment from the ships, the 3/20th was unable to make any headway. Despite successive attacks launched under bugle calls, the fighting largely subsided by 18:00. Plans were made for a night attack, requiring time to reorganise the troops.

On Avni's flank, the fighting continued for a little longer. At 21:05, men of the 2/57th managed to advance to the foot of Russell's Top but were unable to dislodge defenders from their positions. Though a mutual exchange of rifle fire continued for a while into the night, silence eventually descended over the front.[143]

After intense close-quarters combat on 1 May, Turkish troops had advanced their front line to within 8 to 10 metres of the Anzac position on the Second Ridge. All units prepared for a renewed assault on the night of 2 May. At precisely midnight, the left flank forces surged forward, followed by the right flank and Central Group around 02:00. However, this coordinated assault also failed to yield any results. Recognising the failure of the operation and the heavy losses, Kemal called off the attacks across the entire front by 03:00.[144] After the attack ended, his primary concern was supplying the men who had been engaged in continuous combat for 24 hours. When Avni was asked about provisions for the men at 03:20, he reported that rice, eggs, grapes, and canned meat had been

---

[143] ATASE: BDH 5384-183-H3-1-4a.
[144] Reşat Hallı, Muhterem Saral, and Remzi Yiğitgüden, *Birinci Dünya Savaşı'nda Çanakkale Cephesi, Vol. 5, Book 2*, 103.

provided. These meals were transported to the front through communication trenches.[145]

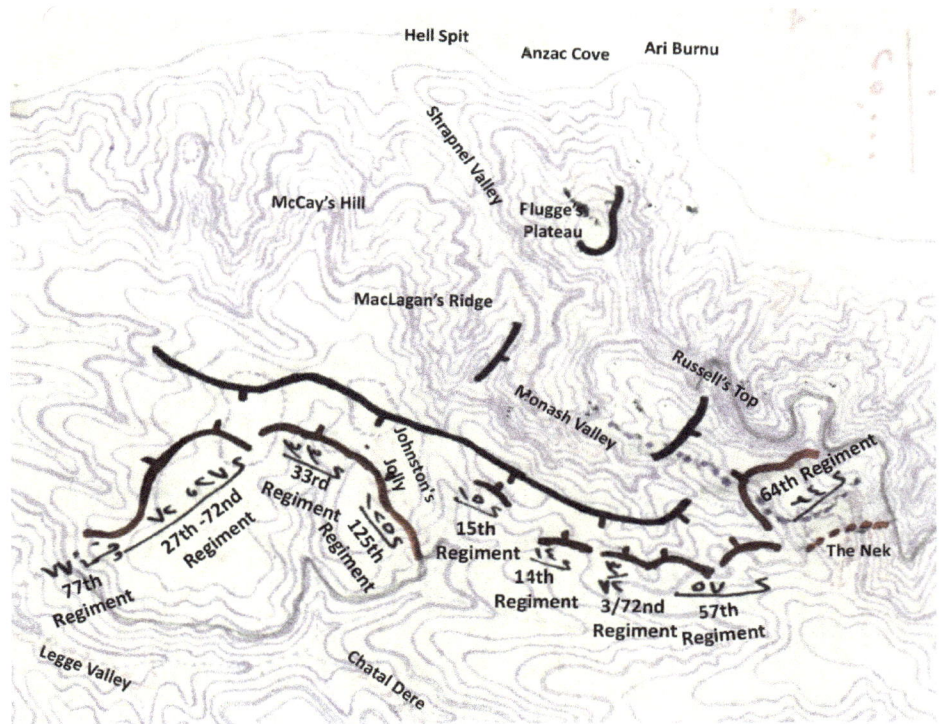

23. Turkish map showing the situation on the evening of 1 May. The red dotted line on The Nek is the final frontline of the 64th regiment on that day. (ATASE 4936-H10-001-12)

In his order sent at 06:30, Kemal instructed that the attack would continue. However, Avni reported that the situation remained unchanged, with the Anzacs firmly entrenched. He noted that his men were exhausted, units were intermingled, and the commanders' ability to maintain command and control was diminishing. Kemal was not hardheaded. In the divisional order issued at 11:00 on 2 May, he outlined the preparations for the attack and specified that it would not commence until they were fully completed.[146] This provided the regiments with breathing space, and time to rest and prepare for both defence and attack.

---

[145] Burhan Sayılır, *Çanakkale Muharebelerinde 57. Piyade Alayı*, 244.
[146] Mustafa Kemal, *Arıburnu Muharebeleri Raporu*, 64–65.

Meanwhile, Avni issued an order requesting battalion commanders to sketch out the positions held by both their own forces and the enemy.

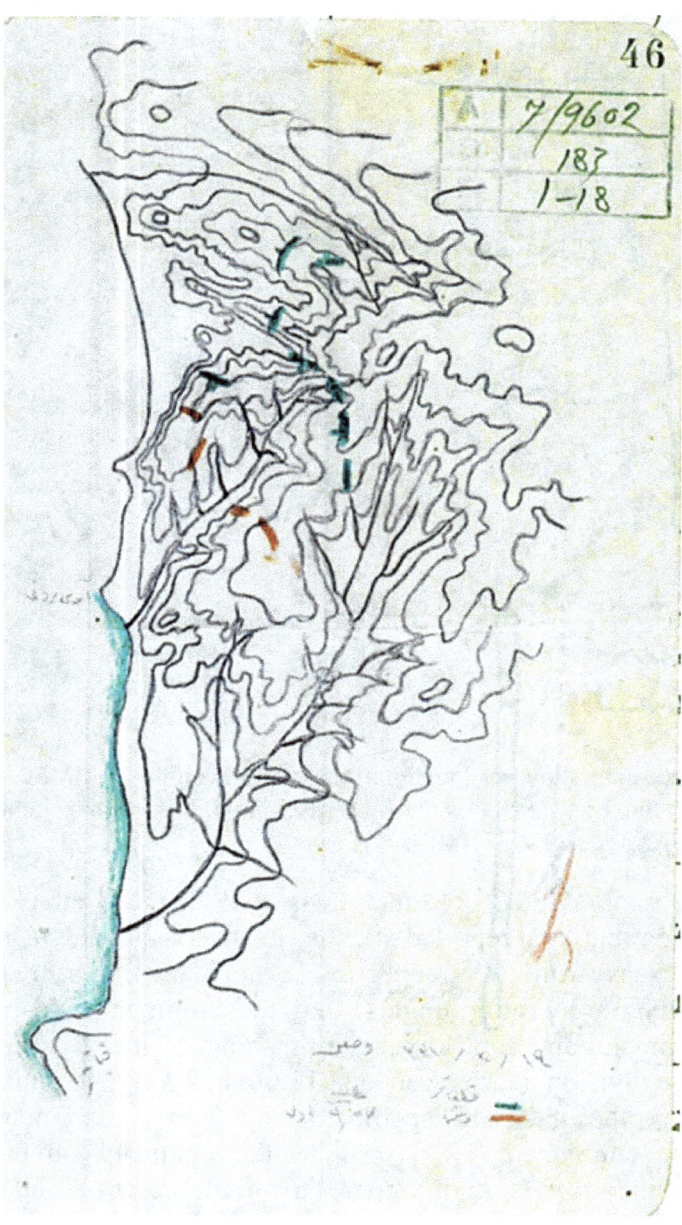

24. An example of sketch maps drawn by the battalion commanders at Avni's request on 2 May. (ATASE 5384-183-H1-1-18)

At 19:25, a naval bombardment began across the entire front. At 21:10, the 57th Regiment's front was attacked following intense machine gun fire. The attackers advanced up to five metres against the trenches held by elements of the 1/64th, 3/57th, and 3/20th Battalions. However, the attack was repelled with grenades and rifle fire, leaving the Allied dead almost piled up in front of the trenches and forcing the survivors to throw themselves into Monash Valley.[147] After the Turkish right flank was shelled for some time by the guns behind MacLaurin's Hill, the attack resumed at 00:50. As the attacks pressed home, Avni issued the following decisive order: 'A soldier never surrenders even a single inch of land to the enemy. Wherever you stand, you will hold on until the very end.'[148] In the small hours of the morning, the second attack had also faltered against the stubborn resistance of the 57th Regiment. Avni reported to the division, 'The attack was completely repelled and halted without the need to deploy reserve forces, but enemy artillery on the beach severely battered the right flank.' He added a resolute statement: 'The enemy is currently in the gully. Hopefully, I will blow their brains out with bombs.'[149]

'A Decoration for Our Regiment'

The morning of 3 May began with a heavy bombardment from Allied ships. Meanwhile, Kemal was busy reorganising his garrison. He ensured that officers and other ranks who had shown courage in battle were duly rewarded and praised:

> Our brave officers, who bolstered our national pride with their extraordinary courage during the 1 May attack, charged into enemy trenches with bared swords, embodying the valour and glory of our ancestors' military achievements and sagas. They set an inspiring example for our brave men, who followed them with spiritual fervour. The sacrifices and heroism of our troops serve as a guiding light for our future success. I trust that our officers and men can drive the enemy into the sea, fighting to the last man. All soldiers fighting alongside me here must understand that there is no turning

---

[147] ATASE: BDH 5384-183-H3-1-5, BDH 5384-183-H3-1-7a; Mustafa Kemal, *Arıburnu Muharebeleri Raporu*, 67.
[148] ATASE: BDH 5384-183-H3-1-8a; CBA: 01000140-1.
[149] Mustafa Kemal, *Arıburnu Muharebeleri Raporu*, 67.

back from our duty to defend the honour of our homeland. I also want to remind all of you that seeking sleep and rest now will deny not only us but also our entire nation this rest forever.[150]

The dearth of company and platoon commanders persisted without replacements. During the night of 3 May, the Allies launched repeated assaults on the regiment's front, only to be staunchly repulsed at a cost to their own ranks. By 4 May, a modest contingent of two squads arrived to

24. Spoils of war in a Turkish trench at Anzac.

repair the ravaged trenches, yet Avni described the work they would do as 'nothing' as many of the shovels they brought with them were broken. Nevertheless, the day's focus centred on fortifying the trenches around The Nek.[151] On 5 May, the day began with another round of attacks. As the sun rose above the horizon, Turkish artillery opened a heavy fire, effectively suppressing the machine guns at Russell's Top. Following Avni's order to attack from the right flank, attacking columns from the

---

[150] Mustafa Kemal, *Arıburnu Muharebeleri Raporu*, 69–70.
[151] CBA: 01000140-1.

1/64th and 3/57th dashed forward with hand grenades and then engaged with bayonets. The Anzac soldiers retreated, allowing the Turks to capture the trench along with 200 rifles and a machine gun. This successful capture reduced the distance between the opposing sides to just 150 metres.[152]

After the initial heavy fighting, the extent of the losses was starting to become clear. Between 25 April and 5 May, the casualties in the 57th Regiment were: 24 officers and 508 other ranks killed, 14 officers and 1,161 other ranks wounded. Additionally, 354 other ranks were reported missing. In total, the regiment incurred 2,061 casualties.[153] As of 5 May, the regiment consisted of 10 officers and 704 other ranks. Due to the significant reduction in numbers, Avni decided to amalgamate the battalions. At 15:30 on 5 May, Avni sent an interesting message to the division, asking for a decoration to be awarded to the regimental Colours:

> To the 19th Division Command
> 5 May 1915
> 15:30
> From the ridges east of Cesaret Tepe [The Nek]
>
> The 57th Regiment has displayed exemplary courage and selflessness since the fighting began on 25 April 1915. Despite losing more than a third of its men, the regiment remains steadfast on the front line, launching relentless night attacks whenever possible to crush the enemy and destroy his trenches step by step. Our regiment has pierced the enemy's heart with bayonets, as evidenced by an enemy coat riddled with holes, recently presented to you. It has distinguished itself among all regiments, demonstrating exceptional prowess in both offensive and defensive operations. The sacrifices of our regiment, which will undoubtedly be etched in the history of war, have been acknowledged and esteemed by all commands. The regiment set an example for future generations to emulate its gallantry and commitment. Therefore, I humbly request that the glorious Colours of our glorious regiment be adorned with a decoration.

---

[152] ATASE: BDH 5384-183-H3-1-16, BDH 5384-183-H3-1-16a.
[153] Arzu Tunç et al., eds., *Çanakkale Muharebelerinde 19. Tümen Cerideleri, Vol. 2*, 231.

Commander of the Right Flank Force and the 57th Regiment Major Avni[154]

Tragically, Avni did not live to see the medal awarded to his regiment, which was eventually attached to the Colours after his death.

At 21:20 on 5 May, the 2/57th received orders to neutralise a machine gun that was persistently harassing the regiment's front. The battalion launched an assault on the machine gun post using grenades and bayonets, managing to capture it after a 20-minute battle. This concluded the day's fighting.[155]

6 May began quietly. Avni presented some of the equipment captured the day before to Kemal with a note, 'I am proud to present it to our distinguished division commander as a historical and valuable gift from the regiment.'[156] When the Turkish forces at Anzac totalled 10 infantry regiments, 3 cavalry companies, and 12 batteries, Kemal had designated all units under his command as the 'Arıburnu Force.' By 6 May, Avni commanded:

    57th Regiment (two battalions)
    64th Regiment (two battalions)
    1/20th battalion
    3/72nd battalion
    3/77th battalion
    3/125th battalion

With a total combined strength of 3,290 men. On 6 May, the Turkish garrison at Anzac was given the name 'Northern Group,' while the garrison at Helles was named the 'Southern Group.'[157]

The Detachment of Volunteers
On the night of 6/7 May 1915, an Anzac attack on the 3/57th front at The Nek was beaten by the 'Sergeant Mehmet's Detachment.' In the early morning, Allied artillery began bombarding the Turkish right flank, prompting Turkish field batteries at Kaba Tepe to retaliate by targeting

---

[154] ATASE: BDH 5384-183-H3-1-16a.
[155] ATASE: BDH 5384-183-H3-1-18; CBA: 01000140-1.
[156] ATASE: BDH 5384-183-H3-1-18a.
[157] Mustafa Kemal, *Arıburnu Muharebeleri Raporu*, 74–75.

the ground between MacLaurin's Hill and The Nek. Following this, Allied ships joined in, bombarding Turkish positions. After a while, both sides ceased firing.[158]

During the day, both sides focused on fortifying their lines. Two major attacks were planned for the night: one aimed at capturing the Anzac trenches near the 3/72nd and 2/57th fronts, and the other targeting the ground known as The Pimple (called Şehitler Tepesi – 'Martyrs' Hill' by the Turks) at Lone Pine with a detachment of volunteers. For the first operation, scheduled for 21:00, the 3/72nd (supported by two companies from the 14th Regiment), 2/57th, and 3/57th battalions would suddenly rush the Anzac trenches with grenades.[159] The second phase of the operation, involving the capture of The Pimple, was crucial for maintaining the stability of the Turkish positions at Johnston's Jolly and Lone Pine. A sudden Allied raid posed a significant risk of losing control over these areas. If that occurred, Anzac troops could potentially advance into Legge Valley (Karayörük Dere). To fortify the position, it was considered essential to secure The Pimple with a detachment of volunteers.[160] In accordance with this plan, Avni wrote to the 3/125th, requesting 50 'brave' privates and one officer. He stated, 'I am sure that all of our soldiers will volunteer,' and asked to be informed of the number of volunteers and the officer who would lead them.[161] A volunteer detachment of 140 men was formed, with 60 from the Left Flank and 80 from the right. First Lieutenant Saffet from the 3/125th volunteered to lead the detachment and was sent to Scrubby Knoll by Avni. There, Kemal personally pointed out the position to be occupied and explained the plan. This detachment was later attached to the 27th Regiment.

The detachment was to rush the Anzac position at Lone Pine during the night. Beginning at 18:00, artillery would intensify its bombardment on the target area. Once the volunteer detachment entered the designated trenches, they would secure the area by opening fire on their front and flanks. The Left Flank units would immediately reinforce the detachment to consolidate the gains. Later, a machine gun would be positioned to

---

[158] Mustafa Kemal, *Arıburnu Muharebeleri Raporu*, 76.
[159] CBA: 01000140-1.
[160] Reşat Hallı, Muhterem Saral, and Remzi Yiğitgüden, *Birinci Dünya Savaşı'nda Çanakkale Cephesi, Vol. 5, Book 2*, 109.
[161] ATASE: BDH 5384-183-H3-1-21.

target other nearby Allied trenches.[162] At 21:15, following an intermittent bombardment, elements of the 3/57th, 2/57th, and 3/72nd battalions on the right flank charged with bayonets after a shower of hand grenades. The defenders on the 3/57 front, overwhelmed by the sudden barrage of grenades, evacuated the trenches and fled. A significant amount of entrenching tools had been captured. The 2/57th also successfully achieved its objective, advancing to the edge of Monash Valley and immediately began entrenching.

On the further side, things didn't go so well. The volunteer detachment sprang into action precisely at 21:00 and stealthily approached the objective. They attacked the position with grenades followed by a bayonet charge. As the defenders quickly responded, the momentum of the attack faltered when the detachment's leader, Saffet, was wounded in the shoulder, and they were unable to secure the objective. Saffet later reported to Kemal, 'The enemy fled their trenches towards the sea, and my men were holding up well. I regret that I did not die in the enemy's trench.'[163]

Crisis and Court-Martial
On the right flank, when two companies from the 14th Regiment, under 3/72nd, showed reluctance to attack and gave various excuses, Avni issued an order and warned the battalion commander that failure to attack would lead to a court-martial.[164] Consequently, the battalion launched its assault at 23:30 and managed to capture a portion of the objective. They captured 50 rifles, 600 entrenching tools, and took a prisoner. In his report to the division at 02:45, Avni wrote, 'A prisoner captured alive has just been sent to you. I believe he is Serbian, as he asked us for water using the Serbian word *voda*.'[165] Avni, who did not speak English but spent most of his life in the Balkans, had mistakenly identified the word 'water' as Serbian.

---

[162] Mustafa Kemal, *Arıburnu Muharebeleri Raporu*, 77.
[163] Mustafa Kemal, *Arıburnu Muharebeleri Raporu*, 78. At this point, it is important to note that Şefik Aker expressed a completely opposite opinion to Saffet, and this raid attempt is not mentioned in any Allied sources, including war diaries. (t.n.)
[164] Avni was the deputy president of the divisional court-martial. (t.n.)
[165] ATASE: BDH 5384-183-H4-1-1.

The day before, on the night of 6/7 May, the 3/72nd front had been attacked. After repelling the attack, Avni ordered the commander of the 3/72nd to counter-attack jointly with the 14th Regiment to capture the enemy trench, which was only 4 metres away, but they failed to do so.[166] When Avni angrily questioned Major Mahmut about the failure, Mahmut defended himself:

> I work day and night to carry out your orders precisely. My purpose is to report what I see, not to express any other opinion. I will work harder to achieve what has been ordered. Success comes from God.

He also complained about the fatigue of his men. However, during the attack planned for the evening of 7 May, the 3/72nd again failed to leave its trenches. At 22:15, Avni sent a message to Captain Ata:

> Have we established contact with the 3rd Battalion of the 72nd Regiment? What's their situation? Are you carrying out joint operations?

Ata Efendi replied:

> I have arrived at the 3rd Battalion, 72nd Regiment. I haven't seen any movement yet. I asked the battalion commander—he gave the order, but when the companies failed to act, he repeated it. They are hesitant to advance. They will reinforce the platoon I sent and then move forward. They don't trust their own men.[167]

Seeing that the companies under the command of the 3/72nd had not advanced, Lieutenant Colonel Ali, commander of the Central Group, telephoned Avni at 23:00. He stated that Major Mahmut's battalion had failed to move forward and asked Avni to warn Mahmut that any further delay would result in severe punishment. Furious at this development, Avni immediately sent a harsh message to Mahmut, stressing that he had provided two companies from the 14th Regiment, that the Anzacs were

---

[166] Arzu Tunç et al., eds., *Çanakkale Muharebelerinde 19. Tümen Cerideleri, Vol. 3*, 208.
[167] Arzu Tunç et al., eds., *Çanakkale Muharebelerinde 19. Tümen Cerideleri, Vol. 3*, 210.

in retreat, and that if they did not attack, he would accuse him of 'treason.' Mahmut replied shortly after:

> I have already given repeated orders to attack as violently as possible. Ata Bey was also present. The attack is already underway. Rest assured, whatever it takes to advance and gain said trench will be done. Nobody accepts being accused of treason. If there was such a stain, what am I doing here anyway? I can assure you I will not refrain from making every sacrifice tonight.[168]

Avni then ordered the 14th Regiment by phone that the 3/72nd was advancing, instructing both companies to move up on the left flank of this battalion. Despite this, the companies of the 3/72nd proceeded slowly and struggled to leave their trenches. Those who managed to advance took only a few steps before being forced back by heavy machine gun fire, preventing further progress. Major Mahmut then requested support from the 14th Regiment, but no assistance arrived. Avni called Major Mahmut at midnight and inquired about their situation. Mahmut reported,

> We moved forward, partially captured the trench. Now attempting to reinforce. Just sent the prisoner we captured.[169]

Despite this, Major Mahmut could not avoid facing a court-martial the next day. Upon learning from the report brought by dispatch riders that Mahmut had failed to lead his men out of the trench and had awaited support from the 14th Regiment, Kemal instructed Avni at 01:15:

> Appoint a brave officer to command the 3rd Battalion of the 72nd Regiment on your left flank, and immediately send the battalion commander to division headquarters for court-martial.'[170]

---

[168] Arzu Tunç et al., eds., *Çanakkale Muharebelerinde 19. Tümen Cerideleri, Vol. 3*, 211–212.
[169] Arzu Tunç et al., eds., *Çanakkale Muharebelerinde 19. Tümen Cerideleri, Vol. 3*, 213.
[170] Arzu Tunç et al., eds., *Çanakkale Muharebelerinde 19. Tümen Cerideleri, Vol. 3*, 213–214.

Avni did not dismiss Mahmut immediately but first requested reports from him and the company commanders of the 14th Regiment. Mahmut stated in his report:

> The left flank of his battalion acted slowly and could not get out of the trench, they kept the men waiting in the trench with bayonets fixed, and they gave their word of honour that they would attack this evening (8 May).

However, he blamed the 14th Regiment for not supporting the left flank and requested their participation next time. The 2/14th reported that the trench Mahmut's left flank failed to capture was actually empty, and upon suffering a few casualties from machine gun fire, they immediately retreated, leaving the sap towards the trench unoccupied. Consequently, Avni requested the 3/72nd to be completely removed from the right flank:

> To the 19th Division Command
>
> I regret to inform you that the situation remains unchanged since the report submitted last night. Due to the cowardice of the officers of the 3rd Battalion of the 72nd Regiment and its commander, the enemy trench in front of this battalion could not be captured. In his report, a copy of which I have attached, the battalion commander blames the 14th Regiment for not cooperating and claims his men will restore their honour tonight. However, it is now obvious that working with this battalion is impossible. The battalion commander placed his responsibility on the 14th Regiment and unfairly blamed them.
>
> In short, the presence of this battalion not only hinders our operations but also negatively impacts the morale of our men. Therefore, I request that a battalion from the 125th Regiment be sent to replace it. I present a sketch showing our current situation, along with two boxes and two strips of enemy machine gun ammunition taken from the trenches captured last night.
>
> Commander of the Right Flank and the 57th Regiment
> Major Avni.'[171]

---

[171] ATASE: BDH 5384-183-H4-1-1.

After reviewing the situation and conveying his congratulations and thanks to Avni, Kemal ordered the 3/72nd to renew the attack at 21:00. Mahmut remained at his post and instructed his companies to prepare for the evening attack. When the time came, they initiated the attack with heavy rifle fire and grenades, but the companies still could not make any progress. Another attempt was made half an hour later. The trench, which had been empty the night before, was now fortified with sandbags. The attackers, facing heavy fire from this trench and area beyond, could only advance a few steps before retreating to their own trenches.

On the morning of 9 May, the battalion was reinforced with 10 volunteers from each of the 57th, 20th and 14th Regiments and the attack was repeated. Company and platoon leaders, and Mahmut himself, advanced the front line to encourage the men. Although some of the men gradually jumped out of the trench after throwing a few hand grenades, those who remained behind did not advance, seeing that those who had emerged were immediately shot.[172] Mahmut reported the situation to Avni after the attack, stating that his unit had been fighting non-stop for 15 days. He explained that the battalion's morale had plummeted after suffering over 500 casualties, and they were struggling even to hold the trenches. He requested that his battalion be relocated. After reading the report, Avni forwarded it to Kemal:

> To Right Flank Command
> 9 May 1915
> 08:20
>
> The battalion has been fighting in the same position for 15 days and has suffered over 500 casualties, which has broken the men's spirit. Despite efforts to encourage them, immediate results have not been achieved. The remaining men are the weaker members of the battalion, both physically and spiritually, so the efforts made do not yield positive outcomes. Guards with bayonets are positioned behind the men holding the trenches, especially at night, to ensure they maintain their position. Continuing this situation is likely to further lower their morale and, God forbid, cause greater

---

[172] Arzu Tunç et al., eds., *Çanakkale Muharebelerinde 19. Tümen Cerideleri*, Vol. 3, 18.

difficulties. Therefore, I strongly request that at least the location of the battalion be changed.

Commander of the 3rd Battalion, 72nd Regiment
Mahmut[173]

Following this message, Avni dismissed Mahmut on the grounds of deserting the battle and sent him to be court-martialled. Captain Halim from the 64th Regiment was appointed in his place.[174] Avni immediately issued the following strict order to the new commander of the 3rd Battalion:

> If any of your men refuse to get into the trenches or desert the battle, you shoot them right away and report it to me. No one is permitted to get away from the front line. And if any of your officers refrain from fighting, send him straight to me so he can be court-martialled, just like his major.

Mahmut went to Kemal's headquarters in the afternoon and was questioned. He complained about his battalion, noting heavy losses since 25 April and fatigue among the men from continuous trench warfare close to the enemy. Kemal reiterated his order to 'capture the Anzac trenches' and declared that 'anyone showing slackness would be disposed of first':

> You are to complete yesterday's attack and capture the enemy trenches directly opposite you. The fresh troops I'll send will relieve you only on this condition. If you fail to mobilise your men to capture and hold the enemy trenches, or if your men behave inappropriately, the relief force will first eliminate you and then take your place.[175]

When Mahmut assured the division commander that he would carry out the orders under all circumstances, he was reinstated to his battalion.[176]

---

[173] Arzu Tunç et al., eds., *Çanakkale Muharebelerinde 19. Tümen Cerideleri, Vol. 3*, 19.
[174] ATASE: BDH 5384-183-H4-1-4a.
[175] Gökşen Özen, 'Çanakkale Muharebelerinde 72'nci Alay' (Master's thesis, Çanakkale Onsekiz Mart University, 2020), 80.
[176] Mustafa Kemal, *Arıburnu Muharebeleri Raporu*, 80.

Avni expressed discomfort with this decision to Kemal, voicing doubts about Mahmut's ability to fulfil his duty. Kemal stated that Mahmut had promised to launch the attack but also noted severe consequences would follow if he hesitated to obey orders again. He demanded that soldiers who attempted to leave their battalion, refused to advance, or fled, be singled out for punishment. However, the attack was not renewed, and Mahmut's wishes prevailed. By 17:30, the 3/72nd had been moved from the right flank to the central sector. They were replaced by the 1/14th, and a decision was made for the 3/72nd to remain in reserve for some time.[177]

On 9 May, Avni sent the Colours of the 57th Regiment to the 3/125th along with its guards, with a message: 'I entrust the protection of my regiment's Colours to you. Let them remain under your care with their guards.' Major Yahya Fehim, commander of 3/125th, replied, 'I have entrusted the Colours of your regiment to the 12th Company of our battalion. They will be safeguarded properly. You can rest assured.' The Colours of the 57th Regiment were now under the protection of the 125th Regiment's 12th Company at Suyatağı.[178]

The strength of the 57th Regiment steadily dwindled over time. The battalions were reduced from four companies to two, with 290 soldiers remaining in the 1st Battalion. In the 2nd Battalion, the 1st and 2nd companies were merged under the command of Captain Şerafettin, while the 3rd and 4th companies were combined under Captain Kadri, bringing the total to 749 privates. Excluding medical and support personnel, there were 663 combatants in total. The Machine Gun Company comprised 116 personnel, including one officer, one gunsmith, and one sergeant major. Of these, one officer and one man were wounded, and 10 men were in hospital.

To compensate for the regiment's reduced numbers, a total of 999 reinforcements were assigned to the 2nd and 3rd Battalions, which Avni organised into their re-formed third companies. At 23:00, the 3/72nd, 1/14th, and 2/57th battalions were attacked. The Anzacs had perceived that the spirit of the Turkish soldiers in this area had waned during the

---

[177] Arzu Tunç et al. eds.*Çanakkale Muharebelerinde 19. Tümen Cerideleri, Vol. 3*, 229.
[178] ATASE: BDH 5384-183-H4-1-4a.

fighting over the previous three days. After midnight, the attack was repeated five more times consecutively, all of which were successfully repelled. According to the reports, the attackers left approximately 600 dead and around 2,000 wounded in front of the Turkish lines. The enfilade fire from the 2/57th played a pivotal role in defeating the attack.[179]

Meanwhile, a party from the 14th Regiment crawled and occupied the trench that the 3/72nd had previously failed to capture. At 14:00, 3/72nd was again placed under the command of the Right Flank. The 3/72nd had significantly diminished, especially after the last fighting, leaving only one captain in the battalion besides Mahmut, the battalion commander. The entire battalion was on the firing line. In his report, Mahmut described the situation: 'We fought continuously through the day and night. All our men are at the front line. They had neither time to eat nor rest.'

Avni immediately pulled the battalion back once again and sent a message to the division, stating that the battalion had only two companies left and urgently requesting the appointment of at least one officer.[180] Kemal was content with the sacrifice and gallantry of the 3/72nd, which successfully repelled repeated Allied attacks following the warnings given to Mahmut. He sent a congratulatory message to the battalion and requested a list of the names of officers and other ranks to be decorated, especially highlighting a private who had bayoneted four Anzac soldiers single-handedly. Avni conveyed Kemal's message to the battalion, extending his congratulations to Mahmut as well. Avni received the names of two officers, a deputy reserve officer, and 13 men from the battalion who would be awarded the Liyakat Medal.[181]

---

[179] Arzu Tunç et al., eds., *Çanakkale Muharebelerinde 19. Tümen Cerideleri, Vol. 3*, 42.
[180] ATASE: BDH 5384-183-H4-1-7a.
[181] Arzu Tunç et al., eds., *Çanakkale Muharebelerinde 19. Tümen Cerideleri, Vol. 3*, 254.

26. Enver Paşa's visit to Gallipoli (24–25 September 1915). The photo includes Enver, Esat Paşa, Lieutenant Colonel Fahrettin, Lieutenant Colonel İsmet, Major Kemal, Corps Artillery Commander Lieutenant Colonel Hasan, and 16th Division Chief of Staff Captain Nazım. (Mustafa Onur Yurdal Collection)

Getting Promoted
In the early hours of 12 May, the roar of Turkish artillery reverberated through the skies over Kaba Tepe. Throughout the day, Avni was busy reforming his 1st Battalion which was now totalled 580 personnel. However, with only two lieutenants and no other officers available, he pulled the battalion back to reserve. Avni then requested the division to send an officer capable of commanding the battalion, or at the very least, a company commander.[182]

---

[182] Arzu Tunç et al., eds., *Çanakkale Muharebelerinde 19. Tümen Cerideleri, Vol. 3*, 253–254.

12 May marked an important day for Avni. Deputy Commander-in-Chief Enver Paşa[183] had visited the front the day before and received a briefing about the ongoing fighting at the 3rd Corps headquarters. Impressed by Avni's gallantry since 25 April, he decided to promote him to the rank of lieutenant colonel.

> To Right Flank Command
> From Kemal Yeri
> 12 May 1915
>
> Deputy Commander-in-Chief [Enver] Paşa visited the Northern Group sector yesterday and expressed great satisfaction with the sacrifices made and being made by all the troops. It was announced that Major Hüseyin Avni, the commander of the 57th Regiment, who had demonstrated an unwavering readiness to sacrifice his life since the beginning of the fighting, has now been promoted to the rank of lieutenant colonel.
>
> Commander of Arıburnu Force and the 19th Division
> Lieutenant Colonel Mustafa Kemal[184]

Kemal issued this message to all units on the front. Alongside Avni, Sergeant Mehmet from the 3/20th fighting under his command was also promoted to lieutenant for his remarkable actions. Avni's promotion received a positive reception from the officers at the front, prompting a flurry of congratulatory messages. Captain Kamil, commander of the Ammunition Column of the 19th Division, was among those who sent their congratulations:

> To Lieutenant Colonel Hüseyin Avni Bey,
> Gallant Commander of the 57th Infantry Regiment
>
> Dear Sir,

---

[183] In the Ottoman Empire, the Sultan traditionally held the title of Commander-in-Chief. Enver assumed the title of Deputy Commander-in-Chief, serving as the Sultan's deputy in military affairs. (t.n.)

[184] Hülya Toker, *Çanakkale Muharebelerine Katılan Komutanların Biyografileri* (Ankara: T.C. Genelkurmay Başkanlığı, 2014), 219.

In yesterday's routine order, I read about your promotion to the rank of lieutenant colonel by His Excellency the Deputy Commander-in-Chief. Words cannot express the joy this news brings to my heart. First and foremost, may your endeavour be blessed. Secondly, I congratulate you on your new rank. I pray to God Almighty that the brave troops under your command will see our wicked and cowardly enemies crushed, defeated and devastated many more times.

I apologise for my fault in not being able to ask about your well-being until now.

13 May 1915

Commander of the Ammunition Column of the Northern Sector and the 19th Division
Captain Kamil'[185]

Dying in the Trenches to the Last Man
On 12 May, 3,000 reinforcements arrived from İstanbul. This brought relief to Avni, as his regiment was augmented by an additional 303 men. However, Captain Ata, who gathered the newly arrived men in the training square and had them do a short drill to understand their training level, reported that they were so raw that they had difficulty even with fixing bayonets and loading their rifles.[186] On the night of 12/13 May, the Allies attempted to advance after a hail of rifle and machine gun fire on the 3/72nd front but were repulsed. In line with Avni's request, this attack was retaliated with by artillery fire.[187]

At 14:20 on 13 May, an hour-long exchange of fire occurred between Allied forces and Right Flank units. Mahmut, the commander of the 3/72, reported to the Right Flank that the remaining 300 men in his battalion had eye problems, poor night vision, were completely incapacitated, and extremely fatigued. Consequently, Avni placed the worn-out battalion in reserve once again, relieving them with the 3/125th:

---

[185] Hüseyin Avni Tanman Collection.
[186] ATASE: BDH 5384-183-H4-1-17a.
[187] Mustafa Kemal, *Arıburnu Muharebeleri Raporu*, 335.

> I have great confidence in your battalion. Since I feel as secure with you as I do with my own regiment, I am entrusting you with this critical duty. I am certain that, given the close contact with the enemy, you will defend with honour and defeat him with bomb and bayonet attacks at night. Show me what you are made of. May God grant you a bright success.[188]

The Allies were reinforcing their trenches more and more every day. The positions consisted of two rows of trenches, one of which was loopholed, with a wall of sandbags to human height. Based on statements from captured prisoners and correspondence, it was estimated that the New Zealand and Australian forces that had landed numbered approximately 20,000 troops in four divisions. Likewise, the number of Turkish troops at Anzac had reached 20,000 with the latest reinforcements. However, due to the inadequate training of the newly arrived troops, it was deemed more appropriate to stay in defence. In the meantime, Kemal requested from the Northern Group the deployment of heavy artillery and the allocation of a fresh division for upcoming offensive operations.[189] When approval came from the corps for the attack, Kemal issued a divisional order:

> I place my trust in God's help and the heroism of our troops to push the enemy into the sea. The 3rd Corps will employ mortars, howitzers, and field artillery to devastate the Allied positions in preparation for our operation. We will prepare for the attack with the aim of either dying to the last man or driving the enemy into the sea to the last man. Report when your preparations are completed.'[190]

While preparations for the attack had begun on the Turkish side, at 01:30, the Anzacs launched three raids at Quinn's Post, as well as targeting the Right and Central Groups, following a heavy burst of fire. The target of

---

[188] Arzu Tunç et al., eds., *Çanakkale Muharebelerinde 19. Tümen Cerideleri, Vol. 3*, 83.

[189] Arzu Tunç et al., eds., *Çanakkale Muharebelerinde 19. Tümen Cerideleri, Vol. 3*, 86–87.

[190] Mustafa Kemal, *Arıburnu Muharebeleri Raporu*, 90–91. Arzu Tunç et al., eds., *Çanakkale Muharebelerinde 19. Tümen Cerideleri, Vol. 3*, 280–281.

the attack was the positions held by the 3/125th, 1/14th, and 2/14th battalions on the right of the Central Group and the left of the Right Flank. The Allies advanced with men carrying entrenching tools and sandbags at the front, followed by a second line, and two lines in close formation behind them. Made aware by the explosions of hand grenades, Avni sent a message to 3/125th at 02:50 to assess the situation: 'What's happening? What are these bombs? Report immediately.' Battalion Commander Yahya Kâzım confirmed that the bombs were thrown by the enemy.

Despite some attackers managing to break into Turkish lines after a fierce dash, those who entered first were dealt with bayonets, and the others were shot. Approximately 300 dead were counted in front of the Turkish trenches, with total Anzac casualties estimated at 1,500. Additionally, more than 200 rifles and a significant amount of equipment, including entrenching tools, had been captured.[191] Avni was especially impressed by the performance of the reserve officers and non-commissioned officers in this fighting. So much so that he sent a name list and message to the division requesting that reserve officers and NCOs in command of platoons who heroically fulfilled their duties be promoted to lieutenant.[192]

While under attack, the Avni made a small-scale lively attempt and sent a patrol from 3/64, 2/57 and 3/57th battalions equipped with hand grenades into Monash Valley. Upon its return, the party of 3/57th brought a pith helmet, two rifles, two books, and four shovels. Avni signed the helmet: 'Captured from the enemy by the Fifty-Seventh Regiment. 13/14 May 1915. Commander of the 57th Regiment, Lieutenant Colonel Avni,' before presenting it to Kemal on the night of 15 May.[193]

---

[191] ATASE BDH 5384-183-H5-1-5a; Mustafa Kemal, *Arıburnu Muharebeleri Raporu*, 91.
[192] ATASE BDH 5384-183-H5-1-2, BDH 5384-183-H5-1-3; Arzu Tunç et al., eds., *Çanakkale Muharebelerinde 19. Tümen Cerideleri*, Vol. 3, 104.
[193] This helmet is currently on display at the Military Museum (Askerî Müze) in İstanbul. It also bears the names and signatures of Mustafa Kemal and the head of the 3rd Corps Quartermaster Office Aziz Cemal. (t.n.)

27. The pith helmet captured by the 57th Regiment on the night of 14/15 May. Avni's note and Kemal's signature can be seen. (İstanbul Military Museum and Cultural Site Command Collection)

The same day, 700 sandbags were sent from the corps depot to the Right Flank. In addition, 10 sets of 1/25,000 maps consisting of seven sheets each were also delivered. Avni distributed the maps to the officers, admonishing them to 'take special care not to let them fall into enemy hands,' and then went to visit the trenches early the next morning:[194]

To Right Flank Units
16 May 1915
09:15
From Cesaret Tepe [The Nek]

It became evident that, in some places, there were no platoon commanders in the fire trenches at all. As a result, the men, left to themselves, fired many unnecessary shots and, when questioned,

---

[194] Arzu Tunç et al., eds., *Çanakkale Muharebelerinde 19. Tümen Cerideleri, Vol. 3*, 98.

claimed that no order had been given to hold fire. It is widely known that such indiscriminate firing undermines the spirit of the men. Moreover, it depletes our ammunition at a time like this. Unit commanders must act prudently. They should consider the source and cost of the ammunition we expend in millions daily. To prevent this, officers must maintain constant supervision over their men. If I do not find the platoon and company leaders in command of their men during my inspections, I will have no choice but to treat them as deserters. Every officer must heed this issue to prevent any negative perceptions.

Commander of Right Flank
Lieutenant Colonel Avni[195]

However, this was not the only issue about the trenches that needed to be addressed. Captain Ali Rıza, the Deputy Commander of the Right Flank, saw the trenches himself and compiled a report indicating several problems.

According to the report, the trenches of the 3/20th battalion were inadequately dug, lacking parapet height suitable for defence, as well as traverses and loopholes. Tree branches were substituted for sandbags in some places, and communication trenches were not deep enough. There were just enough sandbags to line them up in a single row on the parapet in the trenches of the 3/64th. Ammunition chests filled with soil were placed side by side and covered with soil in some sections. Similarly, the trenches of the 57th Regiment were shallow and poorly shaped. Avni initially blamed Captain Hüseyin Naci, the commander of the 11th Division Engineer Company for the situation. Naci refuted the accusations:

> The strengthening of the trenches will proceed diligently as ordered, with additional efforts during the night. A detachment of four squads has already been dispatched. The 11th Division Engineer Company has fulfilled its duties honourably thus far. The company remains resolute and committed to carrying out its

---

[195] ATASE BDH 5384-183-H5-1-8a, BDH 5384-183-H5-1-9.

responsibilities with courage, never accepts any suggestion of cowardice, and is prepared to face death with honour.[196]

Farewell to Kemal Yeri

On 16 May, the Right Flank was tasked with continuously patrolling up to Fisherman's Hut to ensure its security, thus expanding Avni's area of responsibility. Also, the reserve force behind Battleship Hill would be concentrated directly behind the front line. In addition, the 3/125th would be sent to the Left Flank, while the 1/57th would be brought in to replace it, much to Avni's disapproval.[197] Avni was worried that the 1/57th, which would replace the 3/125 h – a battalion that had fought well in this heavily attacked area – would fail to hold on in the front line because it mainly consisted of raw conscripts. Kemal responded to this objection within half an hour, stating that the decision had been made by the corps. The relief took place at 10:30 that night. Except for the occasional exchange of rifle fire, there were no serious attempts from either side throughout the day. Both sides were busy improving their lines until the morning.[198]

17 May was the day of change for the Turkish garrison at Anzac. In a corps order issued from the headquarters at Mal Tepe, Esat stated that the first phase of the battle was now over and that the regiments and divisions had returned to their original numbers with the reinforcements received. Consequently, the corps was reorganised for 'the second phase of the fighting.' To fully assume the command of the operations, the corps headquarters would be moved to Kemal Yeri. Accordingly, the Right Flank would be placed under the command of the 19th Division, the Centre would be placed under the command of the 5th Division, and the Left Flank would be under the 16th Division.[199]

---

[196] Arzu Tunç et al., eds., *Çanakkale Muharebelerinde 19. Tümen Cerideleri*, Vol. 3, 307.
[197] Arzu Tunç et al., eds., *Çanakkale Muharebelerinde 19. Tümen Cerideleri*, Vol. 3, 308.
[198] Arzu Tunç et al., eds., *Çanakkale Muharebelerinde 19. Tümen Cerideleri*, Vol. 3, 311–319.
[199] Arzu Tunç et al., eds., *Çanakkale Muharebelerinde 19. Tümen Cerideleri*, Vol. 3, 131–132.

28. Northern Group HQ, Kemal Yeri [Scrubby Knoll]. From right to left: Chief of Staff Lieutenant Colonel Fahrettin, Northern Group Commander Esat, Major Kemal, Captain Suat, the HQ guard, and Captain Burhanettin. (Mustafa Onur Yurdal Collection)

Thus ended Avni's role as Right Flank Commander. The division ordered that the 57th Regiment, 64th Regiment, 72nd Regiment and 3/45th would be deployed to the gully (Çatal Dere) behind Mortar Ridge. Kemal stated that he would move his headquarters to the east of The Nek by midnight. He also instructed Avni to dig an observation post around Battleship Hill as soon as possible, find a suitable place for headquarters tents, build an artillery position, and dig a communication trench along the shortest route.[200] After issuing a farewell message, Kemal left Kemal Yeri, where he had been for 23 days, at 21:30:

17 May 1915
From Kemal Yeri [Scrubby Knoll]
19:00

---

[200] Arzu Tunç et al., eds., *Çanakkale Muharebelerinde 19. Tümen Cerideleri, Vol. 3*, 130.

To My Dear Comrades in Arms: My Farewell to Command

The growth of the Arıburnu Forces, which I had commanded until now, has necessitated Esat Paşa, the commander of the 3rd Corps and the Northern Group, to assume command and control personally. As I am leaving my post at this moment, I feel compelled to express my gratitude and respect for the 19th Division under my command, which has written a glorious chapter in Ottoman history with its relentless heroic attacks over the past 23 days against the enemy who set foot on our homeland to capture the Dardanelles, the gate to the caliphate and the sultanate. My appreciation and respect also extend to the officers and men of the 27th, 64th, 33rd, and 125th Regiments; the 13th, 14th, and 15th Regiments of the 5th Division; the 5th, 7th, and 9th Artillery Regiments; and the various cavalry, engineer companies, and other units. Thanks to the attacks you gallant soldiers, whom I was pleased to command for 23 days, carried out in a way worthy of the will of God, a force of more than 20,000 of the enemy was destroyed at Arıburnu. The survivors retreated to the safety of their navy, only a few hundred metres from the coast. Those who dared to advance even a single step were badly defeated by your bayonets. I congratulate you. Rest assured, the entire nation joins me in congratulating you.

I am certain that the memory of our arduous and bloody 23-day campaign will be remembered with deep sincerity and respect. I am pleased to inform you that going forward, I will be on the right flank with my division, fighting alongside you and our newly arrived forces, as we unite to crush the enemy and achieve victory. May God grant us His help.

Commander of the 19th Division
Lieutenant Colonel Mustafa Kemal[201]

Until his own headquarters were completed, Kemal visited Avni's headquarters near the head of the Mule Valley and spent some time

---

[201] ATASE BDH 5384-183-H5-1-15, BDH 5384-183-H5-1-15a; Mustafa Kemal, *Arıburnu Muharebeleri Raporu*, 99–100; Arzu Tunç et al., eds., *Çanakkale Muharebelerinde 19. Tümen Cerideleri*, Vol. 3, 322.

chatting there. Later, the commanders of the 64th and 72nd Regiments joined them. Kemal, Avni, Münir, the commander of the 72nd Regiment, and Servet gathered together until late at night. Afterwards, Kemal toured the right flank trenches accompanied by Avni and the battalion commanders. He delivered words of encouragement to the men, provided verbal instructions for the upcoming attack based on the terrain. Later at night, he moved to his new headquarters established southeast of Baby 700.[202] Around the same time, a party of 30 men from 3/57th was raiding the Anzac trench opposite them. Finding the trench deserted, the party rendered it unusable and returned with a significant amount of loot.[203] Avni presented six rifles and three caps captured to Kemal.[204]

The Turkish Attack of 19 May
On 18 May, the 57th Regiment spent the day organising its companies. At 20:10, Esat sent a confidential message to Kemal. The message stated that the enemy positions had been bombarded with artillery fire since the previous evening and that they would be attacked the next morning. The division was instructed to make necessary preparations, ensure the men were well-fed, and to boost their morale.[205] Following this, at 20:45, Corps Order No.15 regarding the attack was issued to all divisions. The order stated, 'Hoping for help from God and the spiritual backing of our Prophet, tomorrow, 19 May, at 03:30, the enemy will be attacked silently with bayonets only and he will be driven into the sea.'

The attack was to be launched from the southern end of Legge Valley, extending northwards up to Hill 122 (Sphinx) all along the front. Each division would target the trenches opposite them, with the 19th Division attacking the Anzac left flank, the 5th Division at the centre, the 2nd Division at Johnston's Jolly and Lone Pine, and the 16th Division at Lone Pine.[206] The 64th Regiment was assigned an advance upon Plugge's

---

[202] Mustafa Kemal, *Arıburnu Muharebeleri Raporu*, 101.
[203] Arzu Tunç et al., eds., *Çanakkale Muharebelerinde 19. Tümen Cerideleri, Vol. 3*, 137.
[204] One of these hats is still exhibited at the Çanakkale Naval Museum. The hat bears the inscription: 'Captured by the 3rd Battalion of the 57th Regiment during a reconnaissance raid on the night of 17/18 May. 19th Division Commander M. Kemal 4-05/03/1331 [17–18 May 1915]'.
[205] Arzu Tunç et al., eds., *Çanakkale Muharebelerinde 19. Tümen Cerideleri, Vol. 3*, 143.
[206] Mustafa Kemal, *Arıburnu Muharebeleri Raporu*, 102–103.

Plateau. The 57th Regiment's task was to attack the Anzac trenches between The Nek and Quinn's Post and drive the defenders into Monash Valley. A battalion from the 57th Regiment would support the 5th Division's attack on Courtney's Post.

For a special mission, Kemal additionally requested that the 57th and 64th Regiments each prepare a 30-man volunteer detachment. The volunteers from the 64th Regiment were to proceed directly to the beach and capture the pier. Meanwhile, the 57th Regiment's volunteers would descend into Monash Valley to cut off the retreating Anzacs, as ordered by Avni:

> Thirty volunteers from the regiment are needed. During the attack, they will descend into Korku Dere [Monash Valley] and capture the enemy fleeing from Hain Tepe [Plugge's Plateau] and our front. Pick ten men, and one corporal from each battalion, under a NCO, and provide me with their names. Equip them with grenades.[207]

The 2nd Division formed the strike force. As the battalions advanced silently, they became entangled in the darkness of the night, unable to spread out across the terrain. Hearing the noise made by the 2nd Division troops, who were completely alien to the front and to the terrain, the Anzacs quickly realised a raid was imminent and stood-to-arms early. At 03:30, the advancing 2nd Division and other units met with a wall of machine gun and rifle fire. Despite heavy casualties, the troops pressed forward in waves.

By 03:40, the attack bugles sounded to boost the soldiers' spirit, thus completely negating the element of surprise. Around the same time, the band of the 2nd Division began playing the 'Regiment March,' and the heartening music echoed across the entire front:
> My mother raised me
> Sent me to these lands
> Placed this flag in my hands
> And entrusted me to God
> Said, 'Don't sit idle, work,
> 'Serve your country, never shirk.

---

[207] Arzu Tunç et al., eds., *Çanakkale Muharebelerinde 19. Tümen Cerideleri, Vol. 3*, 326.

'My blessings you won't receive
'If you don't attack the enemy'.

The 2/57th and 3/5th, positioned in the centre and right flank of the regiment, quietly left their trenches at 03:30 and rushed the Anzac trenches at The Nek. Following a brief and intense skirmish, they successfully captured the first line defended by the Auckland Battalion of the New Zealand Mounted Rifles Brigade. These trenches, still half-finished, were easily overrun due to being only lightly held. Around 03:00, the Anzacs spotted the volunteers of the 57th Regiment attempting to infiltrate Monash Valley and halted their advance with rifle fire. Subsequently, several hundred Turkish soldiers launched an attack on Quinn's Post. Upon noticing the assault, the machine guns of the 1st Light Horse Regiment, positioned on Pope's Hill, immediately opened fire. Only three Turkish soldiers managed to reach the parapet out of the initial group, while the remainder were cut down.[208]

The 1/57th was operating on the left flank of the regiment's front. This battalion, along with the elements of the 14th Regiment had been caught in a hail of rifle and machine gun fire opposite Courtney's Post. The Allied artillery had now come into the fray, bombarding the entire front. Those who dared to leap out of the trenches were immediately shot, causing others to retreat, and forcing the companies to remain in their positions. The moans of many seriously wounded men added to the sombre atmosphere. The Allied wall of fire remained intact and grew in intensity as dawn broke.

Messages and reports began to pour in from the regiments to the 19th Division informing them of the dire situation. Avni urgently called for the guns to be silenced, stressing that despite enemy bombardment beginning an hour after the attack started, the Turkish artillery had yet to respond.[209] Allied artillery batteries positioned on Plugge's Plateau, two New Zealand howitzers, several mountain guns, and numerous machine

---

[208] Charles Edwin Woodrow Bean, *The Official History of the Australia in the War of 1914-1918, Vol II: The Story of ANZAC: From 4 May, 1915, To The Evacuation of The Gallipoli Peninsula, Volume II* (11th Ed.), (Sidney: Angus and Robertson Ltd, 1941), 152.
[209] Arzu Tunç et al., eds., *Çanakkale Muharebelerinde 19. Tümen Cerideleri, Vol. 3*, 146.

guns, had all concentrated their fire on the 57th Regiment. One of these batteries targeted the area between The Nek and Pope's Hill, while another relentlessly showered shrapnel east of Quinn's Post (Mule Valley).

In an effort to boost morale among men pinned down by enemy fire, officers bravely climbed the parapets. Tragically, five out of the six reserve officers, deployed while still studying at the Military Academy in İstanbul, and who had arrived at the front the previous night, were killed by shrapnel as they climbed onto the parapet to encourage their men.[210] The 1/57th remained in its position as the 14th Regiment on its left flank failed to make a headway. Avni reiterated his order to the battalion commander to maintain communication with the 14th Regiment and proceed with the attack together. The battalion's 1st and 2nd Companies endured sustained machine gun and artillery fire, with the 2nd Company almost completely wiped out.

Meanwhile, the 3/57th was forced to abandon the trenches it had captured. The battalion faced enfilade fire from the ridges northeast of Plugge's Plateau, where the 64th Regiment initially advanced but later retreated because of the intense fire.

At 08:00, Major Servet, commander of the 64th Regiment, described the situation in his report to the division:

> I had previously stated that the soldiers who had captured the trench ahead were forced to retreat to their old positions under intense artillery and machine gun fire from all sides. Following this, I wrote twice to the battalion commander in a very bitter and extremely violent tone, insisting that those trenches be reoccupied at any cost and under all circumstances. Three minutes ago, I received a message in which he reported that, despite ordering the commanders of the 9th and 11th Companies to advance, they were unable to do so and came under machine gun fire from Çatal Tepe [No.1 Outpost] For the third and final time, I wrote again, stating

---

[210] Şevket, son of Ömer, 1st Coy 1/57th (born 1891, İstanbul), Mustafa, son of Hasan, 1st Coy 1/57th (born 1877, Manisa), Şevket, son of Ömer Sabri, 1st Coy 1/57th (born ?, Samsun), Hasan, son of Yakup, 2nd Coy 1/57th (born 1893, Trabzon), Ibrahim, son of Mustafa, 1st Coy 1/57th (born 1886, Bursa).

that the trenches must be reoccupied at all costs, even if it meant not a single men remained. If not, I informed him that they would be sentenced to death.[211]

Despite the efforts of both the corps and division commanders, the attack failed to make progress. Volunteers from the 57th Regiment had attempted to descend into Monash Valley at least four times. Finally, at 09:30, 30 volunteers led by an officer advanced to the intersection of Quinn's and Courtney's. A fierce close-quarters battle erupted on the parapet of the fire trench, with even pistol fire exchanged. However, they were ultimately killed by machine gun fire from Pope's Hill, which protected the rear and flank of Quinn's.[212]

The 5th Division suffered the heaviest losses in its attempt against Steele's and Courtney's. Two machine guns, positioned at Steele's and the head of Wire Gully, relentlessly cross-fired for two hours on the attackers as they climbed up Mule Valley. Despite the regiments' daring efforts, no progress could be made, and the trenches became filled with the wounded and dead. Finally, Lieutenant Colonel Fahrettin, Chief of Staff of the 3rd Corps, communicated the group commander's order, via phone, to call off the attack. Fahrettin later recounted:

> Although the attack, which started at dawn, pressed on aggressively, it was impossible to breach the enemy's curtain of fire. The area between the opposing lines had become filled with the corpses of the dead and the wounded. During the operation, when Mustafa Kemal ordered the 14th Regiment on his left to join the attack, I saw with my own eyes more than half of the regiment being decimated as they attempted to advance. By noon, the fighting had ceased spontaneously. Finally, Esat Paşa gave the order to 'stop.' We had tears in our eyes when we learned that our losses for the day were 3,000 killed and 7,000 wounded.[213]

---

[211] Arzu Tunç et al., eds., *Çanakkale Muharebelerinde 19. Tümen Cerideleri, Vol. 3*, 155.
[212] C.E.W. Bean, *The Story of Anzac*, 159.
[213] Fahrettin Altay, 'Fahrettin Altay'ın Çanakkale Hatıraları' *Çanakkale Hatıraları, Vol. 2*. ed. Metin Martı. (İstanbul: Arma Yayınları, 2002), 25.

Meanwhile, Avni, noticing increased activity in the opposing trenches, realised that the Allies had moved their reserves forward and reinforced their lines. He immediately set to work to prepare for a sudden counterattack.

> To the battalions of the 57th Regiment
> From Cesaret Tepe [The Nek]
>
> It appears that the enemy has brought their reserves forward and reinforced their lines. They may launch a counter-attack sometime after the evening. The regiment has the force, with God's help, to repel any attack, and this force is in your hands. I demand the utmost steadiness and the fierceness from the officers. The reserves must be arranged so that not a single man runs back. Any soldier attempting to run must be killed immediately, without mercy. Each battalion should have a force at hand, the size of a platoon, ready to kill any deserters. All men must either perish in their trenches or defeat the enemy. Commanders of any unit, large or small, who cannot keep their men in the trenches and prevent them from fleeing will be held strictly responsible. In accordance with today's division order, and taking advantage of the current calm, it is necessary to maintain the order immediately. Everyone must designate a replacement in case of death or being wounded. I observe excessive crowding in the trenches, which will definitely cause problems. Men should occupy the trenches to the extent that they can fire freely, any surplus should be held in reserve. In case of unexpected severe pressure from the enemy, the 27th Regiment and a battalion of the 45th Regiment behind us are ready to reinforce us at any time.
>
> By God's grace, the force at hand is sufficient to render the enemy insignificant. However, every officer must demonstrate extraordinary steadiness and courage. In the event of losing officers, units should appoint platoon leaders from among the brave sergeants and corporals. Officers should use the current calm to thoroughly inspect the front line. They should motivate the men with words that will boost their spirits and uplift those who are down. I require information from each unit by evening on the extent to which this order has been implemented.

Commander of the 57th Regiment
Lieutenant Colonel Avni[214]

Mustafa Kemal, on the other hand, was satisfied with the efforts of the troops despite the failure:

> I am grateful that the 64th and 57th Regiments, along with the engineer company, fulfilled our division's duty by storming the enemy trenches as ordered, on time and silently, and successfully completing the first phase of the general attack.[215]

During the 19 May attack, the 57th Regiment suffered losses totalling 2 officers and 90 other ranks killed, 3 officers and 142 other ranks wounded, and 120 other ranks reported missing. The regiment's strength had decreased to 19 officers and 2,618 other ranks. In the 19th Division, casualties amounted to 6 officers killed, 7 officers wounded, 333 other ranks killed, and 748 other ranks wounded.[216] The total casualty figure for the Turkish garrison at Anzac was much more striking: 51 officers and 3,369 other ranks killed, with 97 officers and 5,967 other ranks wounded, totalling 9,484 casualties.[217]

On the night of 19 May, a sudden burst of fire erupted from the Anzac trenches, targeting the left flank of the 57th Regiment and the front of the 14th Regiment, lasting until 02:00. When the firing ceased, the 2/57th Battalion launched a surprise attack, catching the Anzacs off guard. Startled, the Anzacs bolted, shouting, 'The Turks are coming!' Assistant Sergeant Major Kemal, recently promoted, led three squads in pursuit of the retreating enemy into the darkness of the night, never to be heard from again.[218]

The Anzacs retaliated with a lively counter-attack after four machine guns on the high ground unleashed a continuous fire. Trapped in their

---

[214] ATASE: BDH 5384-183-H5-1-19a, BDH 5384-183-H5-1-20.
[215] Arzu Tunç et al., eds., *Çanakkale Muharebelerinde 19. Tümen Cerideleri, Vol. 3*, 169.
[216] Mustafa Kemal, *Arıburnu Muharebeleri Raporu*, 107.
[217] Reşat Hallı, Muhterem Saral, and Remzi Yiğitgüden, *Birinci Dünya Savaşı'nda Çanakkale Cephesi, Vol. 5, Book 2*, 137.
[218] Kemal, son of Mehmet (born 1884, Kastamonu). 4th Coy, 2nd Battalion, 57th Regiment. Confirmed KIA.

trenches, the men of the 2/57th Battalion fought gallantly until they exhausted their ammunition. Resorting to desperate measures, they even used stones to defend their position. With Kemal missing, Sergeant Hüseyin took command of approximately 50 remaining men in the trench on the left side, while Lieutenant Aziz[219] led a group of 40 men in the

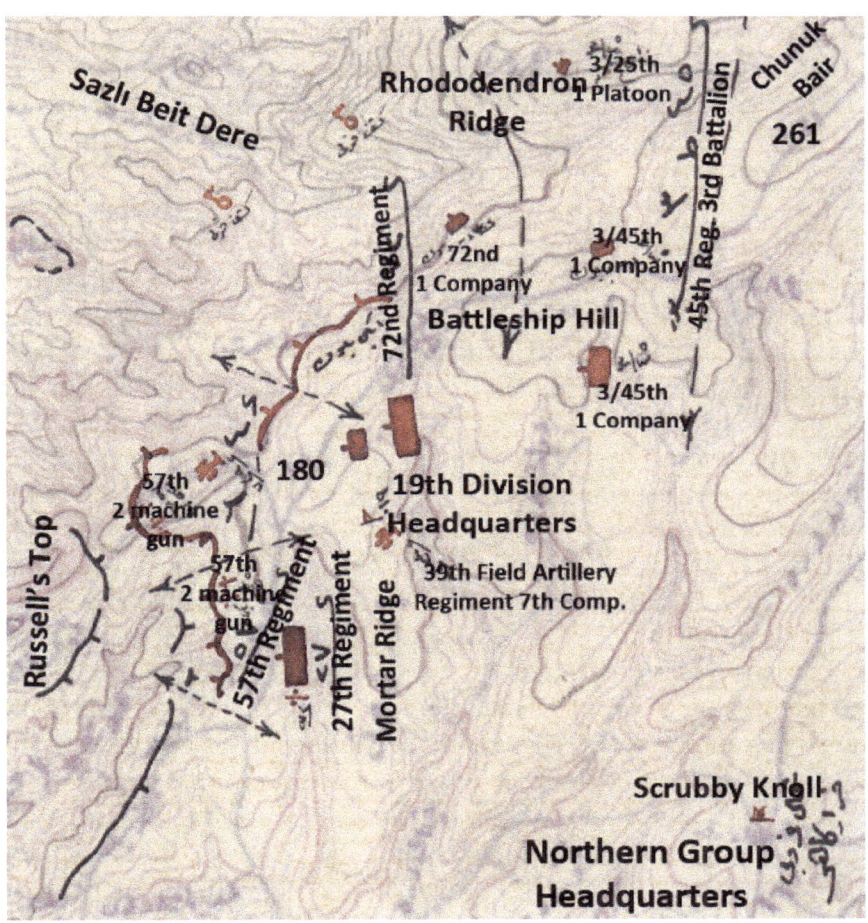

29. Map showing the disposition of Turkish troops at Anzac on 20 May 1915. (ATASE 4936-H15-001-017)

---

[219] Aziz, son of Ahmet Hamdi (born ?, Mecca). Took command of the 3rd Coy, 2/57th on 23 May. KIA 27 May.

right trench. Ata later praised these soldiers for their bravery and steadfastness:

> If the enemy trenches on our right flank, captured and subsequently abandoned by the 3rd Battalion, are not reoccupied, defending our current position will be impossible. Nevertheless, I am confident our troops will hold on to the last man. I recommend that Lieutenant Aziz and Sergeant Hüseyin, who commanded their men who has shown great endurance during numerous enemy counterattacks in shallow trenches under artillery and machine gun fire, be decorated.[220]

The Truce of 24 May
On the morning of 20 May, the Allied artillery began pounding the trenches held by the 2/57th. The bombardment began in the evening and continued until sunset, seriously damaging the 57th Regiment's trenches. Esat, watching the bombardment from Scrubby Knoll, witnessed an unusual incident. He noted a Red Cross flag raised at Steele's Post, followed by several individuals approaching the Turkish lines. In response, Fahrettin issued a strict order on behalf of Esat that no one was authorised to negotiate with the enemy without permission. Esat then instructed the 13th Regiment to raise a Red Crescent flag and allowed the medics to leave the trenches. Shortly after, Esat noted another Red Crescent flag raised at the front of the 57th Regiment, where a few Turks and Anzacs were seen chatting upon the parapet. He strongly objected to this, considering it a serious mistake, and insisted that only the 13th Regiment was authorised to engage in negotiations. Esat would go on to open an investigation to determine those responsible for the incident.
Meanwhile, Mustafa Kemal, who was visiting the firing line of the 2/57th at the time, promptly clarified via phone that the meeting with the enemy was not conducted by the 57th Regiment but by the 14th Regiment.[221]

What really had happened was as follows: Some Turkish prisoners reported during their interrogation that there were wounded Anzac

---

[220] Barış Borlat, *Askerî Kayıtlara Göre Çanakkale Cephesi'nde 19 Mayıs 1915 Türk Taarruzu, Vol 2* (Ankara: Çanakkale Savaşları ve Gelibolu Tarihi Alan Başkanlığı Yayınları, 2020), 150.
[221] Barış Borlat, *Askerî Kayıtlara Göre Çanakkale Cephesi'nde 19 Mayıs 1915 Türk Taarruzu, Vol 2*, 143–146.

soldiers in the trenches near the head of Wire Gully. Hearing this, Lieutenant Colonel Owen, commander of the 1st Australian Battalion, intended to evacuate the wounded from there. When the Red Cross flag was raised, it was hit by a Turkish bullet and fell. However, a Turkish soldier suddenly jumped out of the trench known as the German Officers' Trench, approached the Anzac lines, and said that the men were ignorant and unaware that the Red Cross flag should not be fired upon, effectively offering an apology. This incident led to an informal truce, after which Esat permitted the 13th Regiment in this sector to meet with the Anzacs.

Subsequently, flags were raised on both sides, and Captain Avni, surgeon of the 3/13th, along with Captain İsmail and Regimental Aide-de-camp Şükrü, came out of the trench. They walked halfway between the trenches carrying the Red Crescent flag to ascertain the intentions of the Anzacs. Brigadier General Walker, commanding the 1st Australian Division, happened to witness the event and informed Birdwood. He then walked into no-man's land to ensure that the ceasefire did not provide any advantage to the Turks. Afterwards, he approached the officers of the 13th Regiment, conversing with them in French while exchanging cigarettes.[222]

The Anzacs requested a 6-hour ceasefire to bury the dead and collect the wounded. Captain Avni relayed this proposal to the 5th Division. When the Anzac delegation was informed that the offer could be accepted if a formal request was made in written form, the parties agreed to reconvene at 20:00. Eventually, the division opted not to proceed with a formal agreement.[223]

The short-term informal truce to save the wounded in no-man's land was considered deceptive by both sides, as it developed spontaneously without the front line troops being aware. When it was observed on both sides that the front line trenches were full of soldiers with bayonets attached as a precaution, suspicions of a deception grew, and the guns and rifles fired once again. The wounded and dead who could not be collected posed a new threat, especially to the Anzacs. Over time, the

---

[222] C.E.W. Bean, *The Story of Anzac*, 166.
[223] Barış Borlat, *Askerî Kayıtlara Göre Çanakkale Cephesi'nde 19 Mayıs 1915 Türk Taarruzu, Vol 2*, 157.

stench and flies emanating from the rapidly decomposing bodies under the hot sun made the situation unbearable. With the wind blowing from

30. Collecting the dead in no-man's land on 24 May 1915.

land to sea, the Anzac trenches had become untenable. Consequently, a formal truce became inevitable.

On 22 May, Avni visited the division headquarters to arrange the promotion and decoration of 3 officers from the 1/57th, 11 other ranks, and several privates from the 2/57th, who had bravely managed to enter the Allied trenches on 19 May. He also sought information about the planned truce. While there, he had a long conversation with İzzettin, the chief of staff, and brought him a gift: a British whistle.[224]

After the negotiations, a formal truce was scheduled for 24 May. Kemal issued an order entitled *Conditions regarding the truce signed with the British on 24 May 1915*:

> Tomorrow at 07:30, the firing will cease, and in accordance with the corps order, no one is to show themselves, either in the front line or in the rear..[225]

The battalions of the 57th Regiment reported that the wounded had been collected and the burials completed by 16:20. The regiment was then 'ready for fighting again in 5 minutes.'[226]

31. The British whistle presented by Avni to İzzettin on 22 May 1915. (İzzeddin Çalışlar Collection)

The 57th Regiment Relieved

After the ceasefire ended at 16:30, the fighting continued throughout the night. On 25 May, the 1/57th Battalion reported 57 wounded and 5 dead. In the 2/57th Battalion's sector, an Anzac trench that was captured had been improved, with loopholes constructed.[227]

The logistical challenges were causing Avni significant concern. When he was denied the sandbags needed to construct an observation post, he expressed his frustration: 'We urgently need sandbags to build an observation post, but we don't have a single one. Our men have been sent back and forth for two days, only to be told by the administration that there are no sandbags available.' Seeking a resolution, he appealed to

---

[224] İzzettin Çalışlar, *On Yıllık Savaş: Org. İzzettin Çalışlar'ın Not Defterlerinden Balkan, Birinci Dünya ve İstiklal Savaşları*, ed. İzzeddin Çalışlar (İstanbul: Türkiye İş Bankası Kültür Yayınları, 2010), 107.
[225] Burhan Sayılır, *Çanakkale Muharebeleri'nde 57. Piyade Alayı*, 355–356.
[226] Arzu Tunç et al., eds., *Çanakkale Muharebelerinde 19. Tümen Cerideleri, Vol. 3*, 389–390.
[227] Burhan Sayılır, *Çanakkale Muharebeleri'nde 57. Piyade Alayı*, 385.

Kemal and asked for definitive orders to secure at least a hundred sandbags.[228] In response, the 11th Engineer Company was sent to the regiment to construct dugouts, and posts, dig communication trenches, and improve the existing ones.[229]

After the recent fighting, the Turks had obtained some advantageous points on their right flank. So much so that the Allied bivouac in the gully below the far right of The Nek was completely visible from the old forward Anzac trench there, newly captured by the 64th Regiment. A machine gun was placed in the trench by the 57th Regiment Machine Gun Company and a sudden raid was made at 04:30 on 27 May. The Anzacs immediately responded with artillery. A shell struck through the loophole of the trench, killing Sergeant Major Mehmet Şevki, the platoon commander.[230]

During these days, the 57th Regiment, which had been fighting non-stop since day one, finally had an opportunity to rest. Upon the division commander's assessment, the regiment was slated for relief once the trench improvements on the right flank were finished. After two days of intense labour, the battalions completed the necessary work. Following Avni's inspection, orders came for the 57th Regiment at 11:30 on 27 May to hand over their trenches to the 27th Regiment. At 19:10, the 27th Regiment relieved the 57th in complete silence. The new accommodation for the 57th Regiment would be the second gully running south from Battleship Hill. As of 27 May, the regiment comprised 25 officers, and 3,266 other ranks armed with 2,621 rifles and 2 machine guns.[231] During the regiment's rest period, Kemal proposed granting Avni permission to visit İstanbul and spend a few days with his family. However, Avni felt it inappropriate to leave his regiment as it was stationed in one of the most critical sectors of the front, and decided to stay.[232] Avni and Mustafa Kemal had a close and enduring friendship which is also reflected in the accounts of other officers. Lieutenant Alaattin, Avni's aide, later provided a detailed account about their friendship in his memoirs:

---

[228] Arzu Tunç et al., eds., *Çanakkale Muharebelerinde 19. Tümen Cerideleri, Vol. 4*, (Ankara: Genelkurmay Askerî Tarih ve Stratejik Etüt Başkanlığı Yayınları, 2017), 5.
[229] Arzu Tunç et al., eds., *Çanakkale Muharebelerinde 19. Tümen Cerideleri, Vol. 4*, 12.
[230] Mehmet Şevki, son of Hilmi (1882, Kırklareli), posthumously promoted to lieutenant. The place of death was recorded as 'during the raid on the enemy camp'.
[231] Arzu Tunç et al., eds., *Çanakkale Muharebelerinde 19. Tümen Cerideleri, Vol. 4*, 41.
[232] Quoted by Zehra Gülfiliz Arıburun Tanman from Tekin Arıburun.

After the intense and heated days of the first phase of the fighting, we started communicating with our families by sending letters via İstanbul. Gift packages from the families of officers and men began arriving at the divisional and regimental headquarters. Even the German and Austrian Red Crosses would send small parcels containing chocolates, socks, handkerchiefs, pens, notebooks, calendars, and postcards. For this purpose a torpedo boat would depart for İstanbul once a week, travelling overnight. The next morning, another torpedo boat would arrive from Istanbul, docking at the Akbaş pier, where the mail and gifts would be distributed to the regimental and divisional liaison officers. During this time, our regiment commander [Avni Bey] often received packages containing food, socks, and underwear from his family, relatives, and friends.

When gift packages or baskets arrived, both officers and men would receive their share. Sometimes, the baskets full of fruit and candy were distributed so quickly that even the commander wouldn't get a taste. However, as an aide, I would discreetly save a small handful or two of fruit and candy, occasionally bringing them out when distinguished guests visited.

Avni Bey would share some of his favourite dishes, desserts, and pastries with Mustafa Kemal Bey, the division commander, all specially prepared for him, as he and Mustafa Kemal Bey had been friends for a long time, dating back to their time in Salonika and Bitola. I usually personally delivered these in special tiffin carriers, accompanied by our commander's greetings. On one occasion, a tiffin carrier arrived containing Bitola-style stewed beans and a pudding called Presipka. Mustafa Kemal Bey was very happy when he received it. He turned to me and said:

- 'Hey, child, today you have brought me a meal as precious as a victory. I'm sure you have never tasted these before. Don't leave without trying.'

He then called our commander Avni Bey and expressed his thanks with great cheer. For a long time afterwards, he made jokes by speaking with a Rumelian Accent. This sight brought tears to my eyes, and I thought to myself, 'Oh Lord, they are good friends, as if they were not famous commanders who had won great victories, but like young lieutenants, cheerful and playful. I guess this is why all of us, soldiers, admire them more, for their genuine and heartfelt behaviour.'[233]

After a seven-day rest, the 57th Regiment took over the 5th Division's trenches opposite Courtney's and Steele's Posts on 3 June. The 1/57th settled on the left, while the 3/57th occupied the 1/15th battalion's trenches on the right. The commander of the 3/57th kept two companies in reserve in Mule Valley, and the other two manned the front line, each with a box of 50 hand grenades. On the first day, the regiment suffered casualties one dead and six wounded from enemy bombs. Avni's headquarters had now been moved behind Mortar Ridge, with the 2/57th in reserve in the same place.[234]

It was soon realised that the trenches taken over from the 5th Division were merely ditches. Captain Ali Hayri inspected the trenches and found that they had become shallow and wide ditches. While requesting support from Avni to repair and improve them, he was shot in the head. Before being taken to the hospital at Akbaş for treatment, he appointed the commander of the 1st Company Captain Nuri to take his place.

When the Deputy Commander of the 1/57th, Captain Ali Rıza, came under enemy machine gun fire, he realised the need for at least 600 sandbags and an engineer unit to make major improvements in the trenches. Reports from the battalions indicated that 20 to 30 men were becoming casualties daily due to bombs and rifle fire. To prevent further casualties, Avni decided to cover the fire trenches as soon as possible, which required timber and sandbags. Additionally, the second line trenches on Mortar Ridge had no loopholes and were unsafe. Avni asked the division to send an engineer unit to address all these issues.[235] In the afternoon, the division assigned this unit to the 57th Regiment under the command of Lieutenant Zühdü, and Avni immediately dispatched it forward to begin work.[236] The 3rd Corps decided that the trenches would

---

[233] Tekin Arıburun, 'Arıburun Savaşlarının 66. Yıldönümünde Kahraman Kumandan Şehit Hüseyin Avni Bey'i Anarken,' *Yeni Düşünce Dergisi*, 5-13, (1981): 11.
[234] Burhan Sayılır, *Çanakkale Muharebeleri'nde 57. Piyade Alayı*, 399.
[235] Burhan Sayılır, *Çanakkale Muharebeleri'nde 57. Piyade Alayı*, 403–405.
[236] ATASE: BDH 5384-183-H7-1 a.

be given numbers, and enemy trenches would be marked with letters effective from 3 June. Reports were to be arranged accordingly.[237]

The Fight for Trenches Nos. 31 and 32

Around 23:00 on 4 June, a heavy fire suddenly broke out, rendering the 57th Regiment's trenches almost untenable, particularly those on the right of Merkez Tepe (German Officers' Ridge). Avni hurried to the phone in his headquarters:

> At 11:05 on the night of 4/5 June, the enemy opened heavy fire on the trenches. The battalion commanders were immediately asked about the situation by phone. They confirmed the enemy was firing and that they were responding to the enemy. It was ordered to cease fire immediately. The 1st Battalion ceased fire, and the 3rd Battalion eased somewhat. At 12:00, a private from the 3rd Battalion arrived, claiming that the enemy had broken into our lines. Since this man came directly to me without the authorisation of anyone from his battalion, I immediately contacted the battalion commander by phone to verify the news. The battalion commander assured me unequivocally that it was absolutely not true and that there had been no incident in the trenches to cause concern. At 12:30, the commander of the 27th Regiment asked about the situation on the phone and I explained it. He said that trench No. 31, which is adjacent to the left flank of his regiment, was partially evacuated by our men. I called the deputy commander of the 3rd Battalion to the phone again and asked him. 'Not true, it's nothing. The trenches have not been abandoned,' he replied. I forwarded this to the 27th Regiment commander and we were relieved to some extent. At 01:00, the fire intensified again. I contacted the 27th Regiment commander. He informed me that there was nothing on his front and that trench No. 31 was occupied by the enemy. I asked the battalion commander again, but this time he was unable to offer a definitive opinion. 'I'm investigating,' was all he had to say. I immediately sent my aide to him. The enemy was thought to have partially entered the trench as the three men sent there were instantly killed. The same happened in the attempt made by the 27th Regiment from the right. At that moment, the battalion commander had filled the nearby trenches with reserves to the point

---

[237] Burhan Sayılır, *Çanakkale Muharebeleri'nde 57. Piyade Alayı*, 399.

where there was no room for anyone to move. He then summoned the company I had previously sent to occupy the trenches on the Edirne Sırt [Mortar Ridge], adding it to his own reserve force. The company commander informed me about this by phone. Instead of this company, I had to dispatch the companies of the reserve battalion to the Edirne Sırt. At 01:20, I instructed the 3rd Battalion commander to clear the communication trenches and support lines he had blocked, to ascertain the situation, and to launch a strong attack if trench No. 31 was found occupied by the enemy. After partially clearing the congestion in the mentioned trenches, he had trench No. 31 reconnoitred. As anyone approaching the trench was killed, the situation began to clarify to some extent. The situation could not be entirely clarified because there was a possibility that our men might have fired on their own or were fired upon from enemy trenches. This time, I gave the order to establish a common password with the 27th Regiment and then to advance at both ends of trench No. 31. However, this attempt also failed as two or three men approaching the trench were immediately shot. The situation was still uncertain until 03:05 when it finally became clear to the battalion commander that the enemy had indeed occupied trenches No. 31 and even No. 32.'[238]

Bombs had begun to rain into the trenches of the 3rd Battalion, resulting in Captain Celal, the commander of the 11th Company, being wounded. Some of the men from the 3/57th, battered by the explosions, abandoned their trenches and retreated to the left, creating a gap between them and the 27th Regiment. At 03:30, the Anzacs launched an attack across the entire front of the 19th Division. During the assault at Quinn's, the attackers successfully captured trenches No. 31 and No. 32 and, despite joint efforts with the 27th Regiment throughout the night, the 57th Regiment was unable to retake the lost ground. Avni wrote in his report:

> The commander of the 1st Battalion reported by telephone that the enemy had attacked trench No. 47, but it was beaten after ten enemy soldiers were killed in front of the trench and two upon the parapet. At 4 o'clock, news came that the enemy had attacked our trenches Nos. 31, 32, and 47. Although the enemy was again

---

[238] ATASE: BDH 5384-183-H7-1-5, BDH 5384-183-H8-1–5a, BDH 5384-183-H8-1-6.

defeated in front of trench No. 47, I informed the division commander by telephone that trenches Nos. 31 and 32 were in enemy hands and that we would attack to recapture them. I decided to proceed immediately with a company from the reserve battalion. I took the company to the front line and prepared for the attack. First, a violent bomb attack commenced from the support line.

I went to see the commander of the 27th Regiment to find out to what extent he could assist in the attack. He said he could help with enfilade fire, which was effectively suppressing the enemy. As I returned, an attack order had been given by the division commander. Preparations for the attack were made by fixing bayonets and distributing sufficient bombs to the bombers, with the order to first throw all the bombs following the whistle, and then advance with the bayonet. While this order was being communicated, I also sent my aide-de-camp to inform the commander of the 27th Regiment that we were about to attack and ask him to cease his fire.

Meanwhile, fierce enemy fire continued, with artillery, grenades, and mortars exploding all around. Just as the preparations were completed and the whistle for the attack was about to be blown, the regimental aide arrived. He informed us that the 27th Regiment had begun entering trench No. 31 and suggested that if we joined this movement from the end of trench No. 32, the trenches could be retaken more easily, reducing our casualties. This method was indeed more practical. I immediately called off the frontal attack and ordered a bomb attack with individual men from trench No. 32. I informed the division commander.

At 06:50, news arrived that the 27th Regiment had occupied a four-squad portion of trench No. 31. Approval from the division commander came at 07:05. With the help of God, trench No. 32 was completely captured by our soldiers. None of the British inside could escape, and they were all cut to pieces by bombs. Contact was established with the 27th Regiment. As soon as our men entered the trenches, they found them full of British dead and the loopholes destroyed. They had a difficult time inside the trench due to enemy fire coming from the flanks and the front.

At this moment, the order was received to attack the enemy at 07:30 and to consult with the commander of the 27th Regiment. The 27th Regiment commander and I met with the division commander to explain the situation. The commander evaluated that the enemy's trenches were now strongly held and that an attack would not be worth the casualties, so the attack was abandoned. Thus, the fighting ended in this manner.[239]

Kemal, who had recently been promoted to colonel, came to Avni upon learning that the trenches were lost. After assessing the situation, it was

32. Colonel Mustafa Kemal in a trench west of Baby 700, June 1915.

---

[239] ATASE: BDH 5384-183-H7-1-6, BDH 5384-183-H7-1-6a, BDH 5384-183-H7-1-7.

decided to launch a counter-attack with the support of the 27th Regiment's reserve battalion. Kemal also ordered a battalion from the 72nd Regiment to stand by behind Mortar Ridge as a reserve and instructed the 64th and 27th Regiments to hold their positions at all costs, even at the risk of annihilation.[240] Lieutenant Colonel Şefik, the commander of the 27th Regiment, formed a bombing party consisting of only three men from his regiment. This small party managed to eliminate the Anzacs who had entered the trenches of the 57th Regiment using hand grenades. He then brought forward the 4th Company of the 3rd Battalion of the 27th Regiment.

The 57th Regiment launched another attack on the lost trenches around 05:00. Trench No. 31, filled with Anzac dead, was completely recaptured by 06:00. At 07:25, both regiments mounted a joint attack and regained trench No. 32, capturing many weapons and pieces of equipment, including trench periscopes never seen before.[241] İzzettin noted the events in his diary:

> News arrived that the enemy had taken the 57th Regiment's trenches Nos. 31 and 32. Upon hearing this bad news, we hurried to the 57th Regiment headquarters. The order was given to retake the trenches with a counter-attack at all costs, even if it meant total annihilation of the regiment. The 27th Regiment took appropriate precautions and blew up our trenches, while the 57th Regiment moved forward to regain the lost positions. The enemy incurred the wrath of God. Returned to headquarters at 11:00.[242]

The same day, an unusual incident occurred. 11 privates, tasked with delivering captured equipment to the regimental headquarters, mistakenly took them to the 3rd Corps headquarters. Despite their mistake, Esat warmly welcomed the men, rewarded them with money, and sent his compliments to their battalion commander for his efforts.[243]

---

[240] Necati Ökse and İrfan Tekşüt, *Birinci Dünya Savaşı'nda Çanakkale Cephesi (04 Haziran 1915 – 09 Ocak 1916), Vol. 5, Book 3* (Ankara: Genelkurmay Askerî Tarih ve Stratejik Etüt Başkanlığı Yayınları, 2012), 54–55.
[241] Mustafa Kemal, *Arıburnu Muharebeleri Raporu*. 117; Necati Ökse and İrfan Tekşüt, *Birinci Dünya Savaşı'nda Çanakkale Cephesi, Vol. 5, Book 3*, 55–56.
[242] İzzettin Çalışlar, *On Yıllık Savaş*, 112.
[243] ATASE: BDH 5384-183-H7-1-7.

After two days of intense fighting in the trenches, only three officers remained in the 3/57th. On 5 June, Avni decided to relieve the battalion with the 2/57th. He instructed the officers of the 2/57th to familiarise themselves with every section of the position they were about to take over in daylight. He ordered the 3/57th, now placed in reserve, to regroup immediately and to keep a company ready to stand to arms at any moment. Avni's first message to the 2/5th was:

> Apparently, the enemy took advantage of the darkness and the men's lack of awareness, approaching and climbing onto the covered trenches undetected. From there, they threw bombs, and terrorised our men, forcing them to flee. A soldier who is so heedless as to let the enemy get to the top of his head should not be considered a human being with the right to live. Therefore, I strongly urge every man, especially officers and sergeants, to always remain extremely vigilant. I am confident that the 2nd Battalion will mind this advice.[244]

Two companies of 2/57th took over the trenches silently before sunset. However, the relief of the trench known as Hüseyin Ağa Trench, right across from Courtney's Post, was postponed until the evening. Still, casualties could not be avoided during the relief, as the Allies began hurling grenades one after another, resulting in one man killed and five wounded.[245]

What happened during the loss of trenches No. 31 and No. 32, along with the heavy casualties suffered to retake them, deeply shook Avni. He sent an order to 3/57th to prevent any further vulnerabilities:

> To the Deputy Commander of the 3rd Battalion of the 57th Regiment
>
> Immediately report the names of the platoon leaders, sergeants, and corporals commanding the men in trenches No. 31 and No. 32 who abandoned their positions during yesterday's enemy attack. This

---

[244] ATASE: BDH 5384-183-H7-1-2a.
[245] ATASE: BDH 5384-183-H7-1-2, BDH 5384-183-H7-1-2a, BDH 5384-183-H7-1-3a.

issue is critical and cannot be delayed, but it must be carefully examined and accurately reported.

Commander of the 57th Regiment
Lieutenant Colonel Avni[246]

On the night of 6 June, the Anzacs managed to penetrate the left side of trench No.35, also known as Hüseyin Ağa Trench, with a force of two squads. However, this time their attempt was briskly countered, and the occupied portion of the trench was swiftly recaptured. During this period, hand grenades had become significant trouble for the regiment. Another 20 men from the 2/57th were wounded in a single day due to constant bombing. Trenches Nos. 31 and 32 were particularly in an awful situation. In his morning message on 7 June, Avni urgently demanded that the trenches be deepened and immediate repairs to be carried out in the areas that had been destroyed. Despite his ongoing requests to the division for sandbags, none had been sent thus far. The divisional aide assured Avni that sandbags would finally be dispatched by evening. Avni also sought the deployment of the division's engineer company commander to help minimise further losses.[247]

This time around 23:00 on the night of 7 June, trenches No. 31 and No. 34 came under attack. When the Anzacs encountered rifle fire, they did not press on. They then renewed their attack on trench No. 32. Despite briefly occupying a small section the size of two squads, the attackers were eventually driven back thanks to the stout resistance of the 2/57th.[248]

My Regiment's Steadily Melting Away
The focus of the Anzacs on attacking the same place for several days had caught Avni's attention. When he went to tour the trenches during 8 June, he observed that the trenches taken over from the 5th Division were in

---

[246] ATASE: BDH 5384-183-H7-1-8a.
[247] ATASE: BDH 5384-183-H7-1-8, BDH 5384-183-H7-1-8a, BDH 5384-183-H7-1-9.
[248] Arzu Tunç et al., eds., *Çanakkale Muharebelerinde 19. Tümen Cerideleri, Vol. 4*, 156–157.

33. Map showing the opposing lines at Anzac.

poor condition. Repair work was constantly interrupted by Allied artillery's intense fire, especially at night:

To the 19th Division Command
8 June 1915
16:50

The enemy's penetration into trenches Nos. 31 and 32 on two consecutive nights drew my attention to these positions, which I inspected myself. When we took them over from the 5th Division, we believed them to be well built. However, what I found did not resemble proper trenches at all. Although I have been trying to improve them continuously since the day we arrived, progress has been hindered by inadequate resources. The so-called trenches are nothing more than widely dug ordinary ditches.

The overhead cover was neither constructed in accordance with regulations nor with proper durability. It was supported by ordinary sandbags, which had torn over time. The trench roof is burnt, extensively damaged, and a significant portion has collapsed. In some places, logs and pieces of wood are sporadically positioned in a way that poses a risk of men being crushed.

The trenches in question are constantly exposed to bombs due to their proximity to the enemy which causes the men to become casualties in dozens. We are currently digging a second line behind them. However, it is necessary to seriously repair these ditches as soon as possible and to make them into a state that can be called trenches, by making every sacrifice necessary to prevent them from falling into enemy hands at all costs. An officer, particularly the engineer officer who appears to have come just to have a look last time, will not suffice for this task. It is essential that the trenches receive secure protection after a diligent and courageous officer with a thorough understanding of the science behind the job thoroughly examines this matter. I have come to the conclusion that we cannot do this with the men and officers at hand. If it is desired to hold these trenches, it is necessary to complete their improvement, taking into account the importance of the matter.

Commander of the 57th Regiment

Lieutenant Colonel Avni[249]

Until the morning of 9 June, efforts were concentrated on improving and deepening the machine gun post and trenches Nos. 31 and 32, as well as repairing the damaged loopholes. Additionally, a second line was being dug behind trench No. 31. The Anzacs, aiming to hinder the work, attempted to attack trench No. 32 on the night of 8 June, but failed.

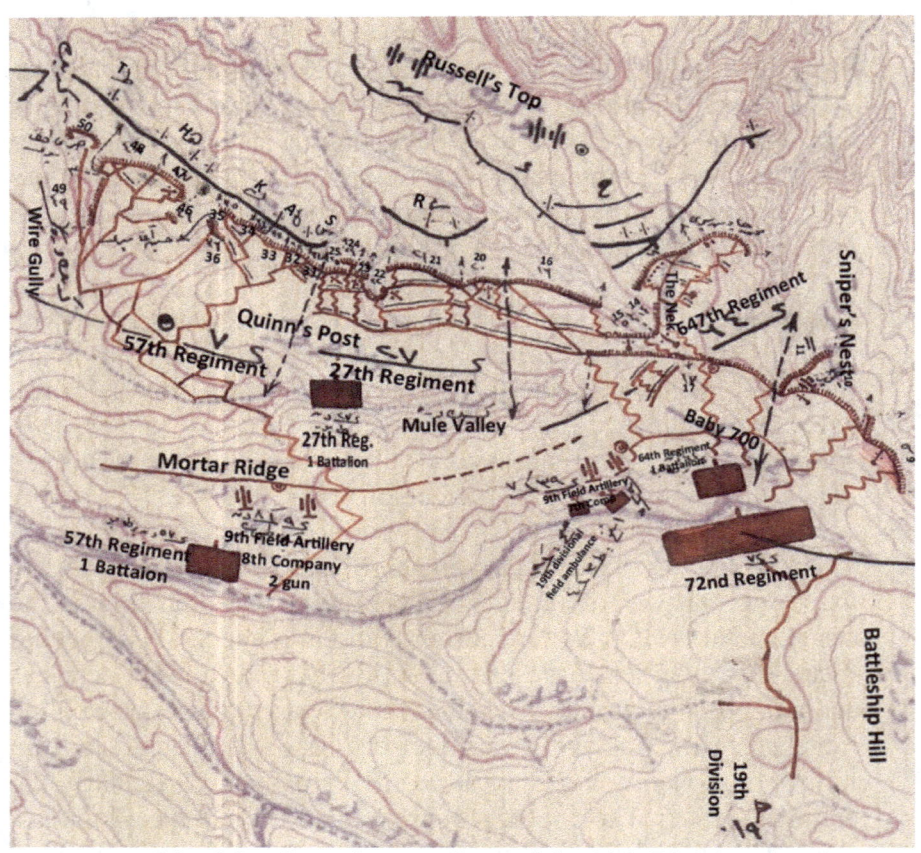

34. Map from the war diary of the 19th Division showing the front held by the division at Anzac in June 1915. (ATASE: 4936-H21-001-010)

On 10 June, upon discovering that a machine gun was positioned in trench No. 47 (German Officers' Trench) on the 1/57th Battalion's front, the Anzacs placed three machine guns opposite trench No. 47 and raked

---

[249] ATASE: BDH 5384-183-H7-1-12, BDH 5384-183-H7-1-12a.

both this trench and No. 48 to heavy fire. At 01:00, a patrol was spotted ahead of trench No. 50 and was driven away with rifle fire. At 02:10, another attack was launched on the 2/57th Battalion's trenches, Nos.. 31, 32, and 34, at Quinn's Post. After 20 minutes of fighting, the attack was repulsed with some loss to Anzacs.[250] The Turkish trenches opposite Quinn's Post—numbered 30, 31, 32, 33, and 34—were the closest to the Allied post, ranging from 7-8 metres to 10-12 metres away. Despite being covered over to reduce casualties, they had turned into a hellish scene due to the flammable materials thrown by the Anzacs. The Turkish defenders valiantly held onto their trenches with great resilience, enduring fire, smoke, bombs and mine explosions.[251] The Anzacs, with their backs against a cliff, clung to their trenches, named 'S' and 'A' by the Turks, with equal determination.

The total length of the trenches held by the 57th Regiment in June 1915 was 758 metres, as follows:[252]

Trench Number	Length (metres)	Distance to the Allied Trench (metres)	Name of the Allied Trench	Name of the Allied Position
31	80	8–10	S	Quinn's Post
32	90	10–15		
33	70	10–20		
34	105	15–25		
35 (Hüseyin Ağa Trench)*	80	20–35	A	Courtney's Post
36	-	-		
46	17	-	K	Steele's Post
47	73	25–40		
48	91	50–70		
49	74	-		
50 (Sabri Efendi Trench)**	33	50–90	H-T	Old Marine Trench
Total	**758**			

---

[250] ATASE: BDH 5384-183-H7-1-15a, BDH 5384-183-H7-1-16a.
[251] Mustafa Kemal, *Arıburnu Muharebeleri Raporu*, 119.
[252] ATASE: BDH 5384-183-H7-1-24; Burhan Sayılır, *Çanakkale Muharebeleri'nde 57. Piyade Alayı*, 87.

* Named after Assistant Sergeant Major Hüseyin Ağa (born 1889) from the 2/57th, who was killed on 12 May 1915.
** Named after a company leader from the 15th Regiment.

35. A Turkish trench at Anzac. The soldier in the foreground holds grenades in his hand, with a match sheet on his chest used to ignite their fuses.

Under these conditions, as of 11 June the regiment had suffered 468 casualties in only a week:

To the 19th Division Command
From the regimental headquarters at Edirne Sırt [Mortar Ridge]

When the regiment arrived with its two battalions to take over the 5th Division's position, it had a strength of 2,768 rifles. As a result of the fighting that has occurred every night since then, the regiment's strength has now dwindled to 2,300. Only in the area held by the 2nd Battalion, which is the most dangerous, there are 30 to 40 casualties each day, amounting to half a squad daily. The trenches in this area span over 500 metres in length. With the battalion deployed across both the front line and support trenches at its current strength, no soldiers are left behind to rest. For this reason, I would like to request that the necessary reinforcements for the battalions be expedited.

Commander of the 57th Regiment
Lieutenant Colonel Avni'[253]

From the night of 11 June until the morning, efforts were made again to repair the overhead cover on trenches Nos. 31 and 32.[254] At 15:00 on 12 June, Anzac soldiers began raining down bombs, resulting in 49 casualties in trench No. 34. The daily toll of casualties significantly depleted the strength of 2/57th, leaving them without reserves. Later that night, a company from the regiment's reserve battalion, 3/57th, was assigned to the 2/57th as a local reserve. Once again, trenches Nos. 31 and 32 were heavily damaged by a shower of over 150 bombs, rendering their overhead covers and sandbags useless. On 13 June, Avni finally relieved the battered 2/57th Battalion with the 3/57th. After the officers of the 3/57th saw the trenches for themselves, the relief began at 17:00 was completed in complete silence within two hours.[255]

Within 10 days of taking over the 5th Division's front, the 57th Regiment had lost a third of its strength. When casualties soared to a hundred in a single day, Avni returned to the trenches during the relief of the 2/57th.

---

[253] ATASE: BDH 5384-183-H7-1-16.
[254] ATASE: BDH 5384-183-H7-1-18a.
[255] ATASE: BDH 5384-183-H7-1-19, BDH 5384-183-H7-1–20, BDH 5384-183-H7-1-20a.

He summoned the corps engineer captain, showed him the situation on-site, and later penned another report to the division commander:

> To the 19th Division Command
> From Edirne Sırt [Mortar Ridge]
>
> I visited the trenches again after learning that we suffered more than one hundred casualties from the continuous enemy bombing last night. The situation in trenches Nos. 31 and 32 remained essentially unchanged since my report dated 8 June 1915. As they are in no state to be called a trench and had been left uncovered for a considerable time, they were further devastated tonight, resulting in such heavy losses. Although our engineers were supposed to cover these trenches with timbers tonight, they were unable to do so. They cannot work today because they are discouraged by the losses they have suffered and their strength has decreased. I invited the engineer captain, who came and witnessed the situation with his own eyes. I would appreciate it if information is gathered from him regarding the situation. These trenches have been left in the lurch. If the casualties cannot be prevented with serious measures and technical efforts, the strength of battalions will dwindle to nothing within a week. To provide some relief to the 2nd Battalion, I had to replace it with the 3rd Battalion again today. No replacements arrive for the casualties of the battalions; whose numbers decrease every day. The 57th Regiment is in a deplorable state because of this great trouble that the 5th Division caused us without making any effort. I kindly request that my concerns be taken into consideration.
>
> Commander of the 57th Regiment
> Lieutenant Colonel Avni[256]

Trenches 31, 32, and 34, initially widened to be covered with timber by the 5th Division but ultimately left uncovered, had nearly lost their function as trenches due to a continuous rain of bombs, resulting in dozens of casualties each night. Upon reading Avni's report, Kemal immediately informed the Northern Group about the situation. He requested the corps engineer battalion to provide sufficient engineers to

---

[256] ATASE: BDH 5384-183-H7-1-21, BDH 5384-183-H7-1-21a.

the 57th Regiment and to remain at Avni's disposal until the repair work was completed.[257] Amid the harsh conditions in the trenches, life went on. Lieutenant Alaattin later described the routine of sleeping in the trenches: 'Our biggest problem was lack of sleep, but eventually, we got used to it. The sounds of bombs exploding and rifles cracking became so familiar that we'd hear them in our sleep and just keep dozing until, of course, a bomb or bullet landed dangerously close. Then, we'd quickly look around to see if anyone was hurt. If everyone was alright, we'd mutter a strong curse in thanks, then fall back asleep as if nothing had happened.'[258]

Empty Bullet Cases Should Not Be Trodden
The regiment's ordeal continued on 14 June. The 3/57th Battalion had suffered 69 wounded and 4 killed in 24 hours. The Anzacs' use of a forward sap to hurl bombs across trench No. 34 caused the most casualties. Although Avni suggested to the division that the sap be shelled, Kemal disagreed, 'It's not possible to shell that area, as our own trenches might inadvertently be hit.'[259]

Upon this, Avni instructed the 3/57th to dig a counter-bombing sap.[260] Later, he went to see the work himself. There he was furious to find empty bullet cases being trampled underfoot, as all war materials were of paramount importance, especially in this time of scarcity:

> To the Battalions and the Machine Gun Company
> 15 June 1915
> From Edirne Sırt [Mortar Ridge]

I find it hard to believe that there is an officer in my regiment who is so careless and unaware of how the ammunition is procured and transported to our front lines. The order to collect and return the spent bullet cases had been repeated multiple times. Yet, during my inspection of the 3rd

---

[257] Arzu Tunç et al., eds., *Çanakkale Muharebelerinde 19. Tümen Cerideleri, Vol. 4*, 219–220.
[258] Arıburun, Tekin, 'Arıburun Savaşlarının 66. Yıldönümünde Kahraman Kumandan Şehit Hüseyin Avni Bey'i Anarken,' *Yeni Düşünce Dergisi*, 5-13, (1981): 11.
[259] ATASE: BDH 5384-183-H7-1-21a, BDH 5384-183-H7-1-22; Arzu Tunç et al., eds., *Çanakkale Muharebelerinde 19. Tümen Cerideleri, Vol. 4*, 229.
[260] ATASE: BDH 5384-183-H7-1-22a.

36. Entrance of a covered trench at Gallipoli.

Battalion's trenches today, I once again saw many bullet cases scattered on the ground beneath their feet. I deeply regret this situation. I hope that this must have caught the attention of one of the 3rd Battalion officers. I resent the officer who saw this and did not bother to give necessary orders. For the last time, I gave the order for them to be collected. I consider anyone who treads on them to be unscrupulous.

I order you to ensure that no bullet cases, especially loaded ones, are ever trampled underfoot, and that anyone who sees them collects them immediately.
Commander of the 57th Regiment
Lieutenant Colonel Avni[261]

The trenches held by the 1/57th Battalion on German Officers' Ridge were also in trouble. On 16 June, Avni informed the Divisional Engineer Company that the trenches and dugouts were highly vulnerable to bombs

---

[261] ATASE: BDH 5384-183-H7-1-23a.

and requested immediate measures be taken. In addition to measures related to engineering and sapping, other solutions were being developed. Lieutenant Ali Rıza, aide to the 3rd Corps Artillery Commander, designed a device capable of throwing hand grenades over long distances. During testing, one grenade reached 60 metres and another 300 metres. The Army Corps approved the device, and production began. When Lütfi, the gunsmith of the 2/57th, returned to regimental headquarters on Mortar Ridge after observing the test at Avni's request, he reported that he had seen the device, found it simple, and believed he could make a better one. Avni then informed the division that they were working on a more effective tool:

> This device requires approximately 20 grams of gunpowder and generates significant smoke when fired. Another device is under development which is simpler, suitable for both camouflaged and non-camouflaged firing, does not use gunpowder, and can propel a grenade up to 150–200 metres based on the strength of the internal spiral spring.[262]

On the same day, news came from the 19th Division that 300 armed reinforcements had arrived for the regiment. Nuri, aide-de-camp to the commander of the 2/57th, was tasked with escorting these men, who were brought to Bigalı village. However, he managed to gather only 270 of the 300 men, who had neither raincoats nor ammunition. Of these, 90 were allocated to the 2/57th, and 179 were given to the 3/57th.

Covering the Trenches
The Engineer Company worked through several nights to cover trenches Nos. 31 and 34, using thick-trunked pine trees cut from the surrounding area and transported to the trenches by pack animals. The digging of the second line trench also progressed. As the trenches became more fortified and protected, the Anzacs made vigorous and continual attempts to ruin them. On 20 June, they used demolition charges, causing the loopholes of trench No. 31 to be blocked and breaking the sandbags. Additionally, the timbers over trench No. 32 had collapsed.

On 21 June, two mountain guns were placed in concealed, loopholed emplacements on the western slope of Mortar Ridge, their barrels aimed

---

[262] ATASE: BDH 5384-183-H7-1-25.

at Courtney's and Steele's Posts. At 09:00 the next morning, the guns opened fire to silence an Anzac machine gun, which was constantly harassing trenches Nos. 31 and 47. The Anzacs spotted the smoke rising from these previously unknown guns and their loopholes. They, too, had placed a mountain gun in a tunnel at the Courtney's Post (opposite No. 35 'Hüseyin Ağa Trench'), to the left of the machine gun. As soon as the first shell from Mortar Ridge was sent, the tunnel mouth, covered with sacks, was suddenly opened, and the gun began firing rapidly. The guns, almost directly facing each other, were separated by no more than 350 metres as the crow flies. One of the shells fired by the gun, manned by Indians under Lieutenant J. H. Thom, found the left gun, destroying its shield and forcing its withdrawal. Another shell damaged the right gun's shield and sights, forcing its removal as well. The Indian gun was eventually silenced when the artillery at Scrubby Knoll intervened.[263] The guns and their emplacements at Mortar Ridge would later be repaired, frequently damaging the Anzac trenches at Courtney's Post.

Avni inspected the work of the engineer company again on 22 June. He was furious to find that the dugouts ordered for the safe accommodation of the battalion reserves had not yet been built:

> Would company officers and battalion commanders not regret it if a bomb came and wiped out one or two platoons? Isn't it pity for these poor men? Anyone who pretends not to understand this issue will be accused of being a traitor. This is your last warning.[264]

The following night, the Turkish artillery laid down a heavy bombardment along the Anzac line between Lone Pine and The Nek. Captain Zeki, the commander of the 1/57th, who had been injured on 25 April and had recently returned to duty, arrived at the regimental headquarters at 02:00 to report on the battle. He found Avni at the observation post above the regimental headquarters, watching the bombardment. While they watched the shells hit Lone Pine, one of the observers saw a cloud of dust at Courtney's Post. Realising parties of Anzacs had moved between Steele's Post and Courtney's Post and were

---

[263] Charles Edwin Woodrow Bean, *Gallipoli Mission* (Canberra: Australian War Memorial, 1948), 256. Arzu Tunç et al., eds., *Çanakkale Muharebelerinde 19. Tümen Cerideleri, Vol. 4*, 290.

[264] ATASE: BDH 5384-183-H8-1-6, BDH 5384-183-H8-1-6a.

heading towards Plugge's Plateau, they quickly sprang into action. According to Avni's report, about four squads of Anzac soldiers made it through, but the rest were prevented from making any further movements.[265]

On 24 June, First Lieutenant Münip, the aide-de-camp to the commander of the 125th Regiment,[266] visited the 1/57th Battalion's front to reconnoitre the Anzac trenches between Steele's and Courtney's Posts. He was shot dead while walking the trenches with Zeki:

> The aide-de-camp to the commander of the 125th Regiment was coming up to my sector on Merkez Tepe one day for a reconnaissance, and wanted to look over from the machine gun position on the northern side of my trenches. You [Anzacs] had the gun awfully well marked by then, and it seldom fired. The sergeant with the gun told him not to look over. He insisted on doing so and was hit through the middle of the forehead and killed.[267]

A War Underground

According to intelligence gathered by Ottoman spies in Egypt, the Allies were busy digging mines at all their positions on the Gallipoli Peninsula. Before this was confirmed, the decision to take precautions against mines or to dig countermines had been left to the regimental commanders. Subsequently, the 5th Army issued orders to dig mines on all fronts. An order issued by the 19th Division on 17 June made it clear that the Allies were mining extensively, and the regiments were instructed to dig countermines to hinder Anzac efforts.[268]

---

[265] ATASE: BDH 5384-183-H8-1-7a, BDH 5384-183-H8-1–8.
[266] First Lieutenant Münip (born in Edirne) was originally with the 4th Company, 1/125th but was serving as aide-de-camp to the commander of the regiment at the time of his death on 24 June 1915. His place of death was recorded as 'Gedik Dere' (Wire Gully).
[267] C.E.W. Bean, *Gallipoli Mission*, 165.
[268] Arzu Tunç et al., eds., *Çanakkale Muharebelerinde 19. Tümen Cerideleri, Vol. 4*, 257.

The first offensive mine at Anzac had been blown by the Turks on 29 May.[269] This was followed by a mine detonated by Australians on German Officers' Ridge on the morning of 25 June. At Gallipoli, explosive charges in underground galleries were now added to the rain of shells and grenades from above. When the Anzacs discovered the tunnel dug by the 1/57th to intersect with the gallery they had driven against trench No. 31, they exploded it at 04:30. The ground swelled in a four-metre diameter, surface cracks emerged, and the sandbags on the trench parapet were damaged. Later, upon realising that a gallery and sap had been driven from trench No.35, over 50 hand grenades were hurled into the trench, tearing apart the sandbags on the parapet.[270] At 15:00, hand grenades began raining down on trench No. 34 once again, setting fire the timbers covering the trench. Over three hours, nearly 300 hand grenades were thrown by the Anzacs at the men attempting to put out the fire.[271]

At 21:45, the Anzacs detonated another mine in front of trench No. 32. Immediately afterwards, a bombing party advanced against the trench, which was repelled with bombs and rifle fire. Around the same time, the Anzacs blew up another Turkish gallery leading towards their lines from trench No. 47, causing the overhead cover of the trench to collapse. Several men from the Turkish garrison trapped beneath the debris were later rescued alive. Meanwhile, another gallery between trenches Nos. 47 and 48 was counter-mined and collapsed.

Despite Avni's repeated requests to the division for artillery bombardment of the Anzac trenches opposite trenches Nos. 31 and 32 as a precaution, his appeals were once again met with refusal.[272] The same

---

[269] This operation was conducted by the 14th Regiment at Quinn's Post. Sixty volunteers under Reserve Officer Vasıf had prepared two mines. The first mine inside a 15 metres long gallery was charged with 90 kilograms of explosives, while the second, laid down inside a 8 metres long gallery, contained 45 kilograms of explosives. The Turkish ends of the tunnels were tamped up at midnight, and the mines were detonated at 03:30 with a great noise, causing significant damage to the Anzacs and were followed by an attack. M. Mutlu Karakaya, *Çanakkale Savaşı'nda 14. Alay* (Ph.D diss., İstanbul University 2017), 173–174.
[270] ATASE: BDH 5384-183-H8-1-9.
[271] C.E.W. Bean, *The Story of Anzac*, 252.
[272] ATASE: BDH 5384-183-H8-1-10a, BDH 5384-183-H8-1-11, BDH 5384-183-H8-1-13.

day, Anzacs noticed another gallery driven from the overcovered communication trench at the junction of trenches Nos. 31 and 32 and blew it in. To guard against Anzac soldiers who might emerge from the hole thus formed, Avni placed men equipped with grenades at its entrance. At 19:30 last evening, the enemy destroyed the gallery that was being driven against their own from the communication trench at the junction of trenches Nos. 32 and 31. One of our men working in the gallery was lightly wounded, he reported to the division at 08:30 next morning.[273]

At 14:30 on 26 June, the mines the Anzacs were digging towards trenches Nos. 31 and 32 were exploded, but only damaged the timber supports of the trenches. During this critical period, the regiment was experiencing a severe shortage of hand grenades. Avni urgently requested three boxes of grenades, as they had completely exhausted the supply. However, only 50 grenades were delivered. In response, at 18:35, he wrote another report to the division, insisting that at least enough grenades be sent to maintain a supply at the regimental headquarters.[274]

For several days, the Anzacs had been trying to erect screens of wire netting in front of their parapets to protect their positions opposite trenches Nos. 31 and 32 from grenades. The Turks used hooks to pull the screens down as a countermeasure, which was repeated frequently.[275] By 27 June, the 57th Regiment's ranks included 31 officers and totalled 3,091 men. The regiment was armed with 1 machine gun, 3,592 rifles, and had 105 hand grenades and 511 boxes of small arms ammunition.[276]

Despite being the location of the closest trenches and the site of the fiercest fighting on his division's front, Kemal did not attach strong importance to Quinn's Post. The capture of this position from the Anzacs was not considered vital enough to force their withdrawal from the Gallipoli Peninsula in the short term. However, he surmised that an attack on Russell's Top via The Nek could be a game-changer. By capturing

---

[273] ATASE: BDH 5384-183-H8-1-15, BDH 5384-183-H8-1-15a.
[274] Arzu Tunç et al., eds., *Çanakkale Muharebelerinde 19. Tümen Cerideleri, Vol. 4*, 339.
[275] ATASE: BDH 5384-183-H8-1-16.
[276] Arzu Tunç et al., eds., *Çanakkale Muharebelerinde 19. Tümen Cerideleri, Vol. 4*, 353.

this area, the Turks would look down both on the landing beaches and the camps in Monash Valley, thus resulting in driving the Anzac forces to the sea. Kemal was of opinion that this plan could be effectively executed with the newly arrived 18th Regiment. This well-trained and fresh unit would be deployed between Baby 700 and Quinn's Post in accordance with the planned attack. Even a tunnel had begun to be dug towards The Nek for this operation, to get the men secretly and safely to their jump-off points. However, this tunnel would not be completed by the time of the attack. In addition, the commander of the regiment, Lieutenant Colonel Abdülkadir, who was known as a brave leader and popular among his men, was shot in the head while visiting the trenches with Major İzzettin.[277] The regimental commander's death did not lead to a change of plans. An attack was scheduled for the night of 28 June. However, the events that took place that night would led the operation to be postponed for 24 hours.

The calmness of the day on 28 June made Avni suspicious, prompting him to send a message to the 1/57th:

---

[277] İzzettin later wrote that he was with Abdülkadir when he was shot. According to his account, he was visiting the trenches with Abdülkadir and a few other officers and explaining the rules to be followed during the relief of the position. Abdülkadir, feeling the tension of his first action, impulsively decided to fire towards enemy. He took the rifle of one of the men in the trench and began firing through a loophole. Although the private, who had loaned his rifle to Abdülkadir, warned and even begged him many times to get out of there, Abdülkadir ignored him. It is likely that he was hit by a sniper's bullet while at the loophole. He was later evacuated to the hospital in Kocadere village, where he succumbed to his wounds. See: Erkan-ı Harbiye Kaymakamı İzzettin, 'Arıburnu Muharebatından İstihsal Edilen Tecarib' *Askerî Mecmua,* 13 (1336/1920): 6. However, in the diary he kept during the campaign, İzzettin stated that on 11 June, he took Abdülkadir and his battalion commanders to the trenches of the 64th Regiment at The Nek and that Abdülkadir was fatally wounded there two days later.
C.E.W. Bean, on the other hand, mentions a Turkish officer who was shot by a sniper at The Nek in June. Although this implies that the Turkish officer may have been Abdülkadir, this view does not match İzzettin's account. The 7th Australian Battalion had noted that this officer, who wore a dark blue uniform with braid shoulder straps, came to the firing line every day, and fired a few shots. (C.E.W. Bean, *The Story of Anzac,* 307.) This detail strengthens the possibility that the officer shot by the sniper was in the 64th Regiment. According to Turkish records, it appears that the officer in question may have been Captain Mehmet Ali from the 3rd Company, 1st Battalion, 64th Regiment, who was killed on 28 May.

Due to suspicious enemy activity observed since evening, a thorough reconnaissance and observation of the front and flanks, particularly the left flank, is necessary. Skilled NCOs, not just privates, should be sent out for reconnaissance. The 125th Regiment was also notified by phone to conduct reconnaissance towards the 1st Battalion on their right flank.

At around 20:30, machine gun fire commenced, followed by an outburst of rifle fire that lasted for some time.[278] Later, at 23:30, a second round of heavy fire started, lasting for a full 15 minutes. Meanwhile, the Anzacs ignited rags in some sections of their lines and fired several flares into Wire Gully. Simultaneously, they cheered and created a commotion, waving their tunics from their trenches. It soon became evident that these actions were merely demonstration.[279] 'The night of 29 June fell very dark,' as noted by Charles Bean, Australian official historian. A violent storm broke out in the evening, and the wind whipped up dust so thick that it resembled fog, severely limiting visibility on both sides. When it was thought that an attack was underway, a wild rifle and machine gun fire was opened along the entire Turkish front. The 1/57th on German Officers' Ridge believed that a mine had exploded, mistaking a flare fired near Lone Pine, which set fire to scrub and caused flames to rise into the sky amidst the swirling dust. Mountain guns stationed at Mortar Ridge and Scrubby Knoll had also opened on the Anzac lines. In response, the Anzacs also began firing, especially targeting the 1/57th.[280] Avni called Zeki to the phone during this uproar:

> An urgent message came from regimental headquarters,' he told us, 'asking for information.' Though I did not know it, Mustafa Kemal, the divisional commander, had an important attack at The Nek planned for next morning, and probably he was most anxious. Our regimental commander, Avni Bey, telephoned to me: 'What has happened?' I said: 'I don't know – I can only tell you that I see nothing but dust, and there is a great deal of noise!' Just then a soldier who had been sent from the right sector of my front trench came in with a report from a young and nervous officer there. It said: 'The English are advancing by bounds.' 'I knew this was

---

[278] ATASE: BDH 5384-183-H8-1-18.111
[279] Mustafa Kemal, *Arıburnu Muharebeleri Raporu*, 121.
[280] C.E.W. Bean, *The Story of Anzac*, 309.

wrong.' he said, 'because your men too were shooting – they must have been at their loopholes ready to fire upon any attack by us.' But as Avni Bey pressed for report, I said: 'I can only send on a report that I have just received from the 12th Company, which I don't believe, but here it is…' and I repeated it, and added that I would go up to the front myself and report. My headquarters was on the rear slope of Merkez Tepe, and I went up the trench to the front line and saw that nothing of importance was happening. Your men were not in our trenches, but many newspapers were blowing over wildly to our trenches. The soldiers gave them to me and I took them and returned. They were papers of old date. I telephoned that it was only a storm. Meanwhile an order had arrived and been written down by my adjutant: 'If the Australians attack,' it said, 'advance and meet them in no-man's-land with the bayonet.' An order had also been sent to one of the battalions, on my left to counter-attack at once and re-establish the position. But as there had been no attack there was no counter-attack. 'Some minutes later the C.O. of our sister battalion at Bomba Sirt rang me up: 'I've been ordered to attack,' he said. 'Be prepared to help us in an hour or two's time, in case of need-with enfilade fire.' I asked the Regimental C.O. about this – what was the reason? His answer was, 'Yes, that battalion at Bomba Sirt is going to make an attack, and the 18th Regiment at the head of Korku Dere is going to make an attack.[281]

After midnight, mountain guns on Mortar Ridge bombarded Russell's Top for about 20 minutes. This was followed by heavy rifle fire opened by the 1/57th and 3/57th battalions. When the firing ceased, the men of the 18th Regiment surged forward, the famous war cry 'Allah Allah!' echoing through the night. Although initial reports indicated that the Anzac front line had been breached, the voices from the front soon fell silent. The flares sent up by the Anzacs illuminated the entire battlefield, both preventing the attackers from retreating unseen and reinforcements to cross no-man's land undetected. Those who managed to retreat disappeared into the pits and unused ditches in no-man's land. Nearly a force of one and a half battalions was almost wiped out in this attack.[282]

---

[281] C.E.W. Bean, *Gallipoli Mission*, 167.
[282] C.E.W. Bean, *Gallipoli Mission*, 169.

When the 18th Regiment launched its attack, Avni immediately ordered the 3/57th forward to draw enemy fire. However, everything was rushed. The timbers covering the trenches of the battalion at Quinn's Post could only be hastily lifted in certain places, allowing the Anzacs to easily target and pick off the men emerging one by one.[283] The attack was called off at 01:35, with casualties in the 3/57th totalling 12 dead and 70 wounded. Among the wounded was Captain Ali Hayri, commander of the battalion, who refused to leave his post.[284]

Defence of Trench No. 47 and the Crater at German Officers' Ridge
30 June was a quiet day. Avni visited the trenches to inspect the engineer company's work. Upon seeing that the trenches were not yet up to standard, he expressed strong disapproval. The commander of the engineer company explained that they had to prioritise covering the trenches to protect themselves from grenades before proceeding with repairs and improvements.[285] In subsequent days, the Anzacs attempted to ignite fires by hurling bottles filled with kerosene followed by hand grenades to burn the timber coverings of the trenches. On 2 July, kerosene-filled bottles were thrown into the trenches, but were swiftly returned before catching fire. Hand grenades continued to bombard the 1/57th trenches at German Officers' Ridge throughout the night. Opposite Quinn's Post, trench No. 31 suffered partial damage, while trench No. 32 was completely ruined.

Around 22:30 on 4 July, the Anzacs blew up a mine to the left of trench No. 47. The explosion not only damaged the firing line of the 1/57th but also damaged support trenches, and destroyed the machine gun post, rendering the weapon unusable. Eight men were killed and eight others wounded as they were buried under soil and timbers during the blast:[286]

> All the communication trenches were filled with dust and all the men were crouching in their shelters. A great crater was formed.

---

[283] C.E.W. Bean, *Gallipoli Mission*, 170.
[284] The commander of the 10th Coy, Captain Süleyman Cavit (born in İstanbul in 1879), was mortally wounded in this attack and died two weeks later in Gülhane Hospital in İstanbul. ATASE: BDH 5384-183-H8-1-20.
[285] ATASE: BDH 5384-183-H8-1-22a, BDH 5384-183-H8-1-23.
[286] ATASE: BDH 5384-183-H9-1-3.

The front part of the trench bordering on it was wholly blown away. The trench had been lightly garrisoned – only fifteen men in that position. Five of these were not seen again. We filled the great gap in the trench wall, where it looked into the crater, with a grid of barbed wire.'[287]

The Anzacs named trench No. 47 'German Officers' Trench' after observers at Steele's Post reported seeing two officers they believed to be Germans there. The machine gun positioned in this trench could sweep the entire slope from this position to Quinn's Post. The Anzacs made persistent efforts to neutralise this machine gun, which was positioned a mere 50 metres from their own lines. Ultimately, they drove a mine gallery beneath the machine gun post. Zeki, the defender of the position, sought advice from German engineer officers when the underground digging was heard. As a precaution, he devised a tactic of digging a counter-gallery to direct the force of any mine explosion and keeping the front line with as few men as possible. Hearing the digging near trench No. 47, he had ordered a counter-gallery to be dug. Upon realising this, the Anzac miners changed their direction and continued their work. They halted three metres from trench No. 47 and eventually detonated a 68kg charge, forming a large crater. Zeki's precautions proved effective: only the front wall of the trench collapsed, preventing total destruction. A grill made of barbed wire was later placed in the collapsed section of the trench. Despite the limited damage, this incident had infuriated Avni:

> Neglecting to properly secure the gallery and being lax in this matter led the way to disaster tonight. We have held this position for a month now. By this time, galleries could have been dug in front of all the trenches across the entire front. Rest assured, if this continues, all the trenches will soon be blown up one by one.

He sternly cautioned the battalion commanders, warning them, 'Allowing this to occur is tantamount to treason.'[288] At 16:30 on 5 July, trench No. 31's overhead cover caught fire again from the grenades. Men worked tirelessly, battling flames while also hurling bombs back. After a great effort, they managed to extinguish the fire. Meanwhile, a section of trench No. 34 on the left, roughly the size of two squads, was completely

---

[287] C.E.W. Bean, *Gallipoli Mission*, 174.
[288] ATASE: BDH 5384-183-H9-1–3, BDH 5384-183-H9-1–3a.

engulfed by the explosion of grenades and subsequently burnt. Simultaneously, a nearby mine exploded, completing the devastation of this section. A gallery under construction there had also collapsed, burying the men working inside. Despite overnight rescue efforts, only one sergeant and six men could be dug out alive. Five others taken out of the collapsed gallery had already died, while a sergeant and four men remained unreachable due to their deeper entrapment.[289]

On the evening of 7 July, the Allied artillery laid down a heavy bombardment on the lines held by the 2/57th. Concurrently, grenades continued to rain down on trenches Nos. 32 and 34, where efforts were still ongoing to repair the damage from the previous day. Three more soldiers were killed and six others were wounded from the grenades. Meanwhile, the sound of picks and shovels from a gallery Anzacs had driven towards trench No.35 alerted the defenders. As a precaution against the recurrent fires caused by grenades, Avni requested from the division that hydropults be sent to his regiment.[290] On that same day, amidst these routine happenings, an extraordinary incident occurred. A soldier, protected by an iron plate wrapped in a sack, emerged from the Anzac lines and threw a grenade after advancing a few metres. Upon hearing this, Avni immediately sent a message to 2/57th:

> An enemy soldier, advancing with an iron sheet for protection, can be shot from either the right or left. Failure to do this means your men are not observing and firing. This must be taken into consideration. Put your loopholes in a state where the whole front can be enfiladed, and find opportunities to engage the enemy in any case. If we fail to utilise our own firepower, we cannot rely on support from other regiments. It's also crucial to intermittently cover the trenches to prevent fire from spreading across the entire overhead cover. In short, it is necessary to act with courage against the activities of the enemy.[291]

Bitter Fighting in Tunnels

On 8 July, a fire broke out once again in trench No. 32, which had been repaired throughout the day, due to flammable materials and grenades

---

[289] ATASE: BDH 5384-183-H9-1-6.
[290] ATASE: BDH 5384-183-H9-1-8a.
[291] ATASE: BDH 5384-183-H9-1-9, BDH 5384-183-H9-1-9a.

being thrown in. Seeing the soldiers trying to extinguish the fire, the Anzacs turned on them. When the second line trenches responded, the Anzac fire ceased. The fire was finally extinguished at 04:20 in the morning. At noon, the Anzacs attempted to ignite the trench No. 32 again by throwing kerosene bottles and grenades. Simultaneously, they hindered the repair efforts by continually bombing the burnt sections of trench No. 34. Further south, the sounds of voices and digging from underground indicated that a tunnel was being driven from the Anzac lines towards the crater formed in front of trench No. 47 four days ago.[292]

Zeki decided to reconnoitre the crater personally. He took a soldier with him, moved aside the wire entanglement, and slipped into the crater, managing to avoid detection by the snipers:

> I set about exploring the crater, taking a soldier with me. There were a lot of stones in it, and after pulling these away I came upon two wires leading straight back towards the 'English' lines. They led into a mass of sandbags which I found to be closing the mouth of a tunnel, the bags being packed up from its bottom to its roof. I and the soldier drew the bags away, one by one. As we did so, some noise the other side made us think that a sentry with a bayonet was there. We took away bags until we had made a crevice and could see through. By then no one was in the tunnel. The tunnel led away from us. I wondered what to do. At first I thought, 'I'll blow this, place in'; so I had six or seven sticks of explosive brought. But it was the sort of explosive that is used in blowing up railways, and this had failed before in similar tasks; accordingly, I decided not to blow the place. I went out again with a man and we pulled the bags away and made an opening. I told the man to go through, and he did so. There was a tunnel leading about ten feet ahead of us. It led no farther in that direction, but then turned at right-angles to the left. I told the man to go round the corner. He did so and a sergeant with him, I staying at the corner. There were steps leading down to a deeper tunnel, and at the bottom a light could be seen flickering, and someone was there. Then someone from below fired a revolver shot, which hit against the wall at the end of the gallery, where the turn in it was. I afterwards picked up this bullet, and sent it to

---

[292] ATASE: BDH 5384-183-H9-1-11a.

Kemal and Essad as the first shot fired in underground warfare here.[293]

37. Major Zeki on the old battlefield in 1919. Trench No. 47 can be seen behind him. To his right is the crater, and in front of him is the collapse of the tunnel leading to the crater. (AWM: G01924)

The tunnel leading from the Anzac lines to trench No. 47 was periodically illuminated by candlelight. However, the last part where the sandbags were piled remained pitch dark. In fact, as Zeki and his companion were drawing the sandbags away, there was an engineer on the other side whose duty was to constantly listen to the ground. When the engineer heard that the crater had been entered, he ran to the 7th Battalion headquarters to find the battalion commander, Lieutenant Colonel Elliot, and reported that he had heard voices beyond the sandbags. An armed sentry was immediately sent to replace the engineer. After a while, when the sentry saw that a hole had opened between the sacks and daylight was entering through it, he immediately returned to the headquarters and gave the news that there were Turks in the crater. The moment Zeki mentioned, 'There was no one in the tunnel,' was the moment when the sentry went back to report. Elliot immediately ordered the crater to be bombed, the

---

[293] C.E.W. Bean, *Gallipoli Mission*, 174.

sentry to withdraw to avoid being hit, and a party to be organised to drive the Turks out. He then personally went in to see the situation.

Meanwhile, Zeki and his companion had advanced to the point where the tunnel formed a corner. Elliot then entered the tunnel with two sentries. He came to the corner illuminated by candlelight, where the man Zeki had sent ahead was waiting. At that moment, with a flash of light, the cry of the man behind Elliot was heard. The Turkish bullet passed under Elliott's left arm had hit the man behind him. Elliot, pistol in hand, leaned against the right wall and waited. After a brief silence, there was an exchange of fire. The men who removed their wounded comrade from the tunnel believed that Elliott had also been shot. Subsequently, another officer entered the tunnel and found Elliot waiting with his pistol in hand. Elliott then ordered a sandbag barricade to be built there. Sandbags were stacked in two rows up to the ceiling, with a steel plate placed near the top. Zeki, with his returning man, had also started building a barricade. Thus, the tunnel was tamped up from both sides, leaving a gap of a few metres in between.[294] The bullet that Zeki took from the tunnel wall and presented to Kemal as a souvenir was the bullet from Elliot's pistol. Avni subsequently wrote a report to the division about this incident:

> In the 1st Battalion, men were sent into the enemy's gallery, which runs approximately four metres vertically before turning left. Steps leading down to a deeper place were seen about five metres from the corner, and the man sent there was fired upon. A defensive line of sandbags has been established inside the tunnel. Since it is not possible to defend with a Mauser there, the men fire at the British with revolvers and the British respond in the same way.[295]

The sentry placed by Zeki behind the barricade soon reported hearing voices from the other side. Suspecting the Anzacs were mining, Zeki took a German expert into the crater. The expert, listening to the ground, determined the digging was going on two or three metres away. Despite considering immediate precautions, Zeki decided not to do anything, knowing the Anzacs would blow in any countermine as soon as they heard it. However, the Anzacs, observing the Turkish sentry from behind their own barricade, managed to secretly place a powerful charge

---

[294] C.E.W. Bean, *The Story of Anzac*, 333.
[295] ATASE: BDH 5384-183-H9-1-12.

between the two barricades without detection. To avoid damage, they thickened their barricade to 3 to 4 metres. They worried the Turkish sentry might notice the explosive and detonator cables, but they stalled him off successfully, as he only fired in response to sounds.[296]

On the afternoon of 9 July, the mine was detonated. At the time, Zeki was in trench No. 47:

> A few days later there was an explosion. I was in the trenches and was thrown down. The sentry behind the tamping was not found at all; the sentry at the mouth of the tunnel had been blown back over the parados of our front trench and killed; the sentry on the right of the tunnel mouth was killed.[297] The tunnel was still there from the crater to the bend, but the bend of it had been blown in arid a new crater had been made just beyond the bend, beyond where our sandbags had been.'[298]

The part of the tunnel leading to the crater was damaged. Two nearby craters formed between the Anzac and Turkish trenches, connected by a partially collapsed tunnel. Zeki re-entered the large crater on the side of trench number 47, and the stone and soil that filled the tunnel were cleared. He entered through the opened hole and crawled to the new crater:

> So we again cleared away the stones and clods where the elbow had fallen in, until we could see through a crevice between the stones. I myself looked through: and there was a soldier, an Australian, crouching on one knee against the forward edge of the crater with his rifle in one hand on one knee, brushing the earth off the bolt quietly with the other hand, and looking intently over his left shoulder up at me. Perhaps he had heard something. My revolver I had lent to our sentry, and it had been lost with him in the explosion. I ran for another. 'I can shoot that man,' I thought. Then I reflected: 'What's the use of shooting him? We will wait for this evening and capture him.' We needed prisoners.[299]

---

[296] C.E.W. Bean, *The Story of Anzac*, 335–336.
[297] Corporal Selim, son of Hüseyin (1876, Sinop), 4th Coy, 1/57th.
[298] C.E.W. Bean, *Gallipoli Mission,* 175.
[299] C.E.W. Bean, *Gallipoli Mission*, 176.

Zeki returned and immediately informed the regimental commander of what he had seen. Avni agreed with the idea of capturing the enemy.[300] The crater was raided at midnight on 10 July:

> I intended to send over about midnight a few soldiers from the old crater and capture the man. They tried it, jumping out of the large crater, just south of the tunnel mouth. two or three of them; but immediately the first who jumped out was shot and badly wounded. The others ducked back crouching in their crater and stayed there. Later the sentry told me that the hole where the [Australian] sentry was had been shut and a wire entanglement put in the crater.[301]

A few volunteers from trench No. 47 had crawled into the crater, but as soon as they emerged from there to raid the new crater, they were met with fire and the first man to come out was immediately shot dead. The raid ended in failure when a squad of Anzac reinforcements subsequently appeared. During the night, 18 men were wounded and 1 man killed from the mutual bombing elsewhere on the front.[302] Major İzzettin, visiting to inspect the 57th Regiment front, made sure to record in his diary what he witnessed on 9 July:

> The weather is hot and breezy. I visited the 57th Regiment front in the morning. First, I saw trenches 31, 32, 33, and 34 of the 2nd Battalion. Just as I passed trench 32, the enemy blew up a mine beneath us. At first, I thought it was a bomb. A private who was buried inside the gallery was dug out alive. I sat in the tent of the 2nd Battalion Commander Major Murat Efendi for a while. Then I went to the 1st Battalion, Zeki Efendi's front, where I visited trenches 47 and 48. Sat with Zeki for a while and drank lemonade. After that, I went to see 57th Regiment Commander Avni Bey. Returned to headquarters at 15:00. Major Selanikli Nuri came to see us.[303]

---

[300] ATASE: BDH 5384-183-H9-1-12a.
[301] C.E.W. Bean, *Gallipoli Mission*, 176.
[302] ATASE: BDH 5384-183-H9-1-13.
[303] İzzettin Çalışlar, *On Yıllık Savaş*, 120.

On the afternoon of 11 July, a fire broke out once again on the right section of trench No. 31 because of grenades. Despite the extraordinary efforts, the fire could not be extinguished. The hydropults that Avni requested had still not been sent. As a solution, he recommended:

> An order has been given to send water from the reserve battalion. However, it will take some time for the water to arrive. To avoid such difficulties in the future, it is recommended to keep both the barrels in the trenches and those in the battalion full at all times.[304]

The raining of grenades increased even more in the evening. The fire surrounded the entire trench and could not be extinguished by any means. The situation had become grave. On the other side, in trench No. 47, while the sound of the Anzacs digging underground went on, grenades were constantly being thrown into the second crater to prevent them from settling in it. Avni wrote to the division:

> We only had two lightly wounded from the grenades in the past six hours. We are preventing the enemy from settling in the nearby mine crater with bombs. There is no other solution than to drive a countermine from inside trench No. 47 against the enemy who is digging towards the right of this trench. The galleries we dug, about a hundred metres long, were collapsed by the mine we exploded yesterday, and the gallery dug by the enemy in this part of our trenches seems to be very useful to him.[305]

The Large Crater at German Officers' Ridge

At 08:45 on 12 July, a wild machine gun and infantry fire opened from the Allied lines. Opposite trench No. 47, unaware that the crater formed on 4 July had blown away the wall of trench No. 47, the Anzac officers doubted its proximity to the Turkish trench as reported by the engineers who mined it. Lieutenant Colonel Elliot, commanding the 7th Battalion, saw an opportunity to turn the crater into a forward bombing post to target trench No. 47. When volunteers were called for the attack, Lieutenant Norman Greig of the 7th Battalion stepped forward to lead. They suddenly climbed out of the small crater on their side and stormed the large crater. Using grenades, they eliminated the guards and established

---

[304] ATASE: BDH 5384-183-H9-1-13a.
[305] ATASE: BDH 5384-183-H9-1-15.

themselves inside. First Lieutenant Fahri, grabbed a stout stick, and led a squad into the crater, preventing the Anzac party from advancing further.[306] At that moment, Fahrettin, observing from Scrubby Knoll, spotted the Anzacs getting into the crater. He immediately got on the phone: 'Zeki Efendi, the enemy is getting into your trenches. What are going to do?' Startled, Zeki hurried to the front trench and saw his men hurling grenades into the crater. As he went a little further to see how much damage the bombs had caused to the wire they placed between the crater and No. 47, Fahri grabbed his arm: 'Don't go there, it's dangerous. They have been exchanging shots.' Zeki ignored his warning and continued forward. He saw his men looking into the crater, where it appeared the Anzac raiding party were retreating from within.

38. Lieutenant Greig in a watercolour painting illustrating the fight at the crater on 12 July 1915. (AWM: ART02191, P10427.015)

Lieutenant Greig and his party disappeared from sight, and they started calling for reinforcements when they were confronted by Fahri and his men as soon as they established themselves in the crater. The

---

[306] Erkan-ı Harbiye Kaymakamı İzzettin, 'Arıburnu Muharebatından İstihsal Edilen Tecarib' *Askerî Mecmua*, 13, (1336/1920).

reinforcements immediately climbed out of the trench and attempted to advance, but being unfamiliar with the terrain, most of them veered towards the right of trench No. 47 instead of heading towards the crater. Unaware of any planned operation, a machine gun at Russell's Top mistook the men for Turks and turned on them. Caught between the fire from both sides, the party had to retreat with some loss. Unable to receive the reinforcements he had called for, Greig ordered his men to retreat through the tunnel. The last of the volunteers who could pass through the tunnel and reach the small crater later said that Greig was standing at the mouth of the tunnel, that he was wounded in the head, and that he stopped the Turks with his pistol in his hand so that his men could retreat. Greig would not be able to return. Zeki, looking at the crater from the trench, called out to his men: 'Don't kill this man. We want to take him alive!' The men replied that the officer would not allow himself to be taken prisoner. Another grenade was thrown, and Greig fell dead amidst dust and smoke. Zeki later recounted: 'I would have liked to take that officer prisoner; he was a very brave man.' Zeki later had Greig buried in the valley behind the lines 'with more ceremony and care than the Turks usually devoted to their dead opponents.'[307]

First Lieutenant Fahri, who confronted Greig and his party, was awarded a Silver Imtiyaz Medal for his bravery. The belongings recovered from Greig were delivered to Avni, who subsequently sent them to Kemal. Later in the afternoon, the Anzacs tried to place a gun in the small crater but were repelled. The crater would now be protected by continuous bombing and rifle fire.[308]

Celebrating Ramazan at the Front
13 July 1915 was the first day of the Islamic month of Ramazan of that year, the month of fasting for all Muslims. Kemal sent a message to Avni celebrating the Holy Month and praising the 57th Regiment.[309] Avni responded with a message of his own:

> To the 19th Division Command
> 13 July 1915

---

[307] C.E.W. Bean, *Gallipoli Mission*, 178.
[308] ATASE: BDH 5384-183-H9-1-15a, BDH 5384-183-H9-1-16.
[309] Despite researches in the archives, it has proved impossible to find Mustafa Kemal's message – in despite of expectations that it should exist.

> From Edirne Sırt [Mortar Ridge]
>
> I would like to express our humble gratitude for the message sent to our regiment on the occasion of the month of Ramazan, which is celebrated by all believers, and for the commendation that you, our esteemed commander, have shown towards us. May God Almighty grant us many more joyful days like these under your command.
>
> Commander of the 57th Regiment
> Lieutenant Colonel Avni[310]

In the afternoon, the Anzacs detonated two more mines to the right of trench No. 47, spaced half an hour apart, causing significant damage to it. The seven men working in the galleries of the trench were lost, never to be seen or heard of again. Avni urgently requested 500 sandbags from the division to put the place in order. At the same time, he requested artillery support to prevent the Allied activities there so that the trench could be defended. The extensive destruction of trench No. 47 affirmed the concerns he had conveyed to the division just hours earlier.[311]

Fighting for 40 Days
The tunnels dug and mines exploded in the last two weeks had brought the fighting mostly underground. Avni believed that this new development made the defence of the trenches more challenging:

> The enemy's persistent attempts through their tunnels against the front we are responsible for defending diminish our defensive capabilities in proportion to their efforts. You are too well aware of the criticality of this front. I have concerns about the regiment, which has been under constant fire since 25 April, and may not be fully capable of fulfilling its duties when required anymore. I propose that now is the time to reinforce this front more robustly, and therefore, I request that the entire front, naturally divided into two sections, be defended with two regiments, allocating an additional regiment for this purpose.[312]

---

[310] ATASE: BDH 5384-183-H9-1-18.
[311] ATASE: BDH 5384-183-H9-1-17.
[312] ATASE: BDH 5384-183-H9-1-16a.

Kemal, who shared Avni's perspective, penned a more detailed message to Esat:

> 1 – The front held by the 57th Regiment is currently subjected to constant and frequent enemy bombings, as well as recent mining activities. This situation significantly impacts the physical and morale strength of the men. Having defended this front for forty days, the 57th Regiment has suffered daily casualties in the trenches, leading to considerable fatigue that has visibly affected the psychological well-being of the men. Although Bomba Sırt [Quinn's Post] was occupied in turns by the 2nd and 3rd battalions of the regiment, the Merkez Tepe [German Officers' Ridge] front was solely entrusted to the 1st Battalion. The battalion, which has been in this position that requires extreme vigilance at all times for forty days, is of course very tired. The notable remarks of the commander of the regiment in this respect have been presented verbatim for your consideration. The 57th Regiment Commander's request to allocate two regiments to the current front is intended to facilitate the regular rotation of battalions, thereby ensuring continuous readiness and fitness among the men. The division does not have the strength to allocate it for this purpose. Since I have little confidence in the 72nd Regiment, I am unwilling to entrust not only the vulnerable position in question but also any portion of the division's front to this unit. Given the urgent need to replace the 57th Regiment, I hereby request the allocation of a fresh regiment to the front in question.
>
> 2 – The situation of trenches at both Merkez Tepe front and the left flank of Bomba Sırt, is considered more critical to examine than the enemy's situation in the same area. Our front at Merkez Tepe is weak compared to the opposing enemy lines and is overlooked by the enemy line[313] parallel to Gedik Dere [Wire Gully]. A solid and reliable line with an overhead cover was not constructed there in the first place. Now, due to the effects of grenades and mines, defending this position has become even more challenging. Only two platoons can be accommodated here. There is a second line, but it is not suitable for effective fire, and the men positioned there are exposed to the enemy's line parallel to the gully, restricting

---

[313] This trench was called Tambour Sap by the Anzacs. (t.n.)

their ability to act freely. It is not possible to completely mitigate the vulnerabilities along the 57th Regiment front. We must also consider the suitability of the 16th Division's position at Kırmızı Sırt [Johnston's Jolly] for this purpose. The newly established enemy firing line against the 125th Regiment's front there will draw the regiment's fire and may leave the enemy line parallel to Gedik Dere completely free. I am of opinion that it is essential to hold Merkez Tepe with a fresh and reliable body of men. Additionally, we should establish a new front at Kırmızı Sırt overlooking Gedik Dere and assign the unit stationed there to protect our trenches on Merkez Tepe.

Commander of the 19th Division
Colonel Mustafa Kemal[314]

In his reply the next day, Esat acknowledged the efforts of the 57th Regiment and the selfless sacrifices of its officers and men. He noted that the unit sent to the Southern Group (Helles) had not yet arrived and that no fresh forces were available. Consequently, he ordered the 57th Regiment to be reinforced with a battalion from the 72nd Regiment. In addition, he stressed that every regiment was a family, and the land they occupied was their home. This home must be defended to the last man. On 15 July, the 2/72nd, with a strength of 690 men, was placed under the command of the 57th Regiment to take over the trenches at German Officers' Ridge.[315]

The last 10 days of July saw a flurry of mine explosions, relentless grenade attacks, and mutual local assaults. Amidst turmoil, British planes ramped up their activity, taking photographs of the front and bombing selected targets. The attacks were particularly intense on Mortar Ridge and the regimental headquarters. While mountain guns on the ridge endured aerial bombardment, howitzers pounded the reserve areas to the east. On 31 July, a British plane dropped a bomb on the regimental headquarters, but caused no damage. These focused attacks on Mortar Ridge indicated that the Allies had pinpointed the location of the

---

[314] Arzu Tunç et al., eds., *Çanakkale Muharebelerinde 19. Tümen Cerideleri, Vol. 5*, 205–206.
[315] ATASE: BDH 5384-183-H9-1-19.

regimental headquarters and had made it a primary target. İzzettin recorded in his diary:

> 25 July 1915: Enemy aircraft remain active. Reports indicate that the enemy is preparing to launch an offensive in early August.
>
> 26 July 1915: Enemy artillery activity continues.
>
> 27 July 1915: The weather is hot. In the afternoon, I met Captain Cemal, the son of Hakkı Bey, who is my relative. He commands the 9th Company of the 57th Regiment. We visited the trenches of the 57th Regiment together, where we witnessed enemy bombardment. Afterwards, I visited Hayri, commander of the 3rd Battalion. Then I met with Avni Bey and Zeki Bey.[316]

Attack at Lone Pine, 6-7 August 1915

By August, Avni's complaints about trench repairs persisted. Despite his repeated requests for essential materials, they were consistently sent incomplete. When his patience wore thin, he summoned the corps engineer battalion commander to inspect the trenches personally. Subsequently, he penned a stern letter to the division's engineer company commander, urgently demanding hand grenades, sandbags, and timber:

> To the 19th Division Engineer Company Command
> 4 August 1915
>
> The commander of the Corps Engineer Battalion came here. He witnessed first-hand and pitied the state of our trenches. He emphatically stressed the urgent need for a substantial quantity of sandbags. He then said that he would prioritise the delivery of sandbags, timbers, and other essentials here. You don't send anything! At least 500 sandbags and 200 timbers are needed immediately. If these are not provided, work in the trenches will come to a halt. If you doubt this or feel sorry, come and see for yourself. These requested materials are not eaten or drunk, they are used where needed. If you truly wish to serve the nation and protect even an inch of our land, you must make full use of the means and resources available. In the evening, I requested two chests of bombs

---

[316] İzzettin Çalışlar, *On Yıllık Savaş*, 124.

but received only one. These supplies are handed out like alms and guarded as if they were treasures. Today, nothing but bombs can dislodge the enemy who will enter our trenches, God forbid. It is strongly needed that three chests of bombs, 500 sandbags and 200 timbers be sent today.

Commander of the 57th Regt.
Avni.[317]

On 5 August, trench No. 32 was in flames once again. Amongst witnessing the scene was İzzettin:

> In the afternoon, I visited the 27th Regiment trenches with the corps' chief medical officer. I saw the trenches at Boyun [Courtney's Post] from the entrance of a communication trench. During our visit, a fire broke out in our trench No. 32 due to enemy bombs, creating a sight to behold. Afterwards, I went to see Şefik Bey. Abdurrezzak Bey, commander of the 125th Regiment was also present, and we engaged in conversation for a while. News arrived that Warsaw had fallen.[318]

The Allies were poised to execute their plan to seize the Hill 971 – Conkbayırı – Battleship Hill – Baby 700 line, which they called Sarı Bayır. By early August, the Allied garrison at Anzac totalled 37,000 troops, reinforced by the recent arrival of the 13th Division, a brigade from the 10th Division, and the 29th Indian Brigade. On the Turkish side, positioned from Sazlı Dere southward, were the 19th Division (72nd, 18th, 27th and 57th Regiments, respectively) and, to their left, the 16th Division (125th, 47th, 48th and 77th Regiments, respectively). The 5th Division constituted the corps reserve.

---

[317] Cengiz Eroğlu et al., *Bir Kahramanlık Abidesi: 57. Piyade Alayı – Şehitler Alayı*, (Ankara: Milli Savunma Bakanlığı Yayınları, 2003), 55.
[318] İzzettin Çalışlar, *On Yıllık Savaş*, 126.

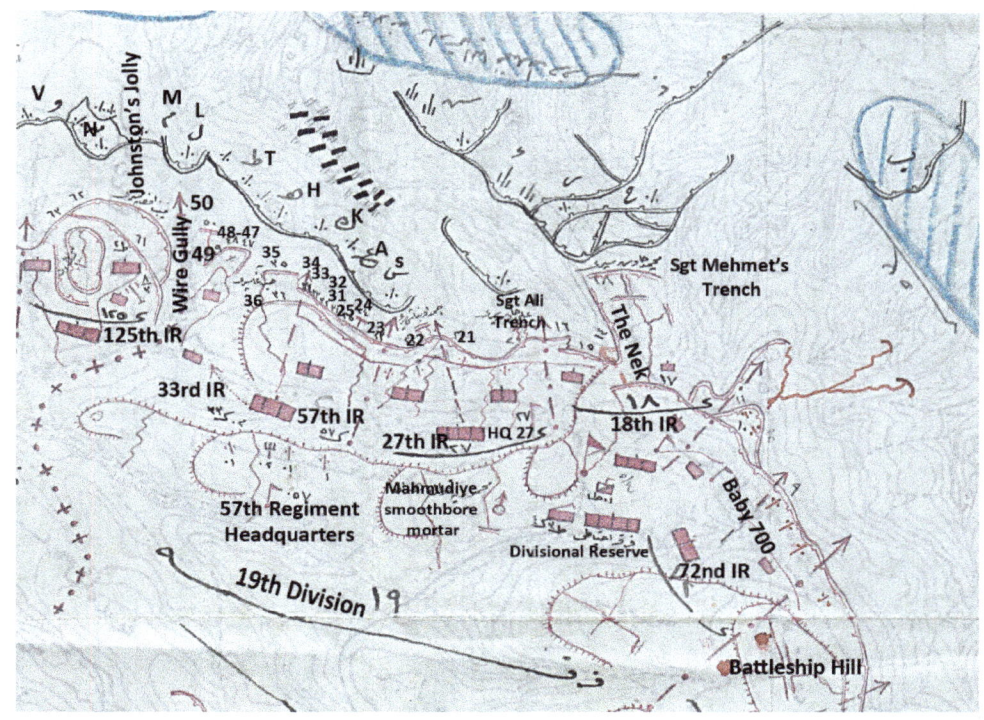

39. Turkish map showing opposing lines at Anzac after August fighting. (BDH-4347-28-12)

The sporadic bombardment from sea and land on the morning of 6 August escalated in intensity through the afternoon. Lone Pine and the left flank of German Officers' Ridge bore the brunt of the heavy shelling. At 17:30, after the artillery fire ceased, four battalions from the 1st Australian Brigade launched an assault on the sixty-metre stretch of Turkish trenches held by the 47th Regiment at Lone Pine, advancing in four waves.

Despite resistance from the few Turkish soldiers who had survived the bombardment unscathed, the Australians established themselves in the Turkish trenches before dark. Esat ordered the deployment of a battalion from the 57th Regiment to reinforce Lone Pine. This occurred on the same day that 1/57th, which had been engaged in continuous

40. A watercolour portrait of Hüseyin Avni, done by the artist Hayri Çizel at the front on 1 August 1915, 12 days before Avni's death. (Haluk Oral, Arıburnu 1915)

combat on German Officers' Ridge for 45 days, was scheduled to be relieved by 2/72nd. The relief was completed under bombardment in the afternoon, and the 1/57th had just withdrawn behind Mortar Ridge when Avni, following Kemal's instructions, ordered the battalion to reinforce the 47th Regiment at once.[319] As the battalion commander, Zeki played a central role in the unfolding events:

> On 6 August, some of these shells burst in the trenches. Coincidentally, that day, by order of Mustafa Kemal, a notice had to be displayed above the parapet of my post announcing the capture of Warsaw. I went up there and put it up myself. We thought that these shells might be an answer to this. From twenty to twenty-four shells had fallen that day around the position, and about five of them had hit the trench direct. The battalion had been suffering so heavily in these last days that our relief had at last been promised; we were to be withdrawn for rest that afternoon. When these shells fell in our trenches I went up to the front myself, and there was the head-cover blown in, and the men lying smashed up and dead. I was very frightened. But now, just when we were to leave, the relieving battalion hesitated. 'We cannot carry out the relief in this bombardment,' they said. The relieving battalion was Arab, one from the 72nd Regiment, in divisional reserve. But I, who had been up to the front line, insisted that they must relieve us. It was always like that, I said and my battalion had been there forty-five days. So the I/57th came out and I went to the regimental headquarters. I was with the regimental commander at Edirne Sırt, and we could see the bombardment which was still going on. We could see that both large and small shells were concentrated on Kanlı Sırt [Bloody Ridge, Lone Pine]. My battalion had just come out and was at that moment assembled behind Edirne Sırt, and I ordered the officer-in-charge at once to be ready to reinforce as they were the nearest reinforcement to Kanlı Sırt. From the regimental headquarters at the back of Mortar Ridge you could see clearly. There was a lot of dust raised by the shells at Kanlı Sırt. I could not see through it, but when the bombardment there ceased we heard infantry fire a little like after thunder you hear the rain beginning; and the observers beside us said, 'The English are getting into our trenches.' Our observation of this bombardment

---

[319] Mustafa Kemal, *Arıburnu Muharebeleri Raporu*, 128.

had given us the impression that the trenches subjected to it would not be in a condition to repel the attack – there had been much damage and heavy loss.[320]

The 1/57th went into fighting immediately upon arrival at Lone Pine and lost heavily in a short time. Meanwhile, at German Officers' Ridge, Avni instructed the officers to keep the men vigilant and fully prepared for a sudden attack. At 00:30, after oily rags were thrown into trench No. 47, howitzers bombarded it together with trench No. 48, and mines were detonated one after another. This was followed by an attack, which the 2/72nd successfully repelled.[321] At 04:50, a mine exploded in front of trench No. 31, burying an entire squad of men. Subsequently, the Anzacs launched an attack with a company-sized force. Avni reported to the division, 'With God's help, the enemy has been laid out in front of our trenches with grenades and rifle fire.' Half an hour later, another attack was made against trenches Nos. 31 and 35, but these half-hearted attempts were repelled without much difficulty. A counter-attack was considered at German Officers' Ridge on the afternoon of 7 August, but no one could get out of the trench due to the intense fire. Finally, at 19:00, Kemal gave up the idea of attacking.[322]

Around this time, Avni received a report from Zeki stating they were in an awful situation and requesting to return to the regiment as soon as possible. Avni immediately asked for permission from the division:

To the 19th Division Command
7 August 1915
18:30
From the regimental headquarters

1 – Yesterday, in accordance with your orders, the 1st Battalion had been sent to reinforce the 47th Regiment at Kanlı Sırt [Lone Pine].
2 – This battalion had just come out from the trenches and was deployed there due to the developing situation before it had time to

---

[320] C.E.W. Bean, *Gallipoli Mission*, 185.
[321] Arzu Tunç et al., eds., *Çanakkale Muharebelerinde 19. Tümen Cerideleri, Vol. 6*, 196; İzzettin Çalışlar, *On Yıllık Savaş*, 127.
[322] Arzu Tunç et al., eds., *Çanakkale Muharebelerinde 19. Tümen Cerideleri, Vol. 6*, 224.

41. A communication trench leading to Lone Pine.

rest and recover. Upon arrival, it found the 47th Regiment in a devastated state, and the battalion soon suffered the same fate.

3 – According to reports from the battalion commander, command and control were lost during the night, resulting in the battalion fighting in a dispersed manner. When the officers attempted to regroup the battalion today, only 300 men from three companies could be mustered.

4 – Regardless of the battalion's current condition, you are aware of our urgent need for men on our front. Many reinforcements have already been sent there. I humbly request that the battalion be allowed to withdraw for reorganisation.

Commander of the 57th Regiment
Lieutenant Colonel Avni[323]

Kemal conveyed this request to the Northern Group Command and requested the return of the 1/57th if it was no longer needed.[324]

At 05:30 on 8 August, the Anzacs were seen fixing bayonets at Steele's Post. This was responded to with heavy fire three times at intervals. An hour earlier, the 18th and 27th Regiments had been attacked, and despite repeated attempts, the Anzacs were repelled with heavy loss each time.[325]

During the day, the 57th Regiment headquarters came under fire from howitzers. There were no casualties, although a few pack animals and men were wounded. The 1/57th had still not returned from Lone Pine. Avni wrote to the division again, reporting that the battalion's strength had been reduced to 400 men and insisting on its return, especially since two regiments had already arrived in that sector. Shortly afterward, he received a call from İzzettin, who informed him that the battalion was in the trenches and would be pulled back as soon as conditions allowed. At the same time, Kemal reiterated his request to Esat for the battalion's return to its regiment. Finally, at 20:50, Esat informed Kemal that the

---

[323] Arzu Tunç et al., eds., *Çanakkale Muharebelerinde 19. Tümen Cerideleri*, Vol. 6, 221.
[324] Arzu Tunç et al., eds., *Çanakkale Muharebelerinde 19. Tümen Cerideleri*, Vol. 6, 223.
[325] İzzettin Çalışlar, *On Yıllık Savaş*, 127.

16th Division had been ordered to send back the battalion.[326] Despite this, the battalion would spent the night of 8 August in the maze of trenches at Lone Pine, Zeki later explained:

> A final order was given [about 9 August] to abandon the attempt to retake Kanlı Sırt, and to entrench our existing front there. As I have told you, the 1/57th had been reassembled at the northern part of the crest [near Owen's Gully] and had been allotted that part to defend. When it was clear that all was safe I wired to the regimental commander: 'If you want this battalion to be entirely worn out and finished, keep us in the trenches.'[327]

A little after 21:00, Avni's aide came to him while he was working at headquarters and handed him the news they had received from the division: Kemal had been appointed to the corps-level Anafartalar (Suvla) Group Command, and had written a farewell message to the regiments:

> I am now moving to assume the command of the Anafartalar Group. Şefik Bey, commander of the 27th Regiment, has been appointed Deputy Division Commander. I bid farewell to you all, believing that I will complete this new task with the fondness and trust you have shown me, just as I have done with the successes you have achieved so far with your efforts and sacrifices.[328]

By 21:45 on 8 August, 1915, Kemal assumed command over all Turkish forces around Suvla and Conkbayırı. This change of command marked a significant moment in both the Gallipoli Campaign and Turkish history. At 04:30 on the morning of 10 August, British forces who had gained a footing just below the crest of Conkbayırı were attacked fiercely by dense waves of several Turkish regiments, and the ensuing hand-to-hand fighting would result in the loss of Conkbayırı for Allied troops once and for all. While this was happening in the northern portion of the front, on

---

[326] Arzu Tunç et al., eds., *Çanakkale Muharebelerinde 19. Tümen Cerideleri*, Vol. 6, 193.
[327] C.E.W. Bean, *Gallipoli Mission*, 184.
[328] Arzu Tunç et al., eds., *Çanakkale Muharebelerinde 19. Tümen Cerideleri*, Vol. 6, 193.

9 August, the 1/57th was gathered behind Mortar Ridge, where they were finally granted much-needed rest.

Chapter Three
THE LOSS OF AVNİ BEY

Celebration and Sorrow

12 August marked the end of a month's fasting and the beginning of the Islamic feast Ramazan Bayramı (*Eid al-Fitr*) in 1915. For a couple of days, the front had remained calm. Following the Allies' defeat on 10 August, the belief began to spread among the Turkish soldiers that they would spend the four-day feast in relative peace. Esat relayed the celebration message from 5th Army Commander Liman von Sanders to the troops and added: 'I would like to celebrate Holy Bayram and express my hope that the troops under my command will be filled with pride in the decisive victories we will achieve.'[329] However, this relative peace would not last much longer. The heavy bombardment that began on the morning of 12 August shattered the silence. The men spent the first day of the feast, now soured, in trench shelters and dugouts under constant shelling.

At 22:30, Avni sent a message to the division with a proposal. He explained that it took time to determine the cause and location of the sudden outbursts of fire at night, and he outlined the measures he had taken as a solution and how they would be implemented: 'Whichever battalion the enemy attacks, that battalion will fire blue/green star shells with the flare gun. If there is a firing raid, a red signal will be given. Battalions will use white signals for ordinary reconnaissance. The artillery and machine guns of my regiment on the Mortar Ridge operate against that front according to this signal.' This method was quickly adopted, and orders were issued for other units to apply it as well.[330]

As the sun rose on 13 August, the sounds of machines filled the air over Anzac, accompanied by observation balloons ascending into the sky. Over the past weeks, these planes had been busy taking aerial photographs of the entire front, reconnoitring the Turkish rear area, and bombing positions and headquarters at Mortar Ridge. The morning brought a more intense bombardment than the day before. Aeroplanes and observation balloons observed the shells falling on specific targets

---

[329] Cengiz Eroğlu, et al., *Bir Kahramanlık Abidesi: 57. Piyade Alayı*, 115.
[330] Cengiz Eroğlu, et al., *Bir Kahramanlık Abidesi: 57. Piyade Alayı*, 115.

42. Lieutenant Colonel Hüseyin Avni in early 1915. (Hüseyin Avni Tanman Collection)

and directed artillery fire. As dust filled the surroundings, soldiers took cover in shelters and dugouts, under the bombardment that marred the second day of the feast.

When the concealed communication trench from Mule Valley to German Officers' Ridge was ruined by bombardment, men moving between battalions were forced to traverse open ground and began to suffer seriously from the machine gun fire from Lone Pine. Avni wrote a report to the division at 12:40, requesting that the trench be reconstructed by the labour companies to mitigate this danger. While this report was being written, Zeki visited the headquarters. He informed Avni that his battalion had relieved the trenches at German Officers' Ridge, trench No. 48 had been repaired, but it was observed that trench No. 47 was still in ruins, and reported near misses of shells came close to the kitchens.[331]

The regimental commander, usually attentive, appeared contemplative and uninterested this time. When Zeki inquired about the reason, Avni shared that he had received a letter from his children that morning: 'I had a letter from home. My children are asking how long this war will last, and whether 'Father' will be with them for the feast, as I had been the year before. They all told me how dreary it was without me.' Zeki stayed with his commander and they chatted for a while longer.[332]

The Last Message
At 13:20, Avni penned his final brief report: 'No notable incidents to report.' Exhausted from two days of bombardment and with his thoughts lingering on his children, he withdrew to his tent to reply to the letter from home and seek some rest.[333] Shortly after, he was informed that a group of officers had arrived to celebrate the feast day. Avni immediately got ready and joined them. The gathering, untroubled by being in the open, had convened near the headquarters to mark the occasion. Meanwhile, the Allied artillery focused its fire on the Turkish rear area, targeting tents and dugouts identified from aerial photographs. Howitzer shells rained down consecutively around Mortar Ridge and the gully behind it (Çatal Dere). Around 14:15, a howitzer shell landed near the

---

[331] ATASE: BDH 5384-183-H11-1a.
[332] C.E.W. Bean, *Gallipoli Mission*, 179.
[333] Ahmet Yurttakal, 'Ramazan Bayramı Şehidi 57. Alay Kumandanı Hüseyin Avni' *Atlas Dergisi*, 53, (June-July 2018): 102.

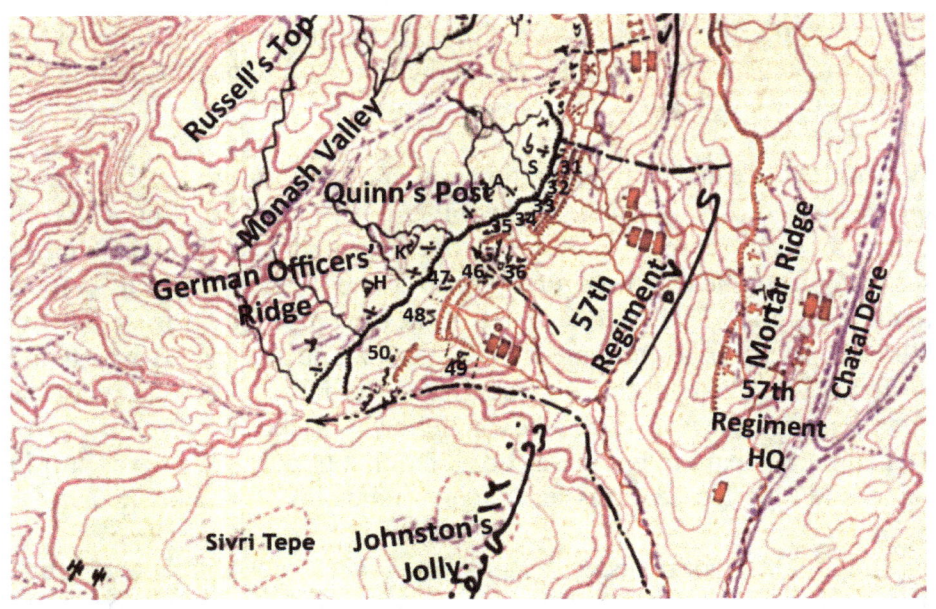

43. Map showing the front and headquarters of the 57th Regiment on 16 August 1915. (ATASE: 4936-H39-H37-1–9)

regimental headquarters, followed by another – a direct hit on the headquarters itself. A thick cloud of dust enveloped the area. As the dust cleared, Avni was seen lying on the ground, seriously wounded. Medics and officers rushed to the scene, but despite the regimental doctor's efforts, it was too late and Avni could not be saved. The command of the regiment was assumed by Major Murat. He was first to inform the division and then the battalion commanders about the death of Avni:

> To the 57th Regiment, the 2nd Battalion 72nd Regiment, and the Machine Gun Company
> 13 August 1915
> 14:30
> From Edirne Sırt [Mortar Ridge]
>
> Our Regiment Commander Avni Bey fell as a result of a howitzer shell that hit his headquarters today. I would like all my friends to be more diligent and vigilant in our duty, striving to take revenge from the ruthless enemy.
>
> Deputy Commander of the 57th Regiment

Major Murat[334]

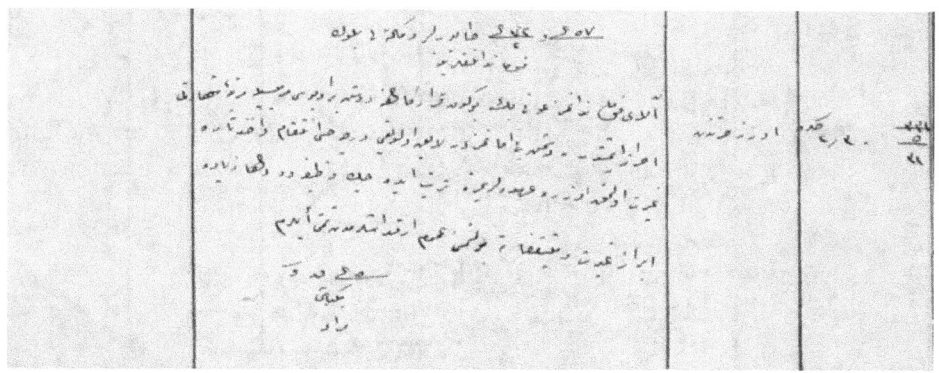

44. The war diary entry about Avni's loss, 13 August 1915. (ATASE: BDH 5384-183-H.11-1-1.)

Lieutenant Colonel Mehmet Şefik, Deputy Commander of the 19th Division, was among those deeply saddened by Avni's loss:

> To Deputy Command of 57th Regiment
> 13 August 1915
> 14:45
>
> The death of Avni Bey has brought profound sadness. Major Murat Bey will assume command temporarily. I trust that the command staff will uphold the remarkable legacy of the 57th Regiment, as achieved under the leadership of the blessed fallen, and will strive to maintain its distinguished reputation with the help of God. My condolences go out to the regiment.
>
> Deputy Commander of the 19th Division
> Lieutenant Colonel M. Şefik.[335]

As the division commander, it fell to Şefik to deliver the news of Avni's death to Esat:

---

[334] ATASE: BDH 5384-183-H.11-1-1.
[335] ATASE: BDH 5384-183-H11-1-1a.

To Northern Group Command
13 August 1915
15:18

At 14:45 [14:15] in the afternoon, Lieutenant Colonel Avni Bey, the commander of the 57th Regiment, fell when a howitzer shell hit the regimental headquarters. Major Murat Bey has been given command of the regiment.

Deputy Commander of the 19th Division
Lieutenant Colonel Mehmet Şefik[336]

'Gallant Commander of the 57th Regiment'
The feast day had turned into mourning day for the entire Turkish garrison at Anzac. Kemal, now the Anafartalar Group Commander, received the news of Avni's death at his headquarters at Çamlıtekke. He paid tribute to Avni's memory in his account:

> I deeply appreciate each officer and man under my command. I remember our sacred fallen, who heroically sacrificed their lives for this noble cause, with boundless respect. I pray for their Holy souls and seek intercession from them. I especially hold the memory of Lieutenant Colonel Avni, the virtuous, devoted, and distinguished commander of the 57th Regiment who was the cornerstone of the defence of Arıburnu, in the highest regard, along with my fallen aide, Lieutenant Kâzım, who greatly assisted me by delivering my orders wherever needed during the most heated times, without paying attention to his wounds.[337]

Kemal's chief of staff, İzzettin, also noted Avni's loss in his diary:

> The weather is scorching. The artillery duel continued. Lieutenant Colonel Avni Bey, commander of the 57th Regiment, fell when a howitzer shell hit his headquarters. Gallant commander of the glorious 57th Regiment![338]

---

[336] ATASE: BDH 4936-H37-1-2a.
[337] Mustafa Kemal, *Arıburnu Muharebeleri Raporu*, 139.
[338] İzzettin Çalışlar, *On Yıllık Savaş*, 129.

Esat also briefly described Avni's death in his memoirs:

> A bomb[sic] hit the headquarters of the 57th Regiment, killing the commander of the regiment and the men around him.[339]

45. Hüseyin Avni's *kabalak* hat, kept by his family. (Hüseyin Avni Tanman Collection)

During his career, Avni received four medals in total[340]: 5th Class Order

---

[339] Esat Bülkat, *Çanakkale Hatıraları,* 713.

[340] According to the 'War Medal (Harp Madalyası) Regulation' officially published on 1 March 1915, those who had not first received the War Medal were ineligible for the Liyakat and Imtiyaz Medals with Swords. (Metin Erüreten, *Osmanlı Madalyaları ve Nişanları Belgelerle Tarihi,* 325, document no.119.) Additionally, after receiving the War Medal, which was awarded to heroes who fought with courage and sacrifice per the Sultan's decree No.8/1028 and the Army Orders No.16 and No. 20, those who continued to distinguish themselves would be subsequently awarded the Silver Liyakat with Swords, Silver Imtiyaz with Swords, Gold Liyakat with Swords, and Gold Imtiyaz with Swords respectively. Regimental and higher commanders could award the War Medal without permission, whereas the Silver and Gold Liyakat and Imtiyaz Medals were subject to the Sultan's decree. According to Order No.19, it was stipulated that individuals who did not receive the War Medal would not qualify for the Gold or Silver Liyakat and Imtiyaz Medals with Swords. (Selahattin Karatamu, *Türk Silahlı Kuvvetleri Tarihi* volume 3, part 6, book 1, İstanbul: Genelkurmay Harp Tarihi Başkanlığı Resmi Yayınları Seri No.2, 337–338) We believe that Avni, who was awarded the Silver Liyakat Medal with Swords on 30 April 1915, should have first received the War Medal. Therefore, the War Medal should be added to the list.

of the Mecidiye (1894), Greek War Medal (1898), Silver Liyakat Medal (1906), and Silver Liyakat Medal with Swords (1915). Additionally, for his service in the Greco-Turkish War of 1897, Avni received a seniority increase of 1 year, 4 months, and 13 days. He earned an additional year of seniority during the Balkan War and an impressive additional five-year seniority during the First World War. Avni's military career, which commenced on 13 June 1889, spanned a total of 33 years, 6 months, and 13 days, including the accrued seniority, and concluded with his death on Friday, 13 August 1915.

The Bloody Uniform
Today, Avni's bloody uniform and some of his personal belongings, which he was wearing at the time of his death, are on display at the Military Museum (Askerî Müze) in İstanbul. His uniform is composed of four pieces: a tunic, trousers, vest, and kabalak hat. Also among his belongings are two photographs and an officer's sword. In section No.15444 of the museum's record book, the following is written under the description titled 'The bloody clothes of Infantry Lieutenant Colonel Hüseyin Avni Bey, commander of the 57th Regiment, who was killed at Arıburnu':

> The uniform consists of four pieces. The tunic is made of khaki-coloured fabric. The remaining pieces include trousers, a vest, an *enveriye*[341] (*kabalak*) hat, and a felt cone hat. All of these items were worn by him at the time of his death and are stained with blood. The uniform and sword were donated to the Military Museum by his son in 1331 (1915).

There are extensive blood stains visible on the front of the tunic, running from the collar downwards. These stains indicate a significant loss of blood, likely caused by a major wound to the head or neck. Additionally,

---

[341] Named after Enver Paşa, *enveriye* (a.k.a. *kabalak*) was the standard headwear of the Ottoman Army during the First World War. (t.n.)

46. The column titled 'The Living Dead' in the 9th issue of the Ottoman War Magazine (Harp Mecmuası), where photographs of fallen officers were featured. Hüseyin Avni can be seen at the top right corner.

the right sleeve of the tunic is marked by numerous blood stains. Avni may have attempted to wipe his face or eyes with his right arm, possibly due to impaired vision from blood flowing from his head wound or the impact of the explosion. Alternatively, he may have put his right on his abdomen, leading to blood contamination in that area as well. The blood stains did not smear on the folds of the tunic, suggesting that either Avni straightened himself up or someone else did so immediately after he was wounded. There is visible damage to the left side of his collar. It appears

47. Hüseyin Avni's tunic. (Military Museum and Cultural Site Command Archive)

that the explosion caused the shoulder board to fall off and tore the collar of his tunic. These damages have naturally been worsened over the intervening 109 years. The vest is cut both from the left shoulder and the waist, suggesting it may have been removed by medics after he was injured. Both the cone hat, likely used as cap comforter, and the enveriye hat bear shrapnel holes and blood stains. The large shrapnel hole on the upper right side of the enveriye hat is particularly notable.

48. Hüseyin Avni's *kabalak* hat and felt cone. Both show visible shrapnel holes and blood stains. (Military Museum and Cultural Site Command Archive)

There are further details about the uniform in the records of the museum:

> The tunic is made of khaki gabardine fabric, has a turn-down collar, a single row of buttons at the front and double slits at the back. It has a pair of curved flap and buttoned pockets at the chest and at

waist level. The collar is made of green broadcloth. A pair of epaulette bridges made of wide brocade tape are sewn on the shoulders. The left shoulder board has fallen off. The right shoulder board is made of a gold braid featuring a star-shaped sunbeam crafted from yellow metal. The inside is lined with chequered cotton fabric. There are ten metal buttons in total on the tunic. The front of the tunic has blood stains, along with moth-eaten spots and tears in the lining inside. There are moth-eaten and torn spots on the kabalak hat as well. The trousers are of the breeches type, made from khaki fabric. It has a flap at the front and a fastening belt at the back. The trouser legs have slits, buttons and ribbons at the bottom. A thin red broadcloth is sewn along both edges. Large tears and holes are visible. The trousers feature a total of three pockets. The vest is made of khaki woollen fabric and has buttons at the front and a fastening belt at the back. It has three pockets and is lined with white cotton fabric.[342]

The officer's sword measures 97 centimetres in overall length, with its steel scabbard measuring 86 centimetres. The hilt, specific to the infantry class, is made of brass with bone plates. The sword features engravings crafted by masters Garabedyan and Mesdciyan, and it was manufactured for the Ottoman Army by the Weyersberg-Kirschbaum Steel and Metalwork Factory in Solingen, Germany.

One of Avni's photographs, held at the Military Museum collection but not on display, was taken in 1907 in Shtip with his children. 'Şehit Avni Bey' is handwritten in the lower left corner on the front of the photograph, likely inscribed when it was given to the museum by his son Tekin Arıburun. On the reverse, it says, 'Father and his two little ones, 1 July 323. 90th Regt, 3rd Bn. Senior Captain Avni.' A full-length photograph of him is on display next to his bloody uniform. This well-known photograph was taken in Skopje in 1912 when he was appointed as the head of the 3rd Branch of the 7th Corps headquarters. There is a handwritten note on the back of the photograph that reads, 'Şehit Avni Bey. Donated by his son. Fell at Gallipoli at the rank of lieutenant colonel.'

---

[342] Military Museum and Cultural Site Command Archive.

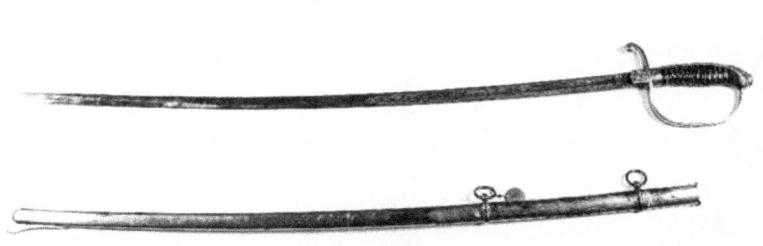

49. Hüseyin Avni's ceremonial sabre. (Military Museum and Cultural Site Command Archive)

Finding the Grave of Avni Bey
The 57th Regiment fought on Second Ridge for an extended period, beginning on 25 April. Avni initially established his headquarters at the head of Mule Valley, approximately 50 metres northeast of today's symbolic 57th Regiment Cemetery. When the regiment took over trenches Nos. 31 to 50 between Quinn's Post and Wire Gully on 3 June, following a seven-day rest at the end of May, the regimental headquarters was moved to the south-eastern slopes of Mortar Ridge. A closer look at Mortar Ridge in the sketch dated 16 August 1915, reveals the regiment's deployment as follows: On the ridge, just above the headquarters, there are two artillery emplacements and a Nordenfelt gun. To the north, there are two machine guns and a mountain gun. The sketch shows the regimental headquarters in a relatively sheltered location on the eastern slope of Mortar Ridge, with reserves stationed in the dugouts on both sides of the headquarters.

In an order he sent to the regiments on 8 August, Kemal mentioned a dressing station attached to the divisional field ambulance was located in the gully behind Mortar Ridge, i.e., Çatal Dere. Divisional dressing stations typically serve as locations where first aid was administered to the wounded and sick, with those in serious condition being transferred to hospitals behind the front lines. These stations were equipped with wards for the wounded patients, stores, baths, and furnaces. Dugouts were also constructed to provide protection against bombardment.

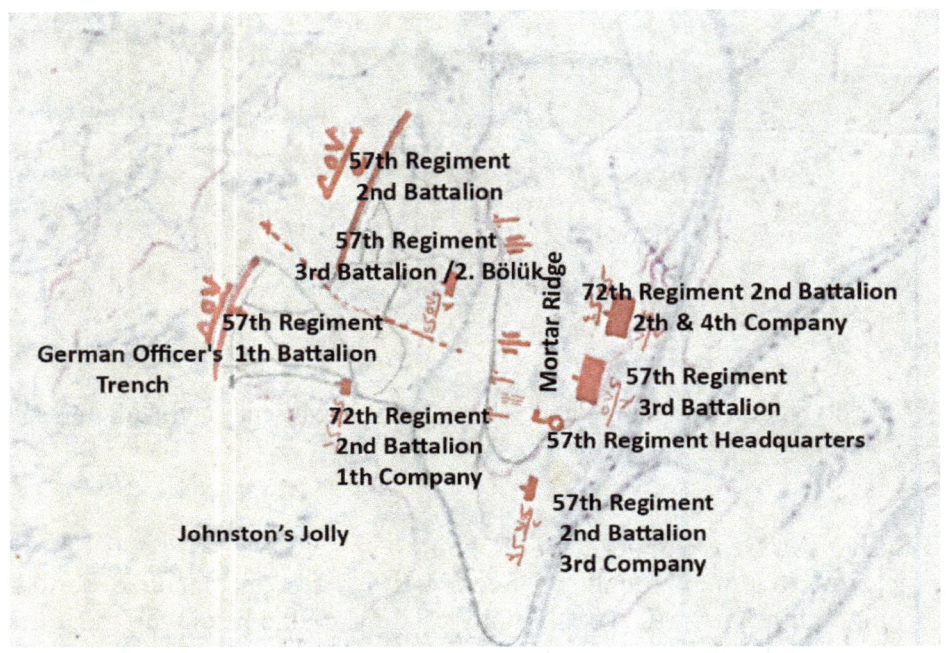

50. Sketch showing the location of the regimental headquarters and the disposition of the battalions. (ATASE: 5384-183-H11-1-4)

According to another map dated 13 August,[343] the dressing station in the gully was located below the headquarters, on the edge of the gully bed used as a communication road, directly across from a cemetery established there. There were one or two wells around the baths and kitchens, established by the engineer platoons responsible for sinking wells. Additionally, there was a fountain called the 'Martyrs' Fountain.' This, likely the only water source in the area, was probably named due to its proximity to both the cemetery and the dressing station. Additionally, a roofed well at the same location can be seen in the photograph numbered G01826 held in the Australian War Memorial archive.

---

[343] ATASE: 4936-H33-001-018.

51. Cemetery and monument in the gully behind Mortar Ridge, 1919. 'X' marks the location of the headquarters. (AWM: G01826)

Avni had described the location of the fountain in a report he wrote on 30 June: 'Martyrs' Fountain is at the starting point of the trench leading to the headquarters of the 27th Regiment, the 18th Regiment, and the 57th Regiment, and the kitchens of all units are nearby.' The trench mentioned had come under fire from an Anzac machine gun at Lone Pine on 13 August. The trench, visible from Lone Pine, likely ran from the southern end of Mortar Ridge through Mule Valley to the 27th Regiment's front at Quinn's Post. Therefore, it can be inferred that the fountain was situated in a sheltered location south of Mortar Ridge, just behind the ridge. In addition to the sketches in the war diary of the 19th Division, a closer examination of the Mortar Ridge section in an aerial photograph taken in July 1915, and in the archives of the Australian War Memorial, reveals the 57th Regiment headquarters, tents believed to be dressing station just below, and the battalions' dugouts.

Tekin Arıburun described Avni's death years later:

> On the feast day, the commanders were visiting the regiments, and during their visit to the 57th Regiment, they gathered at a place close to the regimental headquarters. The 57th Regiment's Commander also joined them. Fahrettin Altay Paşa, the chief of staff of the corps at that time, was the most senior officer present, holding the rank of colonel. All of a sudden, a howitzer shell fired by the Anzacs came whizzing closer and landed about ten metres away from the field hospital[sic]. 'Anyway, all clear!' they said, but another shell came, this time landing directly on the regimental headquarters. The place was engulfed by dust and smoke, making it impossible to see. When the cloud of smoke and dust cleared, they found the commander of the 57th Regiment lying wounded. Fahrettin Altay took him in his arms and noticed a wound to the back of his head. His last words were, 'Tell my family…. Long live the nation.' Then he closed his eyes. They buried him where his grave is now located, near the "three pines."[344]

The place mentioned by Tekin Arıburun, where the first bomb passed over the group and landed 10 metres away from the dressing station, matches the dressing station marked in the sketch. As can be seen from the aerial photograph, the howitzer shell must have passed over the headquarters and landed in the gully bed, a little away from the dressing station's tents.

From the second half of July 1915 onwards, the artillery positions on Mortar Ridge and the dense clusters of tents on its eastern slopes were subjected to fire at various times, by aircraft and howitzers. It can be inferred that the second shell that hit the headquarters on 13 August was directed by observation balloons, having pre-determined the location of the headquarters as a target. The first shell that landed a little further from the target was likely fired during artillery registration. Interestingly, the spot where the second shell landed is marked on the famous Şevki Paşa Map. Two tents can be seen on the side of the communication trench next

---

[344] Quoted by Zehra Gülfiliz Arıburun Tanman from Tekin Arıburun.

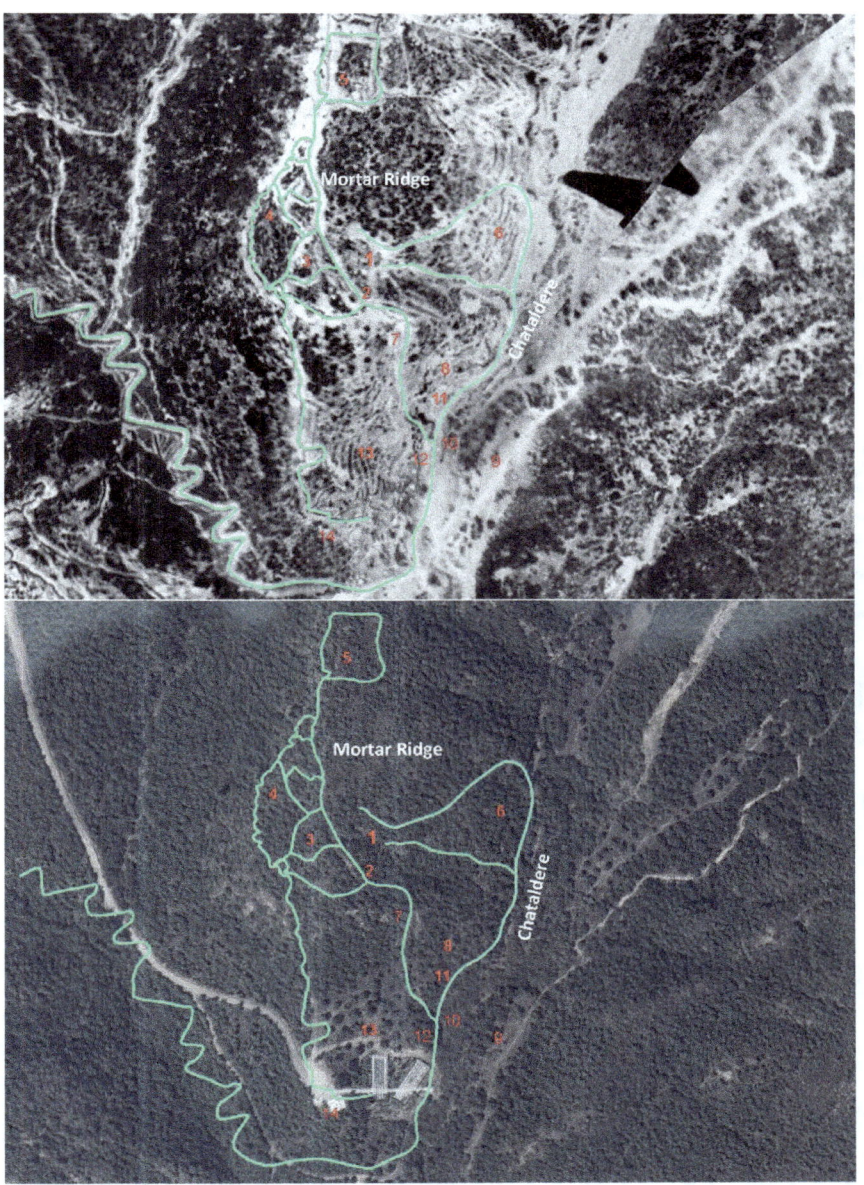

52. 1915 and today, Avni's headquarters and important spots within Çatal Dere. 1, HQ; 2, Possible place where the second shell landed; 3, Nordenfelt gun; 4, Trenches; 5, Gun emplacements; 6, Battalion's dugouts; 7, Tents; 8, Dressing station; 9, Cemetery and monument; 10, Start of communication trench; 11, Fountain; 12, Kitchen/Well; 13, Battalion's dugouts; 14, Avni's grave.

to the headquarters in the aerial photograph mentioned above. When the Şevki Paşa Map and the aerial photograph numbered AWM RC40312 are overlaid, these tents align with the spot that Şevki Paşa marked. It is believed that this was Avni's place and that the officers had gathered either here or in the communication trench nearby.

53. Close-up view of the cemetery and the monument in the gully. The roofed well can be seen on the left. (AWM G01826)

Avni, who breathed his last in Fahrettin's arms, had been laid to rest near a place with 'three pine trees'. Tekin Arıburun searched for this location for many years. Drawing from the recollections of surviving soldiers who served in the 57th Regiment in 1915 and the regiment's aide-de-camp, Alaattin, Tekin visited the battlefield numerous times over the years. Despite his efforts, he was never able to locate the three pines or uncover any clues pointing to the exact whereabouts of his father's grave. While the location of the cemetery was evident, there was no discernible marker on the ground resembling a solitary grave surrounded by stones or marked with a headstone. Even if a grave were identified, determining whether it was Avni's in an area where thousands of soldiers had fallen would be a formidable challenge.

There was a possibility that Avni was buried in a special plot in the cemetery reserved for officers, as it was the closest burial ground to the regiment's position.³⁴⁵ After the war, a monument was erected in the cemetery. However, during the occupation of the Gallipoli Peninsula in late 1918, numerous Turkish monuments were deliberately demolished, possibly including the monument in this cemetery. The 1919 photograph depicts the cemetery with the monument enclosed by barbed wire. To the left, a covered well or fountain is distinctly visible.

Post-war condition of Avni's grave was documented in a report dated 12 July 1922 written to the Ottoman Ministry of War by Lieutenant Colonel Macid, Director of the Depots Department of the Ministry of War Artillery and Transport Section. The second article of the report, detailing the condition of Turkish cemeteries and monuments on the Gallipoli Peninsula, states: 'According to Report No. 221 dated 1 March 1922, the inscription of Lieutenant Colonel Avni Bey, commander of the 57th Regiment, located in the eastern part of Çatal Dere, was shattered into pieces...'.³⁴⁶ Based on the report, it is understood that there was a damaged inscription belonging to Avni's grave located on the eastern portion of the gully, suggesting it was within the boundaries of the cemetery. However, no documentation has been found regarding the exact construction date of the monument and inscription or the precise location of the inscription. Upon examining the photo, it appears that apart from the monument and barbed wire, there are no other structures or visible grave markers in the cemetery.

Since inscriptions on monumental structures or graves typically serve an informational purpose, it is likely that the inscription in question was placed on the monument rather than directly on Avni's grave.³⁴⁷ Taking this further, it can also be assumed that the monument was built over the his grave in memory of all the fallen interred there, with the inscription placed on it. First, the inscription disappeared, and later, the monument itself was taken down. Could it be that the grave Tekin had searched for years was actually beneath this monument? Over the years, the ground was completely covered with thick scrub, and the soil eroded away the trenches and the gully beds used as roads during the campaign. Trees

---

[345] In the Ottoman Army, it was a common practice to allocate separate plots for officers when establishing cemeteries. (t.n.)
[346] ATASE: İSH 1519-3-3/6.
[347] The inscription of the post-campaign Turkish monument erected by the 16th Division at Lone Pine can be cited as an example of this. See: AWM: G01752.

were cut down both during and after the war. Even if the location of the cemetery in Çatal Dere was known, it would not be possible to locate three pine trees, remnants of the monument, or any traces resembling a grave up until August 1952.

54. Commemorations of the 37th anniversary of the Battles of Suvla and Conkbayırı. From right to left: Fahrettin Altay, Melek Arıburun (Avni's daughter), Cemil Conk and Şefik Aker. Çanakkale, 11 August 1952. (Hüseyin Avni Tanman Collection)

On 11 August 1952, the Turkish 1st Army Command organised a commemorative trip to the Gallipoli Peninsula on the steamer *Etrüsk* for the 37th anniversary of the Battles of Suvla and Conkbayırı. Among those invited were veterans, including famous commanders such as Fahrettin Altay, Şefik Aker, Selahattin Adil, Fahri Belen and Cafer Tayyar Eğilmez, along with orphans of the fallen and their families. Avni's son Tekin Arıburun, then a major general in the Turkish Air Force, and his sister Melek were also present. Throughout the visit, Şefik and Fahrettin likely recounted their memories from the campaign and their father's heroic deeds in great detail to Tekin and Melek. Thirty-seven years after Avni's death, his grave would be rediscovered during a poignant moment attended by his children – whom he had spoken of with longing in his final moments – and his comrades who had fought alongside him and laid him to rest. It was Fahrettin himself who accurately pinpointed the exact location of the grave. He recounted how, during Avni's burial, he personally inscribed his name on a gas can with a bayonet and placed it on the grave:

> When we dug a little at the spot pointed out by Fahrettin Altay Paşa, it became evident that it was surrounded by stones. As we continued, we uncovered a grave. Upon further digging, a heavily rusted gas canister was suddenly revealed, flattened like a sheet of paper, with drilled holes, bearing the inscription '57th Regiment Commander Avni'. We had found my father, with a piece of shrapnel lying beside him.[348]

55. Hüseyin Avni's grave in 1973. The back of the photo reads: 'The tomb of my fallen father, reconstructed after the fire'. (Hüseyin Avni Tanman Collection)

---

[348] Quoted by Zehra Gülfiliz Arıburun Tanman from Tekin Arıburun; Perihan Eldeniz Arıburun, *Atatürk'ün Öğretmeni*, (Ankara: Genç Matbaası, 1994), 133–134.

56. The early version of Hüseyin Avni's grave, which Tekin Arıburun had built in 1953.

57. Tekin Arıburun's last visit to his father in 1992.
    (Hüseyin Avni Tanman Collection)

In 1953-1954, after obtaining the necessary permissions, Avni's remains were reinterred at the current site, and the family had a grave built. Tekin explained that the relocation was necessary 'Due to its location in the gully bed, to prevent it from being washed away by floods.' This confirms that the original grave was within the boundaries of the cemetery, near the gully bed. The monument itself was indeed positioned close to the gully bed. The grave, which has undergone several repairs over the years, was last renovated by the Directorate of the Gallipoli Historical Site in 2019, taking on its current form.

58. Hüseyin Avni's grave in 2019. (Ahmet Yurttakal)

Chapter Four
LETTERS

Letter to His Children (14 January 1915)
Tekfurdağı [Tekirdağ]
14 January 1915
To Fehmi
My son,

I received your letter dated 9 January 1915, written in French. Well done! You're progressing well in your French writing. However, you didn't mention anything about the matter with your class. Was there supposed to be a private exam? Were they going to transfer you to another class? What's the news on that?

I kiss your grandmother's hands and feet. And I ask for her prayers. I will send him money and pay my debt at the earliest opportunity. I kiss your [maternal] grandmother's hands. How is that poor thing? Is she sick again? How is your mother? And how are you, I hope you are doing well, right? I kiss your eyes and send my greetings to everyone at home. Don't worry about me, thank God I'm in great health. I am busy training my soldiers day and night.

You say you ate *tarhana*[349]. That made me laugh a lot and I was happy to hear it – what a recipe! If I write to Melek separately, then your mother, grandmother, and aunt will all want a letter too. If I don't send them one, they will feel as offended as Melek did. This is not possible. Tell her not to take offence; I've already sent my regards to her in my letter. And I said 'Well done' for the letter he wrote. Anyway, let me write to her now:

My dear children Melek! You were upset with me, weren't you? Am I at fault? Didn't I say 'Well done' to you in my letter when I received yours? Sorry, my daughter, I can't write separate letters to each of you here. The letter I sent wasn't just for your brother; it's

---

[349] Tarhana is a soup generally consumed in the Balkans, Anatolia and the Middle East. It is prepared with yoghurt, dried red pepper, tomatoe, flour and dried herbs.

for you, your mother, your grandmother, and your aunt. Those letters are for all of you. However, I'm addressing your brother specifically because he's a man. Besides, he's the one who writes me letters, so that's why I write back to him. Otherwise, how could I ever forget about you? Keep writing me like that, and I'll drop you a line or two in my response. Just don't make your letters too long, keep it short, like two or three lines. And give my regards to your aunt too.

May you always be entrusted to God Almighty, my dear children.
Your Father
    Avni

I sent twenty copies of the *Karagöz* newspaper and one copy of the Naval Magazine to both of you separately by mail. You'll enjoy reading them.

Letter to His Wife (20 February 1915)
Tekfurdağı [Tekirdağ]
20 February 1915

My better half,

I haven't received a letter from you this week, feeling a bit down. Hoping for the best from God. Also had some unsettling dreams. I dreamt you were holding a new-born child wrapped in a black cloak. Didn't sit well with me, but I hope God Almighty will turn it around for good.

I kiss my mother's hands and feet and ask for her prayers. I kiss your eyes, Fehmi's, and Melek's too. Send my greetings to Semine Hanım. And pass on my regards to anyone asking about me, and to our neighbours. Pass my greetings to İbrahim Efendi[350] and everyone at home. Let them know I'm asking how they're all doing. Thank God, I'm in good health as you can see. I pray to God Almighty that you stay always healthy and well. I mentioned earlier

---

[350] Husband of Semine, Avni's brother in-law.

59. Senior Captain Hüseyin Avni and his children Fehmi Tekin and Melek, 1907. (Hüseyin Avni Tanman Collection)

that I'd love to have you over if the weather permits, but the current situation doesn't allow it. I am afraid it won't be possible for you to come around this time. Hopefully, things will improve soon, and God Almighty will provide a solution. So don't worry, my darling.

Just this once, instead of myself, a photo of me will arrive with the letter. How's everything going over there? Are you getting what you order? How are things going financially? Write to me – I'm curious to know.

How is Halime Hanım doing? I kiss her hands. Give my greetings to others. I had asked about Mustafa Bey – did he leave? If so, where did he go? You should let me know of these things. May you always be entrusted to God Almighty.
Avni.

To my son Fehmi and my daughter Melek,

How are you, my dear children? I hope you are both in good health. Are you going to school regularly? Fehmi, did you sort out the class thing? Did you get moved to the other class, or did the school manager trick us?

And you, my daughter? Are you getting better at reading and writing in school? Doing any craftwork? Write me a couple of lines in your next letter. I sent you my picture, just like seeing me in real life. I look at your pictures here every day.

May you always be entrusted to God Almighty, my dear children.
Your Father

    Avni

Letter to His Wife (23 April 1915)
Maydos [Eceabat]
23 April 1915

My better half,

I got your letter from 18 April and the one before that. I didn't reply to your last letter because I got really upset when I saw you didn't get the money. I wrote to the postal directorate and the post office here. And for that five liras, I wrote to that treacherous clerk again. I was expecting you to get the money. I was happy to see in your letter today that you received six liras. I hope you get March salary in full, right? You didn't mention it, but I think it was payday when you wrote the letter – I saw it in the newspapers. You should also write that you get the salary.

I kiss my dear mother's hands and feet. Remind her to keep me in her prayers. I kiss your eyes and Fehmi's and Melek's too. Give my greetings to Semine Hanım and everyone who asked about me. I kiss Halise Hanım's hands. Pass my greetings to Mustafa Bey and his children.

You are asking about me, thank God, I am in perfect health and well-being. Today, on the occasion of Holy Friday, I just raised the regimental Colours in front of my tent. We used ammunition chests to make a pulpit, and I had a verse written on the *mihrab*. In short, we built a beautiful mosque and performed a beautiful prayer on the grass with all the soldiers in my regiment. After the prayer, I entered my tent. I slept a little. Just woke up and they handed me your letter. I read it in my tent and I am writing these lines to you in my tent. We are currently staying in tents, not in the town.

We stay at a wooded, lush place, close to water, kind of like Istinye. Do you know what I see from my tent flap? Right in front of me are lush green fields and meadows that shimmer like emeralds. Further out, there are mountains covered in thick green forests. It's all so green, spring is in full swing, and the weather's just perfect. A gentle breeze is blowing, making the tent flap and skirts dance a bit. All my men are spread out under trees, doing their laundry by the water. Most of them have laid out their clothes on the green grass, making it look like a field of flowers.

During the prayer, four enemy planes flew overhead. Our men quickly responded with guns, machine guns and rifles, driving them away after they dropped a few bombs. Thankfully, no one was hurt. Sometimes, enemy planes circle around and drop bombs wherever they see a group of soldiers. But we hear them and are always ready to defend ourselves with guns and rifles. You might hear about all these in the newspapers. We've managed to shoot down a few of their planes. The infidel enemy could not do anything from the sea. He did not dare to land soldiers, so now he is attempting to harass us with planes. But don't worry, it's just a bit of excitement for us.

If you were here to see it, you'd think every corner is like heaven. We're surrounded by breathtaking scenery. My thoughts are only of longing for you. I pray to God Almighty for a good success for our nation and country, so we can soon be together again and live happily. Well, see, this time I am not keeping it short. Are you facing any financial difficulties? It's something I always worry about. But this year, I hope your salaries come through intact without any cuts, and I'll support you as well. Hopefully, you'll find some comfort.

Avni

Telegram from the Front
While the fighting at Anzac was ongoing, Avni's thoughts were with his family. When news of the landings reached İstanbul, his family was deeply concerned. Avni sent a very brief telegram to his family at 12:24 on 29 April 1915, four days after the landings:

I am in good health, do not worry.

Undoubtedly, the family and relatives of Avni, anxiously awaiting news from the front at home in the Fatih district of İstanbul, felt both happy and relieved to receive his telegram.

I Can't Get Enough of Looking at Your Picture
My dear father,

I kiss your hands and ask for your prayers. We are all doing well here, don't worry about us. I pray to God Almighty day and night for your well-being, my dear father.

I kiss elder brother Ahmet's hands. Melek and I were very happy to hear that you are sending him, my dear father.

I am pining for you, my dear father. I can't get enough of looking at your picture. I hope you come back safely, my dear father. I passed my exams and moved up a grade, finishing third. I have twelve ten points, three nines, and three eights, my dear father.

May you always be entrusted to God, my dear father.

    4 July 1915
    Your Son Fehmi

60. Photos of Mehmet Fehmi (Tekin) and Melek, which Avni always carried with him at the front. (Hüseyin Avni Tanman Collection)

Be Entrusted to God Almighty, My Dear Father
To my father Lieutenant Colonel Avni Bey

I kiss your hands and feet and ask for your prayers. I pray to God Almighty for you, day and night. May God grant you a long life and good health, amen. We received the money you mentioned in your letter. Mom gave me one lira and ten *kuruş*,[351] and she gave the same to Melek. Since we're on holiday, she's been taking us out a bit. What should we do at home, my dear father? My aunt seems a bit down. I think she doesn't want an orderly in her room, and that's why she's unhappy.

Always be entrusted to God Almighty, my dear father.

As soon as aunt received the money, she gave me two coins with the lira you mentioned in your letter. Thank you so much, my dear father. Ahmet also arrived. We both miss you dearly. Talking to him felt like I was talking to you. When he left, it felt like you were leaving again, my dear father. I was quite saddened by this. Please send us a soldier too, my dear father. The bakeries here are getting busy again. I went to buy bread in the evening but couldn't get any; we only had half a loaf left at home, so that's what we ate. So we need a soldier here, dear father.

---

[351] Ottoman currency subunit which was worth one gold Ottoman Turkish lira. (t.n.)

Chapter Five
THE FAMILY

'Laid Down His Life Bravely'
It didn't take long for the family to receive news of Avni's death. His uniform, sword, letters found in his tent, photographs, and other personal belongings were sent to them. Among what reached the family was a message from Enver Paşa expressing condolences to the family:

> Imperial Ottoman Army
>
> Lieutenant Colonel Hüseyin Avni, son of Ali, Commander of the Fifty-Seventh Regiment, fell in the Battle of Arıburnu on 13 August 1915, demonstrating the heroism and sacrifice of a true Ottoman soldier. The legacy entrusted by those who laid down their lives bravely in defence of the great religion of Islam and the sacred Homeland is not grief and despair, but rather pride and jubilance. Be assured and take solace in that the precious memory of him, like all his friends, will remain hidden forever in the hearts of not only you, but also his larger family, the army, and that his revenge will be taken from our enemies. I wish God's blessings to all the relatives and loved ones of the honourable fallen, as I extend my deepest condolences and utmost respect.
>
> Deputy Commander-in-Chief
> Enver[352]

To compound the family's grief, they faced financial and emotional difficulties like many families of the fallen. From 14 August 1915, a pension of 1,784 kuruş was allocated to support Avni's family of four, including his widow and mother.

> Commander of the 57th Regiment
> Lieutenant Colonel Hüseyin Avni Bey, son of Ali
> Bitola 1308/94
> Killed in action

---

[352] Hüseyin Avni Tanman Collection.

Killed in action in the Battle of Arıburnu on 13 August 1915. His family lives in house No.29, Değirmen Street, in [Fatih] Kıztaşı, İstanbul.

To Fatih Municipality: This memorandum has been sent to ensure that the necessary investigation is carried out about the family of the fallen whose information is written above, according to the attached civil registry, and that the requested documents and reports prepared and submitted in their entirety.

The salary was calculated and sent to the accounting department for approval. 18 September 1915. 3/3338 9229.

A memorandum was written to the quartermaster branch to cover the expenses. 7 October 1915.

A memorandum was written to the Ministry of Finance. 7 October 1915.[353]

Family record of Lieutenant Colonel Hüseyin Avni Bey, Deputy Commander of the 23rd Regiment, 3rd Corps:
446 son Mehmet Fehmi Efendi
446 daughter Melek Hanım
446 wife Fatma Zehra Hanım
446 mother Fatma Hanım
14 August 1915.

It was reported to the Directorate of Personnel Affairs that salaries were allocated to the above-listed family members of Hüseyin Avni Bey, who was killed in action on 13 August 1915, in accordance with the law, as of 14 August 1915. November 1915.

This official correspondence was deemed sufficient and was added to his personal file. 30 November 1915.[354]

---

[353] Ministry of National Defence –MSB – Archive, Avni's personal service record.
[354] Ministry of National Defence –MSB – Archive, Avni's personal service record.

A Soldier Like His Father

Financial difficulties forced the family to leave Avni's cousin's mansion in Fatih, İstanbul. Fatmatüzzehra Hanım decided to move in with her sister, Semine, in the nearby quarter called Çırçır. This way, they would not be alone, and their pain would be alleviated, at least a little, through family solidarity. Mehmet Fehmi continued his education in secondary school, while Melek was still attending primary school.[355] Mehmet Fehmi submitted a petition to the Ministry of War on 2 February 1916, echoing the plight of countless relatives of the fallen. In his petition, he stated: '

> I am the son of Lieutenant Colonel Hüseyin Avni Bey, Commander of the 57th Regiment of the 19th Division, who sacrificed his life for the homeland and nation in the Battle of Arıburnu on 13 August 1915. After my father's death, I have no one left in the world except my mother and my little sister.

He requested enrolment in Kuleli Military High School, or, if that was not possible, in a boarding school in İstanbul. He highlighted their financial difficulties, explaining, 'Our current situation prevents me from attending one of the boarding schools.'[356] He was only 13 years old when he wrote this petition. On one side of the page, an unidentified officer had penned a note:

> Hüseyin Avni Bey was killed by an enemy howitzer shell while leading his regiment near Bomba Sırt [Quinn's Post]. The regiment made many sacrifices, and its Colours were decorated. The children of such venerable fallen should be protected.[357]

Fehmi's application to Kuleli Military High School was not accepted, but he was deemed suitable for enrolment in one of the civilian Sultani schools. The person who would convey his petition to the Ministry of Education with a cover letter would be the then Undersecretary of the Ministry of War, Colonel Fahrettin, who was his father's commander at Gallipoli, witnessed his death and buried him. Since Mehmet Fehmi

---

[355] Ahmet Yurttakal, 'Paşam Ben Cepheye Gitmek İstiyorum', *Atlas Dergisi*, 54, (August-September 2018): 63–64.
[356] BOA, MF-TLY-00550-592.
[357] BOA, MF-TLY-00550-588.

wished to attend a school in nearby provinces such as Izmit and Bursa, an application form was completed by the headman of his neighbourhood. The form included some details about the family:

Did not apply to the Teachers' School.
Application number: 1/20

Name	Date of Birth	Place of Birth	Hometown	Name and Death of the Father	District, Neighbourhood, Street and House Number
Mehmet Fehmi Efendi	1319 [1903]	Stip	Bitola	Fifty-Seventh Regiment Commander Lieutenant Colonel Hüseyin Avni Bey	Çırçır, Hacı Hasan, Haydar Street, No.39
What is the occupation of the parents? If not alive, what are the place and date of death? Who is the child residing with today?			His father, Hüseyin Avni Bey, was killed in action at Arıburnu, Gallipoli, on 31 July 1331 [13 August 1915]. He currently resides with his mother. She is not employed.		
How much salary and income do the parents have?			His mother, his sister, and himself receive a widows' and orphans' pension of 1,300 kuruş per month. They have no other source of income.		
Does the child have a salary or income? If so, how much is it per month?			He receives a monthly orphans' pension of 440 kuruş. He has no other source of income.		

How many brothers and how many sisters does the child have? What are their occupations? Are any of them accepted to boarding schools? If yes, in which schools?	He has a younger sister who is not employed. She is not studying at a boarding school. She is studying at the İstanbul Girls' Industrial School.
How long has the child been studying? Do they have a diploma? If they are currently studying, in which school and in which grade?	Currently, he is a third grade student at Köprülü Fazıl Pasha Secondary School.

This document, containing the results of the investigation regarding Mehmet Fehmi Efendi's request for free admission to one of the Sultani schools, has been submitted to the Ministry of Education.
 Deputy Headman
 Headman
 Neighbourhood Imam

               23 August 1916

It is verified that the contents of this document are in accordance with the truth.

He desires to attend a nearby Sultaniye school in a nearby region, such as Izmit or Bursa.
 [Signed] Ahmed.

After the correspondence with the Ministry of Education, it was determined that Mehmet Fehmi could be transferred to a school in İstanbul after completing a term at a provincial Sultani school. Subsequently, he was enrolled in Galatasaray High School and after studying there for a year, he chose his father's profession, a profession he had always aspired to, and transferred to Kuleli Military High School. Tragically, the wooden house the family lived in was severely damaged in the great fire of 1918, destroying a significant portion of Avni's mementos.

A Very Young Volunteer
Following the official occupation of İstanbul in 1920, which led to the closure of military schools, Mehmet Fehmi was relocated to a training camp in Ankara and subsequently transferred to Konya Military High School. However, after the Greek Army's failed 1921 campaign into Anatolia, where they aimed to crush the Turkish National Movement, Fehmi's priorities shifted. Instead of continuing his education, he resolved to join the Turkish National Movement. He even planned to escape from the school to see Mustafa Kemal at his mansion in Çankaya. Avni's family maintained close contact with Mustafa Kemal and his sister, Makbule. Kemal took special care of Fehmi, whom he would later nickname *Tayyareci* (aviator), as well as the other members of the family of his fallen comrade.

61. Mehmet Fehmi, 1917.

Fehmi, who escaped from his school, put on his military uniform, which he had kept in his bag, as he neared the area of what is now the Turkish Grand National Assembly (TBMM). He continued his walk towards Çankaya, the foremost district of Ankara. At that time, the surroundings were filled with vineyards, each guarded by armed sentries. Seeing him in uniform, the guards allowed him to approach. 'Hello, little officer,' they greeted him warmly. Fehmi engaged in conversation with them as he approached the mansion's garden gate. Once they recognised him, they ushered him inside. Fehmi knocked on the mansion door. In surprise, Fikriye, Kemal's partner, opened it and exclaimed, 'Fehmi! Where did you come from?' 'I've come to see Paşa,' Fehmi said. Kemal was informed and immediately ordered the son of his fallen comrade to be brought to him. He welcomed Fehmi into his office, where his aide-de-camp Salih Bozok was also present. As soon as Fehmi entered the room, he saluted crisply and took his seat as directed. After exchanging pleasantries, Kemal asked about the purpose of Fehmi's visit. When Fehmi expressed his desire to join the front lines instead of being sent to Konya Military High School, Kemal's fatherly demeanour shifted abruptly. In a stern voice, he asked, 'What's the number one rule to become a soldier?' Fehmi responded meekly, 'It's obedience, sir.' 'So your commanders sent you to Konya, yet you come as far as to me, the army's commander-in-chief, without obeying orders. What sort of discipline is this?' Kemal remarked. He denied Fehmi's request and saw him off, urging him to pursue his education. With this order and life lesson, Fehmi departed for Konya where he continued his schooling in a class designated for the children of the fallen.[358]

62. The photograph of Fehmi signed for his sister Melek on the occasion of the feast day when he was studying at Kuleli Military High School, 25 May 1919. (Hüseyin Avni Tanman Collection)

During their high school years, Fehmi and his classmates were influenced by the *Turanism* (Pan-Turkism) movement, which inspired them to adopt 'authentic' Turkish names. Fehmi chose Gültekin, in honour of Kültigin

---

[358] From the notes of Zehra Gülfiliz Arıburun Tanman.

(684–731 CE), the prince and a general of the Second Turkic Khaganate. Later, he preferred the shortened version Tekin and thus went by Mehmet Tekin. In 1923, Tekin completed his education at Konya Military High School and entered the Military Academy. Shortly afterwards, his mother and sister joined him in Ankara.

Arıburun Family

Fatmatüzzehra Arıburun devoted her life to raising her children. Her daughter Melek Arıburun married Captain İsmail Hakkı Tekçe, Atatürk's aide and the founder of the Presidential Guard Regiment, on 29 July 1926. Melek, who was very fond of cars and skilled in horse riding, actively participated in the training and excursions of the Guard Regiment and cavalry units alongside her husband. She also volunteered with the Red Crescent, contributing to its charitable activities. Due to her husband's position, Melek became part of Atatürk's inner circle until his passing. Following her divorce from İsmail Hakkı in 1947, she lived with her mother in Bahçelievler, a neighbourhood in Ankara.

63. 'To My Dear Brother 14/12/929 Melek & Hakkı.' İsmail Hakkı Tekçe, who served as Atatürk's aide-de-camp for 18 years and founded the Presidential Guard Regiment, with his wife Melek in Ankara. (Hüseyin Avni Tanman Collection)

Melek was known within the family for her cheerful demeanour, childish temperament, and love for animals. Her first-hand experience of political conflicts during the early years of the Turkish Republic instilled a lifelong sense of apprehension in her. She harboured constant anxiety that her every action was being monitored by the National Security Service Organisation (later known as the National Intelligence Organisation – MIT).

64. One Turkish Lira signed by Gazi Mustafa Kemal Atatürk for Melek Arıburun on 5 May 1931. (Hüseyin Avni Tanman Collection)

Even after the establishment of the Republic, Atatürk continued to closely support the family. So much so that the surname 'Arıburun' was bestowed upon the family by Atatürk personally. He emphatically insisted that their surname would not be 'Arıburnu', a geographical name, but 'Arıburun', reinterpreted to signify 'a corner of the homeland purified by the blood of the fallen.' Tekin Arıburun provided the following details about his surname in a letter addressed to journalist Feridun Fazıl Tülbentçi on 26 March 1953:

When the surname law was enacted, Atatürk, as customary, assigned convenient surnames to his relatives and guests during one of his dinner gatherings. Regarding the surname 'ARIBURUN,' he remarked, 'This surname rightfully belongs to Avni Bey and therefore to his children.' The person he referred to as 'Avni Bey' is, of course, Major – later lieutenant colonel – Hüseyin Avni, the commander of the famous and gallant 57th Infantry Regiment, which Mustafa Kemal Bey led to the Kocaçimen Tepe on the morning of 25 April and dealt the first decisive blow to the enemy. Hüseyin Avni Bey was an admirer and friend of Mustafa Kemal Bey, and their families were close, sharing ties as home folks and friends. That evening, during a dinner where members of Avni Bey's family were present, Atatürk bestowed the proud surname upon them. He said, 'Pay attention to my pronunciation. This place, which has an extraordinary heroic epic, is erroneously called 'ARIBURNU', which is a mumpsimus. This name has nothing to do with *arı* [bee] or its 'Nos.e'. It is a sacred place washed with the blood of thousands of heroic Turkish sons and your father, and has become 'pure', that is, *arı*.³⁵⁹ Do not mispronounce this honourable name. I repeat, it is 'ARIBURUN', not 'ARIBURNU!'' There is no doubt that these warnings, remarks, and desires of our Great Atatürk will be an invaluable testament for every Turk who is wholeheartedly devoted to him.³⁶⁰

65. Avni's wife Fatmatüzzehra Arıburun in Ankara in 1950. (Hüseyin Avni Tanman Collection)

---

³⁵⁹ In Turkish, *arı* commonly means 'bee,' but it can also mean 'pure,' though this usage is rare. (t.n.)

³⁶⁰ Haluk Oral, *Arıburnu 1915* (İstanbul: Türkiye İş Bankası Kültür Yayınları, 2007), 295–296. It should be noted that this interpretation either solely belongs to Atatürk himself or originates from the individual who shared the story with Tekin Arıburun. *Arıburnu*, which translates to 'Bee's Point', is not an erroneously known name; it is a geographical name that existed on maps long before the campaign. Understandably, Mustafa Kemal, in his reinterpretation, attributed a different meaning to 'Arıburnu' by transforming it into 'Arıburun'. However, this does not invalidate 'Arıburnu' as a place name. (t.n.)

Fatmatüzzehra Arıburun lived in Bahçelievler, Ankara with her daughter Melek until her ultimate reunion with Avni on 29 April 1962. Melek Arıburun continued to live in their home until her passing on 18 October 1992.

66. Lieutenant Mehmet Tekin with Fatmatüzzehra and Melek on the day he received his pilot badge. Ankara, 1926. (Hüseyin Avni Tanman Collection)

Avni's Son: Mehmet Tekin Arıburun
Mehmet Tekin Arıburun (service number: 1341-1) began his education at the Military Academy in September 1923. During his sophomore year, he was transferred to the air class. He graduated from the Military Academy in June 1925 with the rank of third lieutenant. Officially joining the Air Force in October 1925, he underwent pilot training at Eskişehir Flight School. Upon completion in February 1926, he was promoted to second lieutenant. In December 1926, he earned his pilot badge and was assigned to the 9th Fighter Flight. Tekin played a pivotal role in establishing the Turkish Air Force's first official aerobatic exercises and aerobatics team, which has a notable place in world aviation history in terms of aerobatics.

In June 1926, Tekin was dispatched to England to advance his aviation knowledge and skills. He was promoted to first lieutenant in 1929, and returned home in May 1930 after completing his training in England. Continuing his service in the 42nd Fighter Squadron as a pilot until November 1932, he then entered the Air Force Academy. He was promoted to captain in 1934. The next year, he graduated from the Air Force Academy and assumed the command of the 2nd Air Flight. From March to September 1936, he served in the General Staff Intelligence Department. During this tenure, he was appointed Air Attaché in Berlin, where he served until May 1938. Upon his return, he was given command of the 53rd Fighter Flight in İzmir.

67. Lieutenant Tekin Arıburun in Bristol, England in 1928.

On 6 June 1940, he married Perihan Eldeniz, daughter of Lieutenant General Naci Eldeniz, who had been Mustafa Kemal's teacher at the military high school in Bitola and later took part in the Turkish National Movement after the First World War. They had two children, Gulfiliz and Bintuğ. On 30 August 1940, he was promoted to major and assigned to the Air Training Operations Branch of the General Staff.

He served as the Air Attaché in Washington between 1941 and 1943. Upon his return, he was appointed as the commander of the 2nd Battalion of the 5th Air Wing in Bursa. On 30 August 1944, he was promoted to lieutenant colonel and became the Deputy Commander of the 5th Air Wing. During this time, he attended the San Francisco Conference as the Turkish military delegate, where the United Nations was established in April 1945. Subsequently, he was appointed as an instructor at the Air Force Academy. In 1946, he was promoted to colonel and served as the

Washington Air Attaché for the second time. He returned home in February 1948 and was given command of the 8th Fighter Wing. On

68. Engagement ceremony of Tekin and Perihan Arıburun, Ankara, 25 January 1940. From left to right; Melek Tekçe, Naci Eldeniz, Perihan Arıburun, Aide-de-camp to the President Celal Üner, Captain Mehmet Tekin Arıburun, Naci Eldeniz's wife Makbule Eldeniz, Colonel İsmail Hakkı Tekçe, Fatmatüzzehra Arıburun. (Hüseyin Avni Tanman Collection)

30 August 1950, Tekin was appointed as the Chief of the Air Force Operations Branch with the rank of brigadier general. Between August 1951 and 1952, he assumed command of the 1st Tactical Air Group in Eskişehir. On 30 August 1952, he was promoted to major general and was once again appointed Chief of Air Force Operations. He was then reassigned to the 1st Tactical Air Group. On 9 September 1955, he was appointed Chief of Staff of the Air Force. 21 days later, Tekin was promoted to lieutenant general and became Deputy Commander of the Turkish Air Force.

On 28 August 1956, he was appointed as the commander of the newly established Air Training Corps in İzmir, and in 1957 he became the

Deputy Commander of the Air War Academy. In 1958, he was appointed Commander of the NATO Defence College and went to Paris. While in this position, he was appointed as the commander of the Turkish Air Force on 1 May 1959. He was promoted to full general on 30 August 1959.

Following the coup on 27 May 1960, he was forced to retire as Commander of the Air Force and was sent to prison in Yassıada. He was released in November after spending six months in incarceration. In 1962, he was elected to the General Administrative Board of the Justice Party (Adalet Partisi), and in 1964, he became the İstanbul Senator for the Justice Party. He served the country as President of the Senate of the Republic for two terms between 1971 and 1978, and briefly as Deputy President.

Tekin Arıburun possessed an impressive breadth of knowledge and cultural interests beyond his knowledge of soldiering and military history. His intellectual pursuits spanned literature, philosophy, Sufism, classical Western and Turkish music, cinema and theatre. He was fluent

69. Commander of the Turkish Air Force General Tekin Arıburun, Fatmatüzzehra and Melek Arıburun. 'To My Dearest Mommy and Melek 9.5.1960'. (Hüseyin Avni Tanman Collection)

in English, German, French, Italian, and Hungarian. He also had a keen interest in creating his own music. He demonstrated his talents in this field by composing short songs, especially a lullaby in the *Nihavend Maqam* for his daughter Gülfiliz, among other works he performed at family gatherings with piano. Regrettably, his compositions in the classical Turkish music style were not put into notation. he was a skilled chess player, he also wrote couplets under the pseudonym 'Hüma'[361]. Known for his sociability and warmth, his talks on history, especially with younger people, always left a lasting impression as a valuable lesson.

Tekin Arıburun, the first Turkish officer to serve as Air Attaché in Germany and the USA, had a lifelong wish to die on 13 August, the anniversary of his father's death. His wish came true, and he passed away in İzmir on the night of 12/13 August 1993, at the age of 90. He was laid to rest in Ankara's Cebeci Military Cemetery with a state funeral.

70. Perihan Arıburun and Tekin Arıburun. Ankara, 1990. (Hüseyin Avni Tanman Collection)

---

[361] Hüma, known as 'The Bird of Paradise' in Persian mythology, also holds a place in Turkish folklore. This mythical bird flies at great altitudes without a rest, and its feet never touch the ground.

BIBLIOGRAPHY

Archival Sources
Askerî Müze ve Kültür Sitesi Komutanlığı Arşivi (Military Museum and Cultural Site Command Archive)
Australian War Memorial (AWM)
Birinci Dünya Harbi Koleksiyonu (BDH) (First World War Collection)
Devlet Arşivleri Genel Müdürlüğü Osmanlı Arşivi (BOA) (General Directorate of State Archives, Ottoman Archives)
Genelkurmay Askerî Tarih ve Stratejik Etüt Başkanlığı Arşivi (ATASE) (General Staff Military History and Strategic Studies Directorate)
İslam Tarih, Sanat ve Kültür Araştırma Merkezi (IRCICA) (Research Centre for Islamic History, Art and Culture)
İstanbul Araştırmaları Enstitüsü Arşivi (İstanbul Research Institute Archive)
Milli Savunma Bakanlığı Arşiv ve Askerî Tarih Daire Başkanlığı Arşivi (MSB) (Ministry of National Defence Archives and Military History Department)
Milli Savunma Üniversitesi Kara Harp Okulu Arşivi (National Defence University Military Academy Archive)
Milli Savunma Üniversitesi Müşterek Harp Enstitüsü Komutanlığı Arşivi (National Defence University Joint Warfare Institute Command Archive)
Nüfus ve Vatandaşlık İşleri Genel Müdürlüğü Arşivi (General Directorate of Registry and Citizenship Affairs Archive)
Türkiye Cumhuriyeti Cumhurbaşkanlığı Arşivi (CBA) (Presidential Archive of the Republic of Turkey)

Personal Collections
B. Hakan Arıburun Collection
Hüseyin Avni Tanman Collection
İzzeddin Çalışlar Collection

Books, Theses and Articles
Aker, Şefik. 'Çanakkale Arıburnu Savaşları ve 27. Alay,' *Askerî Mecmua'nın Tarih Kısmı*, 40, (1935).
Alganer, Haydar Mehmet. *Çanakkale Kara Savaşları Günlüğü*. Eds. Erdoğan Öztürk, Zehra Gülbudak, Şeyma Büyükcan Sayılır İstanbul: Deniz Basımevi, 2009.

Altay, Fahrettin. 'Fahrettin Altay'ın Çanakkale Hatıraları' *Çanakkale Hatıraları, Vol. 2.* ed. Metin Martı. İstanbul: Arma Yayınları, 2002.

Arıburun, Perihan Eldeniz. *Atatürk'ün Öğretmeni.* Ankara: Genç Matbaası, 1994.

Arıburun, Tekin. 'Arıburun Savaşlarının 66. Yıldönümünde Kahraman Kumandan Şehit Hüseyin Avni Bey'i Anarken,' *Yeni Düşünce Dergisi,* 5-13, (1981)

Arzu Tunç et al. ed., *Çanakkale Muharebelerinde 19. Tümen Cerideleri, Vols 1–2.* Ankara: Genelkurmay Askerî Tarih ve Stratejik Etüt Başkanlığı Yayınları, 2015.

Arzu Tunç et al. ed., *Çanakkale Muharebelerinde 19. Tümen Cerideleri, Vols 3–6.* Ankara: Genelkurmay Askerî Tarih ve Stratejik Etüt Başkanlığı Yayınları, 2017.

Atacanlı, Sermet. *Arıburnu'nun İllk Müdafaası.* İstanbul: Türkiye İş Bankası Kültür Yayınları, 2015.

Bartlett, Ellis Ashmead. *Çanakkale Gerçeği.* Trans. Yüzbaşı Rahmi, Ed. Muzaffer Albayrak. İstanbul: Yeditepe Yayınevi, 2007.

Bean, Charles Edwin Woodrow. *Gallipoli Mission.* Canberra: Australian War Memorial, 1948.

Bean, Charles Edwin Woodrow. *The Official History of the Australia in the War of 1914-1918, Vol II: The Story of ANZAC: From 4 May, 1915, To The Evacuation of The Gallipoli Peninsula* (11th ed.). Sydney: Angus and Robertson Ltd, 1941.

Borlat, Barış. *Askerî Kayıtlara Göre Çanakkale Cephesi'nde 19 Mayıs 1915 Türk Taarruzu, Vol 2.* Ankara: Çanakkale Savaşları ve Gelibolu Tarihi Alan Başkanlığı Yayınları, 2020.

Bülkat, Esat. *Çanakkale Hatıraları, 3. Kitap* [unpublished typewritten manuscript] İstanbul: Harp Akademiler Kütüphanesi, 1950.

Çalışlar, İzzettin. *On Yıllık Savaş: Org. İzzettin Çalışlar'ın Not Defterlerinden Balkan, Birinci Dünya ve İstiklal Savaşları,* ed. İzzeddin Çalışlar. İstanbul: Türkiye İş Bankası Kültür Yayınları, 2010.

Erkal, Şükrü, Alpaslan Orhon, and Muhterem Saral. *Birinci Dünya Savaşı'nda Çanakkale Cephesi (04 Haziran 1915 – 09 Ocak 1916), Vol. 5, Book 1.* Ankara: Genelkurmay Askerî Tarih ve Stratejik Etüt Başkanlığı Yayınları, 2012.

Erkan-ı Harbiye Kaymakamı İzzettin. 'Çanakkale Muharebeleri 13, 14 ve 18 Nisan 1331 Arıburnu Muharebeleri' *Askerî Mecmua,* 11 (1336/1920).

Erkan-ı Harbiye Kaymakamı İzzettin. 'Çanakkale Muharebeleri Hatıralarından 12 Nisan 331 Günü' *Askerî Mecmua*, 10, (1336/1920).
Erkan-ı Harbiye Kaymakamı İzzettin.'Arıburnu Muharebatından İstihsal Edilen Tecarib' *Askerî Mecmua*, 13, (1336/1920)
Eroğlu, Cengiz, Mustafa Delialioğlu and Murat Babuçoğlu. *Bir Kahramanlık Abidesi: 57. Piyade Alayı*. Ankara: Şehitler Alayı, Milli Savunma Bakanlığı Yayınları, 2003.
Erüreten, Metin. *Osmanlı Madalyaları ve Nişanları Belgelerle Tarihi* İstanbul: DMC Yayınevi, 2001.
Hallı, Reşat, Muhterem Saral and Remzi Yiğitgüden. *Birinci Dünya Savaşı'nda Çanakkale Cephesi (04 Haziran 1915 – 09 Ocak 1916), Vol. 5, Book 2*. Ankara: Genelkurmay Askerî Tarih ve Stratejik Etüt Başkanlığı Yayınları, 2012.
Steel, Nigel and Peter Hart. *Gelibolu; Yenilginin Destanı*. Trans. M. Harmancı. İstanbul: Epilson Yayınevi, 2005.
Karakaya, M. Mutlu. '*Çanakkale Savaşı'nda 14. Alay.*' (Doctoral diss., İstanbul University, 2017).
Karatamu, Selahattin. *Türk Silahlı Kuvvetleri Tarihi, Vol. 3, Part 6, Book 1*. Ankara: Genelkurmay Harp Tarihi Başkanlığı Yayınları, 1971.
Mustafa Kemal. *Arıburnu Muharebeleri Raporu, Genelkurmay Askerî Tarih ve Stratejik Etüt Başkanlığı Yayınları*. Eds. S. Akgül et al. Ankara: Genelkurmay Askerî Tarih ve Stratejik Etüt Başkanlığı 2011.
Oglander, Cecil Faber Aspinall. *Büyük Harbin Tarihi Çanakkale, Gelibolu Askerî Harekâtı, Vol. 2*. Trans. Metin Martı. İstanbul: Arma Yayınları, 2005.
Oral, Haluk. *Arıburnu 1915*. İstanbul: Türkiye İş Bankası Kültür Yayınları, 2007.
Ökse, Necati and İrfan Teşküt. *Birinci Dünya Savaşı'nda Çanakkale Cephesi (04 Haziran 1915 – 09 Ocak 1916), Vol. 5, Book 3*. Ankara: Genelkurmay Askerî Tarih ve Stratejik Etüt Başkanlığı Yayınları, 2012.
Özen, Gökşen. '*Çanakkale Muharebelerinde 72'nci Alay.*' (Master's thesis, Çanakkale Onsekiz Mart University, 2020).
Sayılır, Burhan, Murat Karataş and Barış Borlat. *Çanakkale Muharebelerinde Zabitan İzlenimleri*. İstanbul: Üsküdar Belediyesi, 2017.
Sayılır, Burhan. *Çanakkale Muharebeleri'nde 57. Piyade Alayı*. İstanbul: Bağcılar Belediyesi, 2015.

Toker, Hülya and Nurcan Aslan. *Birinci Dünya Savaşı'na Katılan Alay ve Daha Üst Kademedeki Komutanların Biyografileri, Vol. 3* Ankara: Genelkurmay Basım Evi 2009.

Toker, Hülya. *Çanakkale Muharebelerine Katılan Komutanların Biyografileri.* Ankara: T.C. Genelkurmay Başkanlığı, 2014.

Other Sources
Resimli Tarih Mecmuası
Hayat Mecmuası
Western Mail newspaper
https://www.awm.gov.au
https://recordsearch.naa.gov.au/SearchNRetrieve/Interface/ViewImage.aspx?B=8010260
https://vwma.org.au/explore/people/78143
https://www.naa.gov.au

Index

10th Battalion (AIF), 57
10th Division (Irish), 144
11th Battalion (AIF), 34, 38
11th Division Engineer Company, 86
125th Regiment, 51, 75, 78,89, 123, 127, 142, 144
12th Battalion (AIF), 54, 58, 59, 60
13th Division (Western), 144
13th Regiment, 98, 99
14th Regiment, 64, 71, 72, 73, 74, 75, 76, 79, 92, 93, 94, 96,98, 124
16th Division, 80, 87,90, 142, 144, 151, 171
19th Division, 10, 11, 14, 15, 17, 18, 19, 21, 22, 23, 31, 46, 49, 69, 75, 81, 82, 87, 89, 90, 92, 96, 106, 113, 114, , 117, 118, 121, 123, 139, 142, 143, 144, 148, 157, 158, 167, 186
1st Brigade (AIF), 145
1st Division (AIF), 99
20th Regiment, 9, 10, 45, 47, 48, 51
23rd Regiment, 6, 7, 185
24th Division, 10
26th Division, 10
27th Regiment, 20, 24, 25, 31, 32, 38, 41, 46, 51, 71, 95, 102, 105, 106, 107, 108, 109, 144, 150, 151, 167
29th Brigade (Indian), 144
2nd Field Artillery Battalion, 17
39th Field Artillery Regiment, 17
3rd Army, 3, 16
3rd Army Corps, 16
3rd Australian Infantry Brigade, 54
3rd Brigade (AIF) 32, 34, 60
3rd Corps, 6, 7, 9, 10, 21, 23, 37, 38, 46, 61, 81, 83, 84, 89, 94, 104, 109, 121, 185,
3rd Mountain Artillery Battalion, 17 (AIF), 32
57th Regiment, 9, 10, 13, 14, 15, 16, 17, 18, 22, 23, 24, 25, 27, 29, 30, 31, 32, 35, 36, 39, 40, 41, 42, 43, 45, 46, 47, 48, 50, 51, 53, 55, 62, 67, 69, 70, 76, 78, 81, 84, 85, 86, 88, 90, 91, 92, 93, 94, 95, 96, 98, 101, 102, 103, 105 111, 113, 114, 117, 118, 119, 120, 125, 136, 139, 140, 141, 142, 143, 144, 145, 150, 156, 157, 158, 159, 160, 165, 167, 168, 170, 171, 173, 184, 186
5th Division, 87, 89, 90,91, 94, 99, 104, 111, 113, 117, 118, 144
64th Regiment, 45, 46, 47, 49, 51, 65, 70, 77, 88, 90, 91, 93, 102, 126
72nd Regiment, 10, 17, 21, 29, 39, 43, 46, 49, 51, 73, 75, 77, 88, 90, 109, 141, 142, 147, 156
77th Regiment, 10, 15, 17, 21, 41, 45, 46, 49, 51, 61, 144
7th Battalion (AIF), 133, 137
8th Division, 7

A

Abdurrezzak (Lt-Col, CO 125th Regiment), 144
Abdülkadir (Lt-Col, CO 18th Regiment), 126
Achi Baba, 15
Ağıl dere (Agyhl Dere), 21, 24
Albania, 1,3
Alçıtepe (village), 15
Alexandria, 57, 58
Ali Hayri (Captain), 9, 39, 47, 104, 127, 142
Ali Rıza (Sedes, Colonel), 9, 96, 114, 129
Anafartalar (Suvla) Group, 151
Anafartalar Group, 151, 158
Anzac 20, 23, 25, 32, 37, 46, 47, 49, 52, 60, 62, 64, 68, 69, 70, 71, 72, 77, 79, 81, 82, 87, 90, 91, 92, 96, 97, 98, 99, 100, 101, 102, 109, 114, 116, 117, 122, 123, 124,125, 126, 127, 128, 130, 131, 132, 133, 135, 136, 138, 144, 145, 153, 158, 167, 181
Anzacs, 25, 26, 27, 28, 35, 40, 41, 43, 46, 52, 54, 65, 74, 79, 84, 91, 92, 96, 98, 99, 102, 106, 109, 111, 114, 115, 119, 121, 122, 123, 124, 125, 127,

128, 129 130, 131, 132, 134, 135, 137, 138, 139, 140, 148, 150, 168
Arıburnu, 18, 19, 20, 21, 22, 23, 24, 25, 26, 30, 31, 32, 36, 41, 42 43, 51, 55, 70, 81, 89, 90, 146, 158, 160, 184, 185, 186, 187, 192, 193, 194
Arıburnu Force, 70, 81, 89
Ata (Captain), 9 15, 25, 26, 28, 29, 47, 49, 51, 54, 73, 82
Australian Imperial Force, 59
Azmak Dere, 46

B
Baby 700, 25, 28, 29, 41, 42, 46, 52, 58, 61, 90, 108, 126, 144
Balkan War, 4, 6, 160
Bandırma, 6
Battleship Hill, 27, 28, 30, 37, 41, 43, 46, 54, 58, 87, 88, 102, 144
Biga, 6, 17, 18, 19, 20, 22, 23, 24, 39, 52, 121
Bigalı (Boghali), 17, 18, 19, 20, 22, 23, 24, 39, 52, 121
Bigalı Dere, 17, 23
Birdwood (General), 33, 99
Bitola, 1, 3, 4, 103, 184, 187, 195
Boyun (Courtney's Post), 144

C
Cesaret Tepe (The Nek), 28, 55,69, 85, 95
Chessboard, 29, 40
Conkbayırı (Chunuk Bair), 22, 24, 25, 30, 31, 32, 41, 42, 46, 54, 58, 144, 151, 172
Courtney's and Steele's Posts, 104, 122
Courtney's Post, 29, 62, 91, 92, 110, 115, 122, 123, 144
Çamburnu, 13, 15, 16, 48
Çanakkale, 6, 13, 55, 172,
Çatal Dere, 88, 155, 165, 169, 171, 172
Çatal Tepe (No.1 Outpost), 93

D
Dardanelles Fortified Area Command, 13

Debar, 1, 4
Devanha (troopship), 60
Dik Dere, 25
Duntroon, 58
Düz Tepe (Battleship Hill), 28, 30

E
Eceabat, 10, 11, 13, 14, 16, 17, 19, 46, 48, 180
Edirne Sırt (Mortar Ridge), 106, 117, 118, 119, 140, 147, 156
Ejelmer Bay, 46
Elliott (Lt-Col, CO 7th Battalion), 134
Elston (Lieutenant), 32, 33, 34, 35, 36, 39
Enver (Paşa, War Minister), 81, 184
Esat (Paşa, GOC 3rd Corps), 10, 16, 21, 37, 38, 55, 61, 79, 87, 89, 90, 94, 98, 99, 109, 141, 142, 145, 150, 153, 157, 159

F
Fahrettin (Lt-Col, CoS 3rd Corps), 80, 88, 94, 98, 138, 168, 170, 172, 173, 186
Faik (Captain), 20, 24
Fatmatüzzehra (Avni's wife), 3, 4, 186, 191, 193, 194, 196, 198
Fifty-Seventh Regiment, 54, 84, 184, 187
Fisherman's Hut, 87

G
Gazi Osman Paşa, 3
German Officers' Ridge, 105, 120, 124, 127, 129, 129, 137, 141, 142, 145, 147, 148, 155
German Officers' Trench, 99, 114, 130
Gjirokastër, 3
Godley (General), 32
Greco-Turkish War of 1897, 3, 160
Greig (Lieutenant), 137, 138, 139
Gully Ravine, 22

H
Halep (steamer), 11, 13

Halil Sami (Colonel, CO 9th Division), 21
Hamilton (GOC MEF), 38
Helles, 70, 142
Hill 122 (Sphinx), 90
Hill 261 (Hill 161), 25
Hill 971, 24, 144
Hüseyin Ağa Trench, 110, 111, 115, 122

I
Indians, 34, 35, 122
İstanbul, 3, 4, 6, 10, 18, 82, 85, 93, 94, 101, 102, 103, 160, 181, 185, 186, 188, 189, 197
İzzettin (Major, CoS 19th Division), 21, 37, 126, 136

J
Johnston's Jolly, 62, 71, 90, 142

K
Kaba Tepe (Gaba Tepe), 21, 22, 23, 25, 46, 71, 80
Kanlı Sırt (Lone Pine), 147, 148, 151
Karayörük Dere (Legge Valley), 71
Kemal (Major, 3rd Corps HQ), 37, 80, 88 96,
Kemal, CO 19th Division). 9, 13, 16, 17, 18, 19, 21, 22, 23, 25, 26, 28, 32, 37, 41, 62, 81, 82, 89, 90, 94, 98, 102, 103, 108, 127, 142, 147, 189, 192, 193, 194, 195
Kemal Yeri (Scrubby Knoll), 42, 81, 87, 88
Kilitbahir Plateau, 18
Kilye, 13, 38
Kocaçimen (Hill 971), 24, 193
Kocaçimen Dağı (Koja Chemen Dagh/Hill 971), 24
Kocadere (Kurija Dere), 19, 23, 24, 26, 27, 43, 126
Korku Deresi (Monash Valley), 28, 35, 36
Kör Dere, 25, 42
Krithia (village), 15
Kum Tepe, 22
Kumkale (fort), 10, 15

L
Legge Valley, 71, 90
LemNos., 58, 60
Lone Pine, 62, 71, 72, 90, 122, 127, 143, 145, 147, 148, 149, 150, 151, 155, 167,
Lushington (Private), 35, 36, 39,
Lütfi (CoS 19th Division), 15, 121

M
Macedonia, 1, 3, 4
MacLaurin's Hill, 52, 67, 71
Mal Tepe, 17, 18, 19, 21,37, 46, 87
Maydos (Maidos), 19, 180
McDonald (Captain)32, 33, 34, 35, 36, 37, 38, 39
Mehmet Fehmi (Avni's son), 4, 5, 6, 182, 185, 186, 187, 188, 189
Merkez Tepe (German Officers' Ridge), 105, 123, 128, 141, 142
Millet (steamer), 11, 13
Monash (Colonel), 32
Monash Valley, 28, 29, 32, 33, 35, 36, 47, 48, 49, 64, 67, 72, 84, 91, 92, 94, 126
Mortar Ridge, 46, 47, 62, 88, 104, 106, 109, 117, 118, 119, 121, 122, 127, 128, 140, 142, 147, 152, 153, 155, 156, 165, 167, 168
Mule Valley, 29, 50, 62, 89, 93, 94, 104, 155, 165, 167
Murat II (Ottoman sultan), 1
Münir (Major, CO 72nd Regiment), 49, 90

N
Naci Eldeniz (General), 195
NATO, 197
Nineteenth Division, 54
No.1 Outpost, 93
Northern Group (Turkish), 81, 83, 88, 118, 150, 158
Northern Macedonia, 3, 4
Old Marine Trench, 115
Orhaniye (fort), 10
Owen's Gully, 151
Palamutluk Sırtı (Olive Grove), 46

Pan-Turkism, 191
Patterson (Lieutenant), 54, 56, 57, 58, 59, 60
Plugge's Plateau, 27, 29, 90, 91, 92, 93, 123
Pope (Colonel), 33, 34, 35
Pope's Hill, 34, 92, 93, 94
Pristina, 3

Q
Queen Elizabeth (HMS), 16
Quinn's Post, 40, 49, 84, 91, 92, 93, 115, 125, 126, 129, 130, 154, 165, 167, 186

R
Reading (L/Corporal), 57, 58
Recai (Lt-Col, CO 23rd Regiment), 7, 8
Reşitpaşa (steamer), 11, 13
Ribble (HMS), 60
Robinson (Signaller), 57, 58
Rowlings (Private), 57, 58
Russell's Top, 29, 40, 48, 62, 64, 69, 125, 128, 139

S
Sabri Efendi Trench, 115
Saip (Major, CO 77th Regiment), 21, 49
San Francisco Conference, 196
Sanders (Liman von, GOC 5th Army), 153
Sarafim Farm, 15, 18
Sari Bair, 60
Sarı Bayır (Sari Bair), 144
Sazlı Dere, 61, 144
Scrubby Knoll, 42, 46, 61, 62, 71, 88, 98, 122, 127, 138
Second Ridge, 64, 165
Seddülbahir, 10, 15, 19, 21
Şefik (Lt-Col, CO 27th Regiment), 51, 109, 144, 151, 157, 158, 172,
Sergeant Mehmet, 71, 81
Sergeant Mehmet's Detachment, 71
Şevki (Lt-Col, CO 33rd Regiment), 49, 51, 102, 170
Şevki Paşa Map, 168, 170

Shkodra, 2
Shrapnel Valley, 48
Siege of Plevna, 4
Sinclair-MacLagan (Colonel), 32
Skopje, 4, 12, 164
Soma Depot Regiment, 7, 9, 10
Southern Group (Turkish), 142
Sphinx, 40, 90
Steele's Post, 64, 98. 104, 115, 122, 130, 150
Stip, 3, 4, 5, 187
Suvla, 17, 18, 151, 172
Suyatağı (Su Yatagha), 25, 31, 42, 46, 52, 78

T
Tekin Arıburun (Avni's son), 164, 167, 168, 170, 172, 173, 174, 192, 194, 195, 196, 197, 198, 199
Tekirdağ (Rodosto), 6, 7, 9, 11, 13, 176, 177
Tekke Burnu, 22
The Nek, 28, 29, 32, 40, 41, 46, 55, 52, 65, 69, 71, 85, 88, 91, 92, 93, 95, 102, 122, 125, 126
The Pimple, 71
Third Ridge (Gun Ridge), 46
Thom (Lieutenant), 122
Top Bayırı, 42
Trebishte, 1
Turkish Air Force, 172, 195, 197, 198
Turkish Grand National Assembly (TBMM), 189
Turşun (village), 18

U
Uzunköprü, 11

V-W
Walker (General), 99
Walker's Ridge, 40, 47, 48, 49, 58, 60
Washington, 195, 196
Wire Gully, 94, 99, 127, 141, 165

Y-Z
Yalova (village), 16, 17, 18

Zeki (Captain), 9, 26, 27, 122, 123, 127, 130, 132, 133, 134, 135, 136, 138, 139, 143, 147, 148, 153, 155

www.ingramcontent.com/pod-product-compliance
Lightning Source LLC
Chambersburg PA
CBHW071158070526
44584CB00019B/2838